Journey to Poland

Journey to Poland

Documentary Landscapes of the Holocaust

Maurizio Cinquegrani

EDINBURGH
University Press

Edinburgh University Press is one of the leading university presses in the UK. We publish academic books and journals in our selected subject areas across the humanities and social sciences, combining cutting-edge scholarship with high editorial and production values to produce academic works of lasting importance. For more information visit our website: edinburghuniversitypress.com

Edinburgh University Press Ltd
The Tun – Holyrood Road
12 (2f) Jackson's Entry
Edinburgh EH8 8PJ

First published in hardback by Edinburgh University Press 2018

Typeset in Monotype Ehrhardt by
Servis Filmsetting Ltd, Stockport, Cheshire

A CIP record for this book is available from the British Library

ISBN 978 1 4744 0357 3 (hardback)
ISBN 978 1 4744 6323 2 (paperback)
ISBN 978 1 4744 0358 0 (webready PDF)
ISBN 978 1 4744 0359 7 (epub)

Contents

Figures

Acknowledgements

Journey to Poland: Documentary Landscapes of the Holocaust is about the journeys undertaken by survivors, members of the postgeneration, and filmmakers to the places where the Jews lived before the war and to the places where they were murdered. This book is also the result of my own journey to Poland, and I wish to thank the friends who joined me in exploring the sites of the Holocaust, including Simone Buttazzi, Federico Pagello, Joshua Price, Julia Flood and, in particular, Adam Freeman. For making their films available for viewing I am indebted to Slawomir Grünberg, David Kaufman, Michał Nekanda-Trepka and, in particular, to Kees Hin, Tanja Cummings and Willy Lindwer. Thanks to Luka Vujičić for the inspiring conversations on the subject of this book. Barbara Szewców has helped me with the translation of two films, and it has been a privilege to discuss the historical matters at the core of this book with her. I am also very grateful to Sławomir Nowodworski, with whom I visited the sites of Aktion Reinhard in Eastern Poland; the journey was a major source of inspiration for this book. Similarly, my journey to the former *shtetlekh* of Western Ukraine significantly contributed to my understanding of the events: thanks to Oleh and Sofia. Thanks to Adam Nadolny for inviting me to teach at the Poznań University of Technology; discussing the Holocaust in a Polish classroom has been an invaluable experience. I also want to thank Daw-Ming Lee for inviting me to give a lecture on film and the Holocaust at the Taipei National University of the Arts. I am very grateful to Alicia Kobus for our talk at the Poznań Jewish Community Centre. Ewa Koper at the Bełżec Death Camp Memorial and Olga Rinkus at the Riga Ghetto and Latvian Holocaust Museum have also been very helpful; thank you both. I also wish to thank the team at Grodzka Gate (NN Theatre) in Lublin for their work, and for assistance during my visit to the exhibition. Thanks to Kamila Klauzińska for answering my questions regarding the location of the ghetto in Zduńska Wola. I am grateful to all my colleagues at the University of Kent and in particular to Paul Allain, Aylish Wood and Frances Guerin for their advice. Sally Parrott has read my manuscript and made helpful suggestions; thank you. Staff at Edinburgh University Press, in particular Gillian Leslie and Richard Strachan, have been very supportive and I thank them.

Once in the shadows, the dark forces which fuelled the Holocaust are now emerging again across Europe. This book is dedicated to all the comrades who stand against fascism and against the economic and social inequalities which allow fascism to prosper.

There open up, deep inside a city, reflected streets, streets which are double, make-believe streets. One's imagination, bewitched and misled, creates illusory maps of the apparently familiar districts, maps in which the streets have their proper places and usual names but are provided with new and fictitious configurations by the inexhaustible inventiveness of the night.

— Bruno Schulz, *Cinnamon Shops* (1934)

It is strange how old interiors reflect their dark turbulent past, how in their stillness bygone history tries to be reenacted, how the same situations repeat themselves with infinite variations, turned upside down and inside out by the fruitless dialectic of wallpapers and hangings. Silence, vitiated and demoralized, ferments into recriminations. Why hide it? The excessive excitements and paroxysms of fever have had to be soothed here, night after night by injections of secret drugs, and the wallpapers have provided imagined visions of gentle landscapes and of distant mirrored waters.

The landscape is now like the bottom of an enormous aquarium full of watery ink. Trees, people, and houses merge, swaying like underwater plants against the background of the inky deep.

— Bruno Schulz, *Sanatorium under the Sign of the Hourglass* (1937)

Prologue: Space, Time and the Holocaust

In the autumn of 1941 the SS released orders for the construction of two large labour camps for Soviet prisoners of war to be built on the outskirts of the city of Lublin, in Lesser Poland, and in the village of Brzezinka, near Oświęcim, in Silesia.[1] The barracks and compounds in the *Konzentrationslager* Majdanek and Auschwitz II-Birkenau would eventually resemble those of forced labour camps in the territories of the Reich, including Neuengamme, Mauthausen, Buchenwald, Sachsenhousen, Gross-Rosen and Flossenbürg. There was hardly anything to suggest that both camps would soon be turned into systematic killing tools for what the Nazis called the Final Solution of the Jewish Question. In the months that saw the construction of Majdanek and Auschwitz II-Birkenau, the Jews of Poland were being concentrated in the ghettos and exploited for manual labour. The establishment of these POW camps is unlikely to have been seen by the Jews as a development which would have an impact on their lives. While further east the Nazis had already obliterated hundreds of communities – and despite the fact that early accounts of the executions in Ponary and Chełmno had just reached Warsaw – the idea that both camps would soon combine forced labour with the mass killing of civilians, as well as the fact that camps solely devoted to the latter purpose were about to be built, was still unthinkable. And yet, in less than four years from the creation of Majdanek and Auschwitz II-Birkenau, surviving Polish Jews would emerge from the ruins of Warsaw, from barns and other shelters in rural areas and from the barracks of the camps liberated by the Allies, to face the complete annihilation of their world and the extermination of their people. Most of these survivors left Poland and never went back; some eventually returned to the wreckage of their homes and told their stories; all were irreparably damaged.

Documentary cinema has captured many of these journeys, and has explored a broader range of visits to sites of Jewish life and death invested with different meanings for each category of traveller. As the war catches up with them and tears open old wounds, Jews who return to Poland in search of things past are bound to experience a sense of anguish, loss and displacement in a journey through time and space to a place at once alien and familiar. For the second and third generations, and also for the scholar and the filmmaker, the journey enacts a strategy for the acquisition of knowledge and brings to the present and to reality what had previously belonged to the past and to myth. Documentaries about the Holocaust have explored the connections between personal and collective histories inherent to the act of travelling to the places of one's childhood, to ancestral homes or to the sites of the annihilation of one's people. They have unearthed fragments of the Holocaust and faced the impossibility of piecing together an all-encompassing narrative of the extermination of the Jews. In his recent study of documentary cinema and the Holocaust, Brad Prager has argued that 'today's landscapes and testimonial performances awaken memories of other, older landscapes and testimonial performances' (2015: 25).[2] Filmmakers have used such landscapes and performances to retrieve distant histories of life and destruction, to articulate reflections on mourning, nostalgia, longing, pain and reconciliation, and have thus investigated present-day locations and their revelations about the past. While documentaries have been filmed on the sites of the Holocaust since the immediate post-war years, this cinematic process came to a turning point on a late afternoon one day in 1978:

> I set off again, driving slowly. Then I saw a sign: black lettering on a yellow background that indicated, as though nothing had happened, the name of the village we were approaching: 'TREBLINKA'. Although I had remained impassive before the snowy wasteland of the camp, the standing stones, the memorials, the central blockhouse that purportedly marked out the place of the gas chambers, the sight of this simple road sign utterly devastated me. Treblinka existed! A village named Treblinka existed, dared to exist. It seems impossible to me, such a thing simply could not be. Though I had wanted to know everything, learn everything, about what had happened here, though I had never doubted that Treblinka had in fact existed, the curse that, to me, hung over the name also entailed an almost ontological taboo: it was then that I understood that I had consigned it to the world of myth, of legend. (Lanzmann, 2012: 472)[3]

With these words, in his autobiography *The Patagonian Hare*, Claude Lanzmann recalls his first journey to Poland for the filming of what was to become the milestone Holocaust documentary *Shoah* (1985). The encounter with the road sign at Treblinka caused a sudden shift from myth to reality in the filmmaker's understanding of the events and, as Lanzmann explains, this resulted in the allocation to Poland of the crucial place it deserved in *Shoah* as the main site of the extermination of European Jewry

(2012: 474). As he parked his car near the railway station in Treblinka and observed freight and passenger trains passing by, Lanzmann made the shattering revelation that the juxtaposition of the dreary contemporary reality of Treblinka in 1978 and the terrifying human memories of the events which took place there between 23 July 1942 and 19 October 1943, when as many as 900,000 Jews were exterminated, held the detonator of his plan to capture site-specific testimonies of the Holocaust and of his attempt to bring to the present actions that had previously belonged to the past.

Lanzmann's account of his journey to Poland echoes the claim made by Israeli historian Omer Bartov that 'if there is any true *lieu de mémoire* in Europe, it is in the fields and hills, the river banks and towns of Eastern Europe' (2008: 593).[4] Most scholarship of the Holocaust, argues Bartov, has largely focused on the interaction between the perpetrators and their victims in the territories of the Reich, while the east has remained uncharted territory for most historians, and one that has rarely been systematically studied in relation to memories of Jewish life in the *shtetlekh* and in the cities, and of Jewish death in the camps and in the forests (2008: 557–62).[5] Before Bartov, Lanzmann charted this territory in a film where, as Margaret Olin has argued, topography itself validates the act of witnessing as it relates to the intrinsic power of its narrative and substitutes plot and fictional reconstruction (1997: 1–3).[6] *Shoah* is indeed defined by its locations and by the active role played by these sites in the act of reassessing the Holocaust as an enduring phenomenon with extensive ramifications into the present. This reading of *Shoah* is also supported by the final sequence of the film, where the train used by Lanzmann during the filming in Treblinka continues its ride through the Polish landscape and deprives the narrative of any sense of closure. Accordingly, Stella Bruzzi has argued that, as a documentary journey, *Shoah* is more preoccupied with 'charting moments of encounter and examining the act of journeying than of reaching a fixed destination' (2006: 83).[7] Bruzzi has observed that the idea of journey, implied in the recurring shots of trains, platforms, tracks and stations, is central to Lanzmann's work: 'The film's power stems in part from the central journey being both metaphorical and actual, both concerned with the emotional and intellectual comprehension of the Holocaust and with its physical organisation and execution' (2006: 99). With this multidirectional engagement with the act of journeying, Lanzmann created, in his own words, a quintessentially geographical film where testimonies are validated by the experience of the sites of the Holocaust:

> If you go to Auschwitz without knowing anything about Auschwitz and the history of the camp, you will see nothing, you will understand nothing. In the same way, if you know without having being there, you will also not understand anything. It therefore requires a combination of the two. This is why the issue of the site is so important. I did not make an idealist film; it is not a film with grand metaphysical or theological reflections about why all this happened to the Jews, why they killed them. This is a film from the ground up, a topographical film, a geographical film. (2007: 38–9)[8]

Poland is thus at the centre of the filmmaker's spatial investigation of the Holocaust and at the core of the precarious task of capturing a landscape made of absences, a killing ground where most of the evidence of the extermination was obliterated by the Nazis before the end of the war. Lanzmann has described the Polish locations of *Shoah* as 'non-sites of memory' and thus acknowledged the physical destruction of the camps and the derelict state of places associated with pre-war Jewish life (2007: 15). And yet, according to Pierre Nora's useful distinction, while these locations might not be real environments of memory, or *milieux de mémoire*, they can be discussed as sites of memory, or *lieux de mémoire*, that is, places where memory is seized by history and by the consequent requirement for every group to redefine its identity through the re-elaboration of its own past (1989).[9] Dominick LaCapra has been critical of Nora's work and argued that his polarised conceptions of memory and history, with the latter eclipsing the former, testify to a sense of loss while representing an attempt to neutralise trauma (1998: 18–19).[10] And yet, while sites of memory are not necessarily bound to the evocation of trauma, the chronological overlap between the work of Nora and Lanzmann provides a useful connection between diverse memory cultures, histories and the disappearance of traces. Nora began working on the concept of site of memory in the late 1970s, while Lanzmann was filming in Poland, and the first volume of the collaborative project *Les Lieux de Mémoire* was published in 1984, one year before the release of *Shoah*.[11] Nora later explained the importance of this particular historical juncture:

> Our interest in *lieux de mémoire* where memory crystallizes and secretes itself has occurred at a particular historical moment, a turning point where consciousness of a break with the past is bound up with the sense that memory has been torn – but torn in such a way as to pose the problem of the embodiment of memory in certain sites where a sense of historical continuity persists. There are *lieux de mémoire*, sites of memory, because there are no longer *milieux de mémoire*, real environments of memory. (Nora, 1989: 7)

At the same particular moment in history, Treblinka, Sobibór, Chełmno and Oświęcim emerged from *Shoah* as sites of memory by means of what

Lanzmann calls a journey through time to a place where persistence and disfigurement coexisted and 'wrestled with each other, impregnated each other, chiseling perhaps even more finely, more heartrendingly, the presence of what remains of the past' (2012: 475).

The striking opposition between persistence and disfigurement, between harrowing spaces of extermination and anguishing remnants of Jewish life, as it emerges from a larger cohort of films, is also central to the present investigation. The map of Poland, and its cinematic image, is filled with such places; not only the aforementioned death factories of the Final Solution but also concentration and transit camps, the ghettos and the sites of pogroms. Along with the locations of *Shoah*, the camps in Bełżec, Majdanek, Trawniki, Stutthof and Płaszów, the ghettos of Lviv, Lublin, Białystok, Kraków and Łódź, the graves of Jedwabne and Kielce, among many other places, are sites where the persistence of memory coexists with the disfigurement of the actual locations, with the disappearance of traces or with their monumentalisation. And along with these sites of memory, hundreds of cities, towns, neighbourhoods, villages and hamlets where the Jews lived before the war are now remnants of a past life that appears incredibly remote and yet is profoundly close. Filmic explorations of these locations evoke images of annihilation as well as reminiscences of that Jewish world which was destroyed by the Nazis: railway tracks, fences, watch towers and chimneys, derelict cemeteries, empty marketplaces and courtyards, crumbling synagogues and *mikva'ot*, sparse *mezuzot* and scattered wooden houses are all part of the landscapes of the Holocaust in Poland.

After Lanzmann, with the decline and fall of the Eastern Bloc and the increased ease of movement that resulted from the events, filmmakers from Poland and other countries have set out to explore these landscapes and have created a number of documentaries aimed at capturing spatial narratives of the life and death of Eastern European Jewry. In doing so, they have revealed the complexity of the relationship between Jews and Poles by means of the type of juxtaposition between past events and present sites already articulated in *Shoah*. Lanzmann has claimed that his film 'is the abolition of all distance between past and present' and that, in the making of *Shoah*, he aimed at reliving history in the present (2007: 18). Similarly, the films investigated in this book aim at diminishing the distance between past and present, and are primarily concerned with the ways in which what happened during the war still informs our contemporary world. *Journey to Poland: Documentary Landscapes of the Holocaust* explores the cinematic spaces of these documentaries and, to paraphrase Lanzmann's aforementioned words, I am not writing an idealist book; this is not a book with a grand theoretical reflection on whether writing poetry or making films after the Holocaust should be considered barbaric.[12] *Journey to Poland* is a book from the ground up, a topographical book, a geographical book.

Space and the Holocaust

Nostalgia and longing for a lost world, excruciating pain bound to harrowing memories, individual and collective struggles for survival in the context of the Holocaust are all associated with specific places. However, space had seldom been used as an analytical framework in scholarly discussions of the destruction of the Jews until a very recent surge in this particular approach. In their space-oriented investigation of the Holocaust and the ways in which victims, perpetrators and bystanders interacted with one another, Anne Kelly Knowles, Tim Cole and Alberto Giordano have written:

> The Holocaust destroyed communities, displaced millions of people from their homes, and created new kind of places where prisoners were concentrated, exploited as labour, and put to death in the service of the Third Reich's goal to create a racially pure German empire. We see the Holocaust as a profoundly geographical phenomenon, though few scholars have analysed it from that perspective. (2014: 1)[13]

Paolo Giaccaria and Claudio Minca have also moved from the assumption that the Holocaust was an 'eminently geographical project' and addressed spatial theory and Nazi ideology in an interdisciplinary study reassessing the role of geography in cultural and political histories of modernity (2016: 1).[14] In a similar vein, Joanne Pettitt and Vered Weiss have recently argued that the intertwining of space and time in relation to the shifting topographies of the Holocaust can provide an analytical framework for the comprehension of the most troubled aspects of the genocide (2016: 145).[15] Following this train of thought, *Journey to Poland* unfolds a geographical reading of the events and articulates the idea that documentary cinema has the power to convey, albeit in a fragmented form, the spatial complexity of the Holocaust as it addresses the range of profoundly heterogeneous experiences of victims and perpetrators. The identity of the latter changes depending on whether one looks at the persecution of the Jews in Western Europe, where Germans relied on collaborators from the occupied countries less consistently, or at the extermination of the Jews in the East, where Ukrainians, Lithuanians, Latvians, Estonians and others carried out mass killings under the direction of the Nazis. The predicament of the victims also varies greatly depending on their nationality; the experience of a Hungarian or an Italian Jew taken to a transit camp, deported to

Auschwitz II-Birkenau to be selected by Josef Mengele and then forced to work for the Germans differs from the experience of a Lithuanian Jew trapped briefly in the ghetto of Vilnius and then taken six miles south of the city to the forests in Ponary for execution, or from that of a Latvian Jew forced into the ghetto of Riga shortly before being killed in the woods of Rumbula, eight miles south of the city. Documentary films have traced these diverse experiences of persecution and articulated a cinematic geography of the Holocaust where testimonies are inscribed into specific places and spaces. However, the study of film and the Holocaust has seldom reflected on the spatial ramifications of the events and consistently focused on the experience of the concentration camps and less so on the places inhabited by the Jews before the war and on the variety of spaces created, destroyed and abandoned by the Nazis in the process of the Final Solution. Furthermore, films addressing the dynamics between Jews and German perpetrators have been central to existing scholarship, while the way in which documentary cinema has addressed the relationship between Jews and other groups in Eastern Europe is still a neglected subject of investigation.

More broadly, critical debates on the ethical implications of depicting the horrors of the camps and the gas chambers have dominated this field, while the strategies adopted by documentary filmmakers in order to channel the dissolution of an entire pre-war world as a profoundly spatial phenomenon have played a very minor role in the existing literature. Arguably, the environmental dimension of the Holocaust in film has only been studied in depth in regard to the work of Claude Lanzmann. Gertrud Koch, for instance, has explained that *Shoah* projects the knowledge of the extermination of the Jews into spatial visibility as the film travels to the places of a destruction whose 'spatialization occurs in the present; what remains absent is what is temporally removed, the annihilation itself' (1989: 21).[16] The topographical interplay in the chronology of the film narrative is central to Koch's reading of *Shoah* and to her claim that 'past and present intertwine; the past is made present, and the present is drawn into the spell of the past' (1989: 22). *Journey to Poland* addresses this interaction between layers of time in relation to various cinematic attempts to give spatial visibility to the Holocaust in the territories of what, in the interwar period, used to be the Second Polish Republic, and is today Poland and territories of Belarus, Lithuania and Ukraine. Here, over three million Polish Jews were killed during the Holocaust, half the overall number of victims and almost 90 per cent of the Jewish pre-war population of the republic; about 500,000 Jews were killed by mobile operations, 550,000 in the ghettos, and 1,950,000 in the camps (cf. Hilberg, 1985: 767).[17] Additionally, hundreds of thousands of Jews from other European countries found their death in the extermination camps of Poland, primarily in Auschwitz II-Birkenau (cf. Clarke, 1996: 462–4).[18] The Second Polish Republic thus had the largest pre-war Jewish population and the highest number of victims, and it was also the site of the annihilation of a heterogeneous group of Western and Southern European Jews. On this account, Lanzmann allocated to the country its crucial place in *Shoah* and, on the same basis, documentary cinema and the unfolding of the Holocaust in these territories will be the subject of investigation of this book. As we shall see, despite the outrage that followed the television broadcast of *Shoah* in Poland in 1985,[19] recent years have seen a significant number of documentaries filmed in the former Second Polish Republic and dealing with return journeys of survivors, often accompanied by members of the postgeneration, to the places of their childhood and their youth, as well as to the sites of the extermination of their families and communities. Additionally, several documentaries focusing on Polish bystanders, saviours or betrayers of the Jews have also contributed to the establishment of a cinematic topography of the Holocaust, and will be discussed in the following chapters in terms of comparison with narratives of survival.

Janet Walker has argued that 'physical location matters deeply to the full impact of Holocaust testimonies of return, but so do insights about the psychic dimensions and the unassimilability of place and occurrence' (2012: 271).[20] Accordingly, the present investigation addresses personal processes of transmission of knowledge and uses documentary films in order to construct a space- and place-oriented narrative of the Holocaust as it has emerged in the past four decades, since that distant day in 1978 that saw the arrival of Lanzmann and his film crew to Treblinka. *Journey to Poland* thus focuses on specific locations used in Holocaust documentaries in association with a series of spatial readings of the events and with the remembrance of the life that was destructed by the Nazis. This contribution to the debate on film and the Holocaust also aims to establish a shift from the specific focus on Auschwitz II-Birkenau, which characterises many scholarly contributions on the subject, to the broader landscape of Jewish life and death in Poland. Rob van der Laarse has articulated a useful reading of the role played by Auschwitz II-Birkenau in the historiography of the extermination of the Jews, one that can also be applied to much of the existing literature on film and the Holocaust:

> If Auschwitz has become our common heritage, it is because it was the place where 'our' Jews from Western European cities went to, and from which we know so much because of its many survivors. But what do we know about the experiences of Eastern European Jews and non-Jewish populations? Many of them were already

> dead before the building of Birkenau in 1942, and almost none of the survivors were able to publish war memories. (2013: 214)[21]

Studies of Holocaust cinema have often focused on standard narratives of blue and grey striped uniforms, stars of David and other camp badges, whereas these tropes are representative of the experience of a minority of Holocaust victims, that minority described by van der Laarse as 'our Jews'. With a similar topographical preoccupation, Naomi Mandel has argued that the specific localisation of the Holocaust in Auschwitz can give 'the horror a specific location and a name' and the annihilation of the Jews thus becomes 'localized, abstracted, and isolated, as if the Holocaust is (merely) what occurred at the camps' (2001: 219).[22] Mandel continues:

> But the fact remains that family members, friends, neighbours, co-workers, students, teachers, employers, employees, religious leaders, municipal and government officials, real and imagined allies were all potential betrayers or murderers, and it is this dissolution of an entire network of human relations, not just the killing, that constitutes the Holocaust. (2001: 219)

What occurred in the concentration and death camps was the final part of a process that began in the places where the Jews had lived before the war and continued with the displacement of an enormous mass of people resettled in other neighbours, towns, cities and labour camps. The road to the extermination is a collective history shared by the victims; each instance of survival and return to the familial places from which the Jews were removed is a personal and unique narrative, a prodigy which shatters the foundation of the annihilation project envisaged by the Nazis. Holocaust documentaries have engaged with the complex process of annihilation beyond what happened in the concentration camps, and have also told these site-specific stories of survival and resilience in the background of narratives of an interwar Eastern European Jewish life memorialised in the shadow of its looming destruction.

Documentary filmmakers have faced the disappearance of traces and records of the extermination, and thus the study of film and the Holocaust should take into account the ways in which, amidst these challenges, a lost world and the process of its destruction have been evoked on the screen. The lack of physical traces is intertwined with the ethical question of the representability of the Holocaust: filmmakers have both encountered the challenge to unlock the past on the background of a landscape made of absences, and faced the question of whether it is appropriate to represent the genocide. And yet, recent scholarly works on the subject have addressed a growing suspicion surrounding the idea that the

Holocaust should be beyond representation. Libby Saxton, for example, has observed the presence of an analytical shift 'from the question of whether the event could or should be represented to the question of how it might adequately or responsibly be represented' (2008: 2).[23] Saxton has also reflected on the consequences of the near absence of photographs or film footage of the Nazi machine of mass murder in action, and has suggested that 'Holocaust films may be haunted by these missing images in ways which are not fully articulated or directly represented' and that this void 'has served as a catalyst for aesthetic and ethical innovation, for an ongoing search for more responsible forms of witnessing' (2008: 2). As she has addressed the obstacles to seeing and witnessing the Holocaust, Saxton has argued that filmmakers should respond to 'the attempt by the Nazis to eradicate the visible evidence of their crimes' by accepting 'the task of making the invisible visible and the absence present' (2008: 14). In the wake of the Nazis' attempt, Saxton continues, filmmakers are thus charged with the responsibility 'to reveal what lies beyond the visible: hidden traces, missing bodies, mechanisms of concealment and erasure and the skewing of perception they entail' (2008: 13). The documentaries discussed in the present study have accepted this responsibility and yet, as we shall see, they have had to wrestle with heartrending voids in the landscapes of post-war Poland that ultimately cannot be completely filled.

A number of filmmakers have tried to give presence and visibility to what was hidden by means of various ways of capturing present-day locations in juxtaposition to the act of remembering pre-war and occupied Poland. And yet, a comprehensive study of film and the destruction of the Polish Jews had long been neglected in favour of a focus on the victims from Western Europe until the publication of Marek Haltof's book in 2012.[24] *Polish Film and the Holocaust* was the first monograph to focus on the role of the Holocaust in Polish national cinema and to investigate the relationship between Jews and Poles as it has emerged from fiction films made during and after communist rule. *Journey to Poland* covers the period described by Haltof in terms of 'return of the repressed', which consists of the past four decades and which follows twenty-five years characterised by 'organised forgetting' (2012: 139–86), and is equally concerned with the way in which films have addressed the Polish–Jewish relationships. The space- and place-oriented methodology adopted and the selection of case studies explored in the present investigation, however, depart from Haltof's contribution. The focus of *Journey to Poland* is exclusively on documentaries and on their engagement with environment-based narratives of witnessing, and with the process of unlocking site-specific memories. Case studies include previously neglected feature-length documentaries, shorter non-fiction films made for television and independent productions aimed at the festival circuit. These films are not bound to one particular production context and, rather than using national cinema as an interpretative framework of analysis, the present investigation applies a transnational approach to its subject. As Prager suggests, Lanzmann's international filmic journey between five nations acknowledges the distinctively transnational character of the aftermath of the Holocaust (2015: 24). In a similar vein, personal Holocaust documentaries based on testimonies of survivors, and on cinematic journeys to Poland and other territories where the Final Solution unfolded, have been discussed by Annette Insdorf and Aaron Kerner as a form of transnational travel cinematography (1989: 202–24; 2011: 213–27).[25] Accordingly, the cohort of documentaries discussed in this book was shot in different languages by Polish filmmakers as well as by directors from various other countries (including the USA, Israel, Germany, Canada, Britain, France and the Netherlands) in the course of transnational journeys to the territories of the pre-war republic.

The approach guiding *Journey to Poland* is inspired by Michael Rothberg's definition of multidirectional memory, which he has articulated as a framework of analysis apt to consider 'a series of interventions through which social actors bring multiple traumatic pasts into a heterogeneous and changing post-World War II present' (2009: 4).[26] Multidirectional memory is concerned with individual and collective memory and, as Rothberg suggests, addresses the interaction between agents and sites of memory 'within specific historical and political contexts of struggle and contestation' (2009: 4). With a focus on the relationship between memory and identity in the age of decolonisation, Rothberg has thus investigated the ways in which memory captures 'the individual, embodied, and lived side and the collective, social, and constructed side of our relations to the past' (2009: 4). Beyond the preoccupation with the ways in which the memorialisation of the Holocaust has been used to channel traumatic memories, *Journey to Poland* shares with Rothberg's work a focus on a renewed understanding of transnational relations to the past, memory, testimony, survival and transmission of knowledge. In doing so, this book aims at assembling a mosaic of testimonies of an event whose totality, as the dominant Holocaust historiography suggests, is beyond reach. Linda Williams, for example, has argued that Lanzmann's film has shown that the truth of the Holocaust exists only as a collection of fragments and not as a totalising narrative (1991: 18).[27] Accordingly, *Journey to Poland* gathers particles of the Holocaust emerging from documentary films by means of a study of the relationship between past and present, memory and testimony, in a series of site-specific cinematic inquiries. Each place and each space will be discussed in relation to its contribution to the process of unlocking and exhuming spatially defined memories as part of that perpetually present experience of the past shaped by Holocaust documentaries.

Time and the Holocaust

The aforementioned challenges to the possibility of representing and capturing the destruction of the European Jews on film have been a central concern in the study of Holocaust cinema. Ilan Avisar has argued that the most fundamental problem of any Holocaust representation lies in 'the difficulty of reaching the horrific past from a distance of time and of reconciling the unbelievable atrocity with current perceptions and patterns of thought' (1988: 7).[28] This claim was prompted by the opening sequence of Alain Resnais's *Nuit et Brouillard* (*Night and Fog*, 1955), which was filmed at Auschwitz II-Birkenau, and its incongruous association between a peaceful rural landscape and the knowledge of the horrors which took place there. As Avisar suggests, the juxtaposition of black-and-white archival films of the camp in 1945, with the pervasive violence they convey, and contemporary colour footage of the site emphasises the sharp contrast between the two periods (1988: 13). The intertwining of past and present in documentary film is also central to the current study, which is indebted to one of Avisar's main conclusions:

> Over the years of its happening, the Final Solution ceased to be a dramatic unfolding of unexpected events, a tragically fatal chapter in the story of human history, but became rather a continuous state of affairs, requiring endurance, adjustment, and acceptance of the fact that every day thousands of innocent people were being slaughtered. (1988: 15)

On this basis, Holocaust documentaries can reflect the endurance of the past into the present and can travel beyond a mere description of the actions which unfolded from the day of the Wannsee conference on 20 January 1942, when the implementation of the Final Solution of the Jewish Question was agreed by the Nazis, to the liberation of the camps in 1944 and 1945. Documentaries are about the historical events as much as about the process of coming to terms with them in the present, and they can thus provide means of reflection on Jewish life before the war and on Jewish death during the Holocaust, as well as a meditation on the memorialisation of the genocide in the years which followed. Accordingly, rather than aiming at a spatial history of the Holocaust in Poland told through documentary films, this book is about the act of looking back and aims at addressing personal and collective histories without becoming frozen in the process. *Journey to Poland* thus articulates a temporal reflection on the Holocaust and on the various ways of juxtaposing past and present locations in documentary films, and considers the three main segments of a timeline including the memory of the erased Jewish communities of the inter-war republic, the extermination in the period 1942 to 1945, and the workings of postmemory in the present.

Postmemory is a concept theorised by Marianne Hirsch as a process of transmission of trauma, mediated by imagination and not by recall, from those who witnessed the events to members of the postgeneration for which the traumatic occurrences that preceded their births appear to become memories in their own right. As Hirsch suggests, postmemory 'is not identical to memory: it is "post", but at the same time, it approximates memory in its affective force' (2008: 109).[29] Hirsch continues:

> The 'post' in 'postmemory' signals more than a temporal delay and more than a location in an aftermath. [. . .] And yet postmemory is not a movement, method, or idea; I see it, rather as a structure of inter- and trans-generational return of traumatic knowledge and embodied experience. (2012: 5–6)[30]

In documentary films, postmemory as a structure of return of knowledge can work on two different levels. On the one hand, survivors transmit memories of their traumatic experience to the second and third generations in the diegetic world of the documentary. For the postgeneration, the journey to Poland thus answers the necessity of achieving a higher proximity with the embodied experience of their parents and grandparents. On the other hand, documentaries themselves contribute to the transmission of knowledge from the survivors to the audience. For the viewer, whose engagement with the past can only approximate that of the postgeneration, the cinematic journey can thus contribute to fulfilling what Gary Weissman has described as that 'unspoken desire' of remembering and memorialising the Holocaust expressed by individuals who have no direct experience of the events (2004: 4).[31] Weissman's analysis is critical of the idea of identification and, while documentaries encourage this process, the invitation to take up the position of second- or third-generation descendants of survivors is problematic inasmuch as the viewer's familial connection with the sites of memory can be assumed to be missing. Documentaries thus contribute to fulfilling a desire that is closely related to the idea of postmemory and yet cannot be as firmly experienced as the process of identification represented in the films themselves, as their narratives unfold on the background of landscapes that are vicariously experienced by the audience as sites of postmemory.

In his analysis of testimonial performances, Weissman has also observed that Szymon Srebrnik is the only survivor interviewed by Lanzmann in *Shoah* who is persuaded to return to Poland, specifically to the site of the killing centre in Chełmno, while all other interviews are taken in distant and at times mundane locations. Nevertheless, as Weissman suggests, all testimonies in the film are located on the sites of the death camps 'through the use of voice-over narration and images of present-day sites which, through skilful editing, are made to coincide with the events being narrated' (2004: 192). The testimonies emerging from the case studies explored in the following chapters are also located on the sites of Jewish life and death and were filmed during memory and postmemory journeys or occasionally recorded remotely in the places where the survivors moved after the war. The documentaries investigated in *Journey to Poland* thus juxtapose oral testimonies to the landscapes of the Holocaust and address what Annette Insdorf, in relation to Resnais's *Night and Fog*, has called the 'dual perspective' of the witness (the survivor) and the visitor (the filmmaker), with whom audiences identify as they try to come to terms with the exposure to traumatic memories (1989: 201). Insdorf has also suggested that, while they often rely on archival footage and interviews, documentary films can 'contain a narrative spine, poetic sinews, an edited pulse, and a profoundly personal voice' (1989: 200). This claim resounds in the ways in which the documentaries studied in this book combine present-day images of the sites with oral accounts of the events and, in most cases, with a use of archival photographs and footage that signals an apparent departure from *Shoah*'s rejection of archival images. The promise of authenticity, as Lanzmann's film implies, is highly debatable in the case of atrocity footage, a type of archival material which has largely been deemed unsuitable to enhance historical authority inasmuch as it was shaped by external forces, fabricated as it was by the Nazis or by the liberators. Among others, Toby Haggith and Joanna Newman have also reflected critically on the use of footage of the camps after the liberation and argued that 'the attraction and power of the moving image is its verisimilitude, the medium appears to be a transparent and a true record' and yet these images are not 'an unimpeachable historical record of the Holocaust' (2015: 6).[32]

The narrative discourse articulated in the documentaries considered in *Journey to Poland* departs from the abovementioned rejection of archival films or photographs of the atrocities pursued by Lanzmann on account of the limited testimonial value of sparse existing material.[33] The archival inventory used in most films at the core of the present investigation seldom portrays acts of violence and persecution; on the contrary, this material is largely made of pre-war family photographs and amateur films made by Jews who had migrated to the United States at the turn of the century and went back to Poland in the 1930s with their cameras, unknowingly capturing images of a world on the brink of annihilation. Such mediated images, as Jo Spence and Patricia Holland have explained, can operate at the 'junction between personal memory and social history, between public myth and personal unconscious' (1991: 13).[34] These visual records are unaffected by the taboo of representation of the physical extermination of the Jews and can be seen as remnants of pre-war Jewish life, serving the purpose of unlocking distant memories. Furthermore, as Prager suggests, the taboo associated with the use of archival photographs and footage in Holocaust documentaries has been recently replaced by a tendency to re-evaluate archival images and to 'bring about a reconsideration of how historians have interpreted films and footage from the past' (2015: 11).

The idea of 'archivalness', as Jamie Barton has argued, seems to promise truth-value as it appears directly retrieved from history: 'The sense of the "foundness" of the footage enhances its historical authority because what has been "found" has not (ostensibly) been fabricated or shaped by the filmmaker who repurposes this footage' (2013: 7).[35] Postmemory can facilitate the process of interpreting this material and overcome the ambiguities inherent to the promise of authenticity in archival images. In her investigation of the relationship between family photographs and the processes employed by public institutions to re-embody archival memory, Hirsch argues that family photographs of a world annihilated by force can diminish distance between past and present and contribute to establishing an 'intimate material and affective connection' (2008: 116). Photographs thus capture what no longer exists and provide the process of mourning with a visual referent. Documentaries can integrate these archival images with present-day footage and oral testimonies in order to bridge the separation between past and present by means of the emotional weight of those images described by Hirsch as 'leftovers, debris, single items that are left to be collected and assembled in many ways' (1997: 13).[36] The deceased are often introduced by means of family photographs in documentary films articulating various ways of assembling these fragments and of conforming to what Hirsch has described as an attempt to see the past in the present 'in the form of a ghostly revenant, emphasizing, at the same time, its immutable and irreversible pastness and irretrievability' (1997: 20).

The use of family photographs in documentaries is haunted by death and can emphasise the visual power of what Susan Sontag has called the 'innocence, the vulnerability of lives heading toward their own destruction' in photographic images pervaded by 'the knowledge of how soon all these people were to perish' (1989: 70).[37] Archival images can thus provide a visual referent to the testimonies used in documentary films, to those personal memories of witnesses and survivors which, according to Omer Bartov, are charged with the task of liberating us 'from the dilemmas of "authentic" fictions and polluted documents' (1996: 172).[38] Documentaries have gathered these testimonies and collectively provided a mosaic of experience of death, struggle and survival. As Janet Walker suggests, they can also 'reintroduce individual memory to the sphere of rational history in such a way that the terms are distinguished from one another by their relationship to the actual historical event but are still mutually corroborative' (1997: 822).[39] The documentary thus becomes an answer to what Joshua Hirsch has described as that crisis of representation brought on by the Holocaust which affects both the destruction itself and the image of pre-war Eastern European Jewish life (2003: 11).[40] As *Journey to Poland* aims at demonstrating, by means of combining testimonies, location shooting and site-specific archival images, documentaries can effectively evoke, and yet never fully represent, this lost world while conjuring the process of its destruction.

The witnesses interviewed in documentary films often emphasise the impossibility of providing a clear image of what was erased in the extermination. First-person oral testimonies nevertheless remain central to the process of unlocking memories and unearthing remnants of pre-war Jewish life and, in the light of this exhumation, the annihilation itself. The role played by survivors and bystanders in documentaries relates to that concept of the witness as a social actor which has already been invoked by Rothberg and is also articulated by Bill Nichols in relation to the use of archival material:

> Social actors, witnesses, could speak now about what they know of historical events. The indexical image authenticates testimony now about what happened then. With historical footage from the time recounted appended to it, indexicality may guarantee an apparent congruity between what happened then and what is said now. (1994: 4)[41]

The intertwining of history and memory, past and present, Nichols continues, results in a series of representational strategies where 'we can see in what witnesses say now the continuation of the past in the present, its corporeal incarnation through speech and action' (1994: 4). Following this train of thought, Aaron Kerner has argued that 'when documentaries incorporate witnesses into their narrative, manifesting in the form of testimony, the presumption is that the documentary provides the spectator with unassailable admittance to what "really happened"' (2011: 11). Kerner has explained that documentaries that rely significantly on testimonies often adopt interactive narratives based on the role of the filmmaker as a social actor shaping and interacting with the events that unfold in front of the camera; observational strategies, on the other hand, often apply to films with a focus on the contemporary experience of the Holocaust, while expository narratives are often used for the purpose of historical investigation (2011: 178–9). As we shall see, in the context of the impossibility of assembling the truth or the history of the Holocaust the interplay between these documentary modes allows the viewer to acquire at least *a* truth or *a* history of a Holocaust understood as a historical phenomenon whose memory is subject to constant renegotiations, or as an event that, as Kerner puts it, 'needs to be placed into a continuum of human experience that requires continued re-evaluation' (2011: 203).

In what follows, the endurance of the Holocaust in the present will be investigated by means of a place- and space-specific assessment of documentary practices aiming at transgenerational transmission of knowledge and at the exhumation of a world lost in the midst of the genocide and in the depths of challenges to memory, photographic evidence and testimony. As Tim Cole suggests, the extermination of the Jews 'did not happen in one place but many, and was not one single event (with a single landscape) but multiple events that took place in different ways, at different times, in different places' (2016: 226).[42] Cinematic landscapes can foreground this complexity, and will be addressed in the following chapters by means of a long journey focusing on the ways in which documentary films have explored localised present-day sites by means of travelling to the places that were inhabited by the Jews before the war and to the sites where they were murdered. The first chapter introduces the concept of *shtetl* (pl.: *shtetlekh*) and investigates the murder of Jews at the hands of Poles and its ramification in the present within the context of the former *shtetl* Jedwabne, the Mazovian countryside, and the city of Kielce. Chapter Two and Chapter Three specifically focus on the cinematic *shtetl* as the location of a series of quests for traces and remnants of Jewish life in Gąbin, Suchowola, Brańsk, Luboml, Eishyshok, Delatyn, Opatów, Zdunska Wola, Urzejowice and Pińczów. Chapter Four and Chapter Five investigate the ways in which Jewish heritage and the Holocaust itself are still inscribed in the built environment of Warsaw, Kraków, Łódź and Lviv, as it is revealed by documentaries conjuring with topographical accuracy the memory of the ghettos of these cities. Based on close analysis of a selected number of documentary films, the investigation presented in these two chapters will be triggered by brief reflections on the ways in which popular fiction films have addressed the specific sites of the Holocaust in these four cities. In the final part of this journey, documentaries filmed at the sites of the death camps in Treblinka and Oświęcim[43] will be discussed in relation to the use of specific places within these locations, and to the attempt made by filmmakers to establish a connection between past and present in spaces characterised by physical disfigurement and traumatic memories.

The Jews of Poland were taken from their villages and neighbourhoods, from the places that shaped them, to the largest ghettos or directly to the slave labour and death camps or to other sites of execution, and *Journey to Poland* thus follows the steps of the Jews who saw their physical, familial, affective, religious and cultural world being obliterated. Among them, Polish–Jewish writer Bruno Schulz was killed by Gestapo officer Karl Günther in 1942 while he was walking back with a loaf of bread from the Aryan quarter of the city of Drohobycz, in today's Ukraine, to the ghetto. His short stories, which he wrote in the late 1920s and 1930s, contain the quotations that open *Journey to Poland*. With their references to 'illusory maps of the apparently familiar districts', to a dark past filled with situations that 'repeat themselves with infinite variations' and to a landscape that 'is now like the bottom of an enormous aquarium full of watery ink', Schulz's stories are saturated with omens of what would soon happen to the Jews and with visions of that valley of death which would be visited by survivors many years after the Holocaust (2008: 55, 189, 261).[44] The documentaries investigated in this book are about these survivors and that inky landscape at the bottom of the aquarium, about its darkness and its emptiness. Bruno Schulz and the other six million are at the margins, unreachable in the illusory and gentle landscape they inhabit in memory.

Notes

1. Plans were released by the *SS-Wirtschafts- und Verwaltungshauptamt* (SS Main Economic and Administrative Office). On the construction of Majdanek and Auschwitz II-Birkenau, see Wachsmann, *KL: A History of the Nazi Concentration Camps*, pp. 278–84.
2. Prager, *After the Fact*.
3. Lanzmann, *The Patagonian Hare*.
4. Bartov, 'Eastern Europe as the Site of Genocide'.
5. A number of significant books addressing the Holocaust in Eastern Europe and in territories of the Soviet Union have nevertheless been published and, among other titles, include Patrick Desbois' *The Holocaust by Bullets*;

Richard Rhodes' *Masters of Death*; Christopher R. Browning's *Ordinary Men*; and Yitzhak Arad's *Bełżec, Sobibór, Treblinka*.

6. Olin, 'Lanzmann's *Shoah* and the Topography of the Holocaust Film'.
7. Bruzzi, *New Documentary: A Critical Introduction*.
8. Lanzmann, 'Site and Speech: An Interview with Claude Lanzmann about *Shoah*'.
9. Nora, 'Between Memory and History'.
10. LaCapra, *History and Memory after Auschwitz*.
11. Nora, *Les lieux de mémoire: La République*.
12. Theodor W. Adorno's widely discussed claim reads 'to write poetry after Auschwitz is barbaric'; in Adorno, 'Cultural Criticism and Society,' p. 34.
13. Knowles et al., *Geographies of the Holocaust*, pp. 1–17.
14. Giaccaria and Minca, 'Introduction: Hitler's Geographies, Nazi Spatialities'.
15. Pettitt and Weiss, 'Introduction'.
16. Koch, 'The Aesthetic Transformation of the Image of the Unimaginable'.
17. Hilberg, *The Destruction of European Jews*.
18. Clarke, 'Holocaust topologies'.
19. On the television broadcast of *Shoah* in Poland, its critical reception and the public debate that followed, see Marek Haltof's *Polish Film and the Holocaust*, p. 185.
20. Walker, 'Moving Testimonies'.
21. Van der Laarse, 'Archaeology of Memory'.
22. Mandel, 'Rethinking "After Auschwitz"'.
23. Saxton, *Haunted Images*.
24. Haltof, *Polish Film and the Holocaust*.
25. Insdorf, *Indelible Shadows*; Kerner, *Film and the Holocaust*.
26. Rothberg, *Multidirectional Memory*.
27. Williams, 'Mirrors Without Memories'.
28. Avisar, *Screening the Holocaust*.
29. Hirsch, 'The Generation of Postmemory'.
30. Hirsch, *The Generation of Postmemory: Writing and Visual Culture After the Holocaust*.
31. Weissman, *Fantasies of Witnessing*.
32. Haggith and Newman, *Holocaust and the Moving Image*.
33. On the debate on the total rejection of archival footage and photographs in *Shoah* see, for example, Saxton's *Haunted Images*, pp. 23–45.
34. Spence and Holland, *Family Snaps*.
35. Baron, *The Archive Effect*.
36. Hirsch, *Family Frames*.
37. Sontag, *On Photography*.
38. Bartov, *Murder in Our Midst*.
39. Walker, 'The Traumatic Paradox'.
40. Hirsch, *Afterimage: Film, Trauma, and the Holocaust*.
41. Nichols, *Blurred Boundaries*.

42. Cole, *Holocaust Landscapes.*
43. Throughout *Journey to Poland* I will refer to Oświęcim as the Silesian town in south-western Poland, and to Auschwitz I and Auschwitz II-Birkenau when referring to the two main spaces adapted or created by the Nazis in this area for the purpose of the Final Solution.
44. Schulz, *The Street of Crocodiles and Other Stories*, pp. 55, 189, 261.

CHAPTER 1

Countryside, *Shtetl*, City: The Murders of Mazovia, Jedwabne and Kielce

> 'I remember a lane leading to the house where we lived.'
>
> — Henryk Grynberg, *Birthplace*

An old Jewish man named Jurek returns to his *shtetl* Otwock, in central Poland, wanders in the dilapidated Jewish cemetery at sunset and walks the empty streets of the village, a place at once familiar and yet profoundly alien (Fig. 1.1). This sequence from Małgorzata Imielska's *Powiedz mi, dlaczego* (*Tell Me Why*, 2005) captures a landscape that is emblematic of the destinations of many Holocaust survivors' return journeys to Eastern Europe and of their cinematic image in documentary films. *Tell Me Why* is based on interviews with Jurek and Stella, two survivors who fell in love in 1936 in Otwock and were then separated by the war.[1] Jurek was deported to Auschwitz II-Birkenau and later settled in Israel, while Stella was taken to a labour camp in Germany and then moved to the United States. In 2005, following the recent deaths of their spouses, Jurek suggested they should meet again. The location for this reunion was planned to be the *shtetl* of Otwock, where Jurek returned after more than sixty years while Stella decided to stay in Boston. Despite the unsuccessful attempt to reunite Jurek and Stella, *Tell Me Why* uses the site of the *shtetl* to unlock painful and yet nostalgic memories of pre-war Jewish life, with that ambivalent retrospective look at ancestral locations that characterises the cinematic landscapes of the life and death of the Jews of Poland. In documentaries of return, the transgenerational communication of knowledge is part of a process aimed at filling absences, deciphering flashes of memory, and assessing the conformity of present-day spaces to the recollections of the survivors. These films also define the old *shtetlekh*, their streets, marketplaces, buildings and cemeteries, as cultural paradigms for the transactions of memory from the survivors to the second and third generations and as selected sites for various attempts of reconciliation between Jews and Poles.[2] Additionally, recent documentaries have given

Figure 1.1 *Powiedz mi, dlaczego* (*Tell Me Why*, Małgorzata Imielska, 2005).

Polish witnesses the responsibility of conveying memories of pre-war Jewish communities and their destruction. The present and the following two chapters address these documentaries and, by investigating the ways in which particular locations have been used to exhume distant events, they aim to convey the spatial complexity of the Holocaust from multiple points of view and by means of a polyphony of voices emerging from films about those who return to their towns of birth (the survivors), those who visit their ancestral *shtetl* for the first time (the postgeneration), and those who have never left the country (the Polish witnesses).

In a discussion about their own journey to the city of Chernivtsi in western Ukraine, Marianne Hirsch and Leo Spitzer have addressed the personal, the familial and the cultural memory of the place, and explained that a fundamental motivation for returning to the sites of Jewish life is to be identified in 'the ambivalent desire to recall negative experiences at their place of happening, and to transmit them to sympathetic listeners and co-witnesses' (2003: 84).[3] This is also the motivation behind the journeys recorded in documentaries of return and in their expressions of nostalgia for the destruction of Eastern Europe Jewry. Pervaded by a void, the transnational journeys addressed in these films have seen survivors fulfilling a desire to transmit the knowledge of the events on the location where they originally took place. And along with accounts of persecution and destruction, childhood and youth memories of family homes, schools, playgrounds, market days, holidays and religious celebrations are articulated by the survivors in order to pass on to new generations the knowledge of pre-war Jewish life and transmit an understanding of that world which was erased during the Holocaust, as well as a desire to come to terms with the annihilation itself.

The former *shtetlekh* filmed in the case studies selected in these chapters are now located in Poland, Lithuania and Ukraine, but they were all part of the Second Polish Republic in the interwar years. A Yiddish term for town or village, the word *shtetl* itself, as Jeffrey Shandler has explained, is central to the understanding of the ways in which Jewish culture in Eastern Europe can be conceptualised. And yet, the meaning of this word has very variable characteristics in regard to the size, location, economy, ethnic and religious composition of the villages. Broadly defined as a small multicultural, albeit predominantly Jewish, human settlement, the *shtetl* needs to be understood as both the historical phenomenon of Jewish towns in Eastern Europe before the Second World War and, Shandler explains, as a mythical concept based on the idea and the memorialisation of a vernacular Jewish culture (2014: 1–7).[4] Echoing the distinction suggested by Shandler, Barbara Kirshenblatt-Gimblett has argued that there are two main readings of the concept of *shtetl*. On the one hand, Kirshenblatt-Gimblett suggests, there is the physical space and the notion of Jewish towns in Eastern Europe, with their multicultural complexity; and, on the other hand, the literary and imaginary rendering of the *shtetl* in popular fiction as a hermetic Jewish community (1995: xviii–xix).[5] With a focus on both the peaceful coexistence and the ethnic tensions between Jews and Poles which characterised provincial life before the war, the testimonies presented in the documentaries selected for these chapters reflect the cultural, religious and linguistic heterogeneity of the *shtetl* rather than its imagined hermetic quality. In doing so, they articulate an ambivalent narrative about the role played by the Poles in the persecution of their Jewish neighbours, with both instances of heroism and examples of crimes induced by anti-Semitism.

The post-war struggle to integrate the memorialisation of the annihilation of the Jews into the consciousness of the Polish nation, as well as into its historical and cultural identity, provides a significant narrative strand for the films investigated in this and in the following two chapters and informs their use of site-specific events canalising a larger, multilayered and contested history of Poland as a killing field. With a focus on the juxtaposition between oral testimonies, archival images of the *shtetlekh* and present-day footage of the same places, documentaries have evaluated the impact of anti-Semitism on Polish–Jewish relationships and conjured the intrigues, lies, revelations and fears of reappraisal which characterise cinematic narratives focusing on the crimes perpetrated by Poles against the Jews. Accordingly, a recurring focus of Holocaust documentaries is the context within which the extermination eventually became possible and unfolded. Interwar Poland saw a significant rise in anti-Semitic tensions, with one-third of its Jews reduced to abject poverty by the policy of governments influenced by the anti-Semitic movement *Narodowa Demokracja* ('National Democracy'), the main political force behind boycotts, violent demonstrations and attacks against the Jews (cf. Burleigh, 2000: 323, 574).[6] During the war, anti-Semitism characterised a considerable part of the Polish response to the ghettoisation of the Jews and often defined the active role played by Poles in the persecution of their neighbours. In this historical context, the memories of pogroms and murders at the hands of Polish people emerge painfully from documentary films dealing with the weight of responsibility, with deception, shame and denial, while highlighting persistent tensions between Poles and Jews in today's Poland. And yet, as we shall see in Chapter Three, thousands of Jews were also saved by those Poles who had the courage and compassion to face Nazi terror and even the hostility of their own people and who could ultimately, as Michael C. Steinlauf suggests, see the Jews beyond the process of their dehumanisation and as human beings in desperate need of help (1997: 41–2).[7] In this dual reading of the events which took place in Poland lies an neglected landscape of pain which appears somewhat distant from the more widely discussed scenery of death at Auschwitz II-Birkenau, and yet is intrinsically related to that purpose-built dark world of night and fog.

In *Shoah*, Lanzmann visited Włodawa, a former *shtetl* in Eastern Poland whose Jews were murdered in Sobibór, the death camp located seven miles from the town. In this sequence of the film, shots of the derelict synagogue of Włodawa are edited with Lanzmann's interview with Pan Filipwicz, filmed in front of the Church of St Louis. A Polish bystander who saw the destruction of the local Jewish community, Filipwicz gives an account of the deportation of the Jews to Sobibór and the brutal ways in which they were herded by the Nazis to the local train station. He is taken on a drive through the streets of Włodawa, and while Lanzmann's camera pans over the houses of the former Jewish neighbourhood, Filipwicz provides details about the buildings formerly owned by Jewish merchants, barbers, blacksmiths and shoemakers. This type of cinematic exploration of a former *shtetl*, accounting both for Jewish life before the Holocaust and for its destruction during the war, has consistently been used in later documentaries canalising the void left by the murdered Jews in the cultural and physical landscape of post-war Poland. In what follows, the Holocaust landscapes emerging from these documentaries will be contextualised in relation to the ways in which individual and collective histories can provide an answer to the need for documentation, reflection and discussion of the genocide and its aftermath. These landscapes will be discussed in connection to the documentary practices employed by the filmmakers, including the use of archival footage and photographs, voice-over narration and talking-head interviews, in the context of what Bill Nichols has articulated as the various modes of documentary and, in particular, interactive, expository and observational strategies (1991: 34–56).[8] The towns and villages investigated in these films exemplify the 5,000 *shtetlekh* destroyed by Nazis in the Holocaust. The Germans occupied these places, and systematically established ghettos which were liquidated with the transports to larger cities and to the death camps or with executions on site and near the *shtetlekh*. Details of the course of events in each town are reported in the footnotes; these are repetitive in the information they provide, and as such give a glimpse of the relentless repetitiveness of the destruction of thousands of communities such as those evoked in these films.

During and after the war, Jews were killed at the hands of Poles in a series of individual murders and pogroms which unfolded on the sites where Jewish communities were being destroyed or had already been annihilated by the Nazis. The three documentaries discussed in this chapter address these events and use diverse narrative devices to reflect upon the ways in which the past still informs the landscapes of the Holocaust in the Mazovian countryside, the *shtetl* of Jedwabne and the city of Kielce. *Miejsce urodzenia* (*Birthplace*, Paweł Łoziński, 1992) is a survivor's personal return journey to eastern Poland, where he chases a familial memory and investigates the truth about his father's violent death. Anti-Semitic pogroms in occupied and post-war Poland, as well as their aftermath, are the subject matter of *The Legacy of Jedwabne* (Slawomir Grünberg, 2005) and *Świadkowie* (*Witnesses*, Marcel Łoziński, 1986). Like *Birthplace*, these two films focus on the events of the 1940s as much as on the ways in which the role played by Poles in the annihilation of the Jews has long been a problematic and inconvenient truth that has struggled to find its way in the historical and cultural consciousness of the nation. As they intervene in the debate about Polish responsibilities in the Holocaust, *Birthplace*, *The Legacy of Jedwabne* and *Witnesses* reveal contested personal and collective sites of memory and investigate past events whose persistence in the present is revealed by spatial explorations and by testimonies. Their engagement with specific places inscribes the events into a landscape where temporal boundaries are blurred and where the dead have left an indelible mark on the memories of the living, of those survivors who return to ascertain the impossible, to verify the entire destruction of their world.

The Holocaust landscapes of Poland are filled with unsolved crimes, unanswered questions and frustrated historical investigations intertwined with the impact of anti-Semitism on Polish history, a pervading force addressed in documentary films in relation to the desire to provide survivors and members of the postgeneration with a sense of closure. While Polish pogroms against the Jews were often ascribed to either Nazi or Soviet influences, the large number of individual cases of post-war assaults against Jews reveals ethnic and religious tensions rooted deep into the nation itself and can shed light on the circumstances that caused many Holocaust survivors to flee Poland (cf. Steinlauf, 1997: 43–61). One of these episodes is the subject of Łoziński's *Birthplace*, a documentary about Henryk Grynberg, a writer and Holocaust survivor who returns to Poland from the United States in order to investigate the circumstances of his father's murder at the hands of his Polish neighbours.[9] The themes of Grynberg's novels, plays and poems are bound up with the writer's struggle to come to terms with his own memories and with the forgetfulness of others. *Birthplace* can be read as a visual counterpart to these concerns and as an account of the writer's attempt to find closure during a visit to several villages in the eastern part of the Mazovia province, including Dobre, Drop, Głęboczyca and Radoszyna, the hamlet where Grynberg was born in 1936.

The involvement of Poles in crimes against the Jews had hardly ever surfaced in Polish cinema when Łoziński, who directed the film as part of his degree at the National Film School in Łódź, addressed national responsibilities in a direct and uncompromising way that was barely tolerated within the context of the changed political landscape that followed the end of communist rule.[10] Fears of retaliation against those who provided testimonies in regard to the Polish role in the persecution of the Jews are acknowledged in *Birthplace*, and yet Grynberg succeeds in obtaining the information he seeks, discovering that his father survived the Holocaust and was killed after the war by two Polish brothers to whom he had entrusted his valuables for safekeeping. The older brother was already dead by the time of filming in the early 1990s, while the younger sibling is interviewed on camera as he denies his involvement in the death of Abram Grynberg. With the help of local farmers, the writer identifies his father's burial site and digs up the man's skull, his bones, and the milk bottle Abram carried with him. For Grynberg, the countryside of Mazovia thus becomes the locus of the destruction of his family and community, and simultaneously the space where vague childhood memories can be anchored to some physical evidence. As he captures the expressions of the writer and the interviewees through a series of close-ups and extreme close-ups edited with long shots of the local countryside, Łoziński articulates Grynberg's reacquisition of memory without the use of voice-over narration or archival footage, and follows him unobtrusively as he talks to the eyewitnesses. *Birthplace* thus embodies the idea of bearing witness in an observational manner which, according to Nichols, 'gives a particular inflection to ethical considerations' and is characterised by 'indirect address, speech overheard rather than heard since the social actors engage with one another rather than speak to the camera' (1991: 39).

The opening sequence of the film introduces the journey to a place that for Grynberg had until then only existed in his fading memories. The image of a plane landing on the wintry Polish landscape is followed by a long take of an icy road in the countryside of the Mazovia province, filmed from the car which is taking the writer to his birthplace. In the following shot, Grynberg is seen inside the car in the act of using his hand to clear condensation from the misted side window (Fig. 1.2). As the landscape of his childhood appears through the window and is introduced to the audience by means of a series of point-of-view shots, Grynberg begins a brief voice-over opening with these words: 'I remember a lane leading to the house where we lived. Or to a farmhouse or a manor house. The end of that lane seemed like the end of the world.' The action of clearing the window of condensation, an image which will occur again towards the end of the film, anticipates Grynberg's attempt to clear foggy memories and to find in this landscape the answers he is seeking, the closure is hoping to obtain.

His exploration continues by foot to the centre of a small village. Here, the local marketplace, or *rynek* in Polish, is presented as a key site in the processes of memory and nostalgia, and one that rejects a mythic understanding of the *shtetl* as a hermetic Jewish world and addresses the coexistence of Poles and Jews in the area. An old Polish woman remembers the wedding procession of Henryk's mother, with whom she went to school, crossing the marketplace, with Jewish girls carrying candles and cake to the house where the celebration took place: 'That cake was delicious, I'm telling you. They baked such a good cake for the wedding.' This nostalgic view echoes Grynberg's own memories of a crowded marketplace full of carts, groceries and livestock, and where Jewish merchants traded produce with Polish farmers. The images filmed in 1992 in eastern

Figure 1.2 *Miejsce urodzenia* (*Birthplace*, Paweł Łoziński, 1992).

Mazovia, however, appear incongruous when compared with Grynberg's longing for the lively pre-war marketplace that survives in his memories. David Lowenthal has argued that 'nostalgia is not so much being uprooted as having to live in an alien present' (1975: 2);[11] accordingly, the image of Mazovia unfolded by Łoziński reflects the alien nature of a present utterly irreconcilable with the past. A few carts, a dozen elderly Poles drinking vodka and trading a handful of goods, children staring at the camera in a muddy square, are all that is left of the old core of the *shtetl*. Additionally, the memory of pre-war marketplaces is rendered even more problematic by another episode related to the Grynberg family and reported by one of the Polish witnesses interviewed by the writer: in the village of Jadów, Henryk's younger brother was shot near the market square by a German policeman. The marketplace thus emerges from *Birthplace* as both a site of memory and nostalgia and a place of mourning and pain. In regard to this type of ambivalence in the context of returnees' journeys to the sites of Jewish life and death in Eastern Europe, Hirsch and Spitzer have explained that:

> At each moment of their journey, the past-*positive* is also overlaid by the past-*negative*. *Nostalgic* memory clashes with negative and *traumatic* memory, and produces *ambivalence*. In the act of return, that ambivalence is generative not so much of corrective narrative as of a kind of performance, the creation of a scenario that can hold both sides of the past simultaneously in view, without necessarily reconciling them, or healing the rift. (2003: 84)

Grynberg's visit to Poland thus reveals a dual perspective and an ambivalent engagement with the past and with a landscape where destruction and fond childhood memories coexist and wrestle with one another. This conflict, unhealed and not reconciled, also emerges in the sequence where, before asking about his father's murder, the writer uses an old photograph of his mother to revive the memories of a woman who knew his parents. Grynberg's mother survived the war thanks to Aryan papers and, as Łoziński's camera closes up on the photograph for several seconds, her youthful face and smile contribute to bringing the Polish woman back to the time which preceded the disintegration of a whole world; this image is consistently evoked by the witnesses interviewed throughout the film. In this landscape of wounds torn open by remembrance, Grynberg's return to the *shtetl* and to the alien present of Poland in the 1990s answers the necessity of a spatial experience of the past, a symptom of what Pierre Nora has discussed as a transition from history as a reconstruction of the past to memory as a perpetually actual phenomenon (1989: 7–8). The old *shtetl* thus becomes one of those sites where the absolute nature of memory is challenged by the relative nature of history, a place where reconciliation is sought by means of a space-specific experience of what belongs to the past. This journey to eastern Mazovia aims to find the remnants of a time that has disappeared forever; its temporal and geographical itinerary thus fulfils that transition from history to memory articulated by means of an experience of the problematic ways in which nostalgia for a lost world and the trauma of annihilation perpetually coexist.

Whereas *Birthplace* articulates a private and individual engagement with the persecution and with the question of Polish responsibility, other documentaries investigate physical remnants of the past in the present-day landscapes of the Holocaust while focusing on the sites of large-scale acts of violence perpetrated by Poles against Jews. Grünberg's *The Legacy of Jedwabne* addresses the events of 10 July 1941, when at least 340 Jews were rounded up by their Polish neighbours in the main square of Jedwabne, corralled into a barn located near the Jewish cemetery and burned to death (cf. Levy, 2005: 366–7).[12] *Witnesses*, directed by Paweł's father Marcel Łoziński, is a documentary about the post-war pogrom in Kielce, a city with an interwar population that included almost 25,000 Jews, where on 4 July 1946 members of the armed forces and a mob of local men and women, provoked by false tales of child kidnapping and blood libel, caused an outbreak of violence against the local Jewish community centre which resulted in the killing of forty-two Jews.[13] Nine Poles were eventually condemned to death in connection with the pogrom (cf. Levy, 2005: 398–9).[14] The chronology of the events that took place in Jedwabne and Kielce reveals the temporal ramifications of the Holocaust as a spatial phenomenon which is part of a historical continuum to be evaluated beyond a set date; accordingly, documentary cinema has explored and memorialised the locations of these two pogroms, one of which took place before the beginning of the Final Solution in 1942 and the other over eighteen months after the liberation of the camps. *The Legacy of Jedwabne* and *Witnesses* have shed a new light on Polish anti-Semitism and revealed how the physical voids in the landscapes of the Holocaust haunt the memorialisation of anti-Semitic violence which took place before and after the phase of industrialised killing. These two films address the absences left by the Jews in Jedwabne and Kielce and, in their quest for truth, focus on the controversies surrounding the events and on the Polish struggle to recognise that anti-Semitism was a widespread force before, during and after the war. These themes are captured by means of the use of different narrative devices and modes of documentary, with both observational and expository strategies employed by the two filmmakers. *The Legacy of Jedwabne* uses the testimonies of elderly Polish witnesses, interviews with Jews who left Jedwabne before the war and with their families; *Witnesses* is composed of a number of testimonies given by Polish bystanders who still lived in Kielce at the time of filming, and who provided different viewpoints on the events that led to the pogrom. Both films are largely based on contemporary filming at the sites of the massacres, and make limited use of archival footage and photographs.[15] Grünberg's film relies on occasional use of voice-over narration to establish links between interviews, while *Witnesses* avoids the intervention of a narrator and allows the story to emerge from the words of the men and women of Kielce, thus resulting in a complex mosaic of testimonies and perspectives on the events.

When Grünberg directed *The Legacy of Jedwabne*, the pogrom had already been the subject of two documentaries directed by Agnieszka Arnold, *Gdzie mój starszy syn Kain* (*Where Is My Older Brother Cain?*, 1999) and *Sąsiedzi* (*Neighbours*, 2001). Arnold's films acknowledge the Polish involvement in the action, but it was only after they were made that the events of July 1941 were investigated by the Polish Institute of National Remembrance (Instytut Pamięci Narodowej) and the full scale of Polish responsibility made public. In the context of the debate that

Figure 1.3 *The Legacy of Jedwabne* (Slawomir Grünberg, 2005).

followed the investigation, *The Legacy of Jedwabne* reflects on its findings and acknowledges that the perpetrators of the crime were Polish inhabitants of the town and its environs inspired by the German occupiers. The film opens with an establishing shot including the Jedwabne road sign on the background of the Church of St Jacob the Apostle, and this is followed by images of the old houses of Jedwabne once inhabited by Jews (Fig. 1.3).[16] The opening scenes of the film imply both the absence of the Jews in contemporary Jedwabne, and the fact that Christianity is now the only faith practised in the former *shtetl*. Poland is introduced as a Catholic country with remnants of Jewish life embodying memories to be deciphered in the course of the process of coming to terms with an inconvenient past, with the knowledge of Polish guilt and with its impact on the present. This sequence is immediately followed by footage from a television programme reporting the demolition of the old monument commemorating the massacre, which listed only the Germans as perpetrators. The television speaker announces that a new memorial reflecting the recent findings will take its place; however, she claims that Polish men and women assisted the Germans on the day of the pogrom, whereas the investigation has proved that the killings were carried out exclusively by Poles and the German invaders did not take part in the pogrom. Rather than establishing that sense of historical accuracy associated with the use of found footage, the inclusion of this news report thus emphasises the problematic and divisive manner in which different viewpoints about the pogrom have coexisted since the end of the war and have fuelled ambiguous attempts to memorialise the event.

The built environment of Jedwabne is used throughout Grünberg's film in order to retrieve memories of the pogrom and pre-war life in the *shtetl*. For example, a series of shots of the surviving wooden houses that belonged to the Jews is accompanied by the voice-over narration of former resident Rabbi Jacob Baker and his reminiscences of the town of his youth; this sequence portrays today's Jedwabne as a quiet provincial space juxtaposed with the description of the vibrant pre-war town conjured in Baker's account. The contemporary images of the town engender that type of retrospection which is activated, as Shandler suggests, by an understanding of the *shtetl* as an organising locus for Holocaust narratives and, ultimately, as the epitome of absence (2014: 121–2). *The Legacy of Jedwabne* articulates this sense of loss while providing multiple points of view on the pogrom expressed by means of interviews with local men and women for whom the events of 1941 have different meanings. The former mayor of Jedwabne, Krzysztof Godlewski, was forced to resign because of his support for the new memorial to the victims. The local parish priest, Edward Orlowski, vehemently denies Polish involvement in the pogrom. Antosia Wyrzykowska is a religious peasant woman who hid seven Jews in two shelters built at her farm under the sheep pen, and who was savagely beaten by her neighbours when they found out what she had done; Antosia is still terrified by the thought of the repercussions her actions could have had six decades after the events. Leon Dziedzic is a former Polish resident of Jedwabne whose family saved a Jew during the pogrom, and who was later persecuted for making public his recollection of the events; in *The Legacy of Jedwabne* he meets Rabbi Baker, and together they remember the lost world of the Jewish shops and trades located on Łomżyńska Street. Regina, a Jewish woman who left Jedwabne just before the war broke out and has since lived in Buenos Aires, remembers the pre-war town with nostalgia and wonders whether her house still exists. Brothers Mieterk and Berek Olszewicz, and Berek's wife Elsa, who also live in Argentina and survived the pogrom while being sheltered by Antosia Wyrzykowska and her husband, use old photographs of their murdered relatives to provide a visual referent to their memories and their process of mourning.[17] This polyphony of testimonies articulates a reflection on guilt and responsibility inscribed in the built environment of Jedwabne, its streets and buildings, and reveals a contested landscape of memory that emerges from the process of unearthing fragments of experience. This intertwining of time and space is vocalised further in the account of the journey to Jedwabne undertaken by a group of survivors and their families on the sixtieth anniversary of the pogrom. Their visit to the town facilitates the recollections of the survivors despite the alien nature of present-day sites which are irreconcilable with their memories. In the sequence where Sara Walerstein, a former resident of Jedwabne, identifies the house where she lived in the 1930s before moving to Mexico, memories are conjured on a street that no longer belongs to her living experience.[18] With the Jewish community of Jedwabne almost completely erased, *The Legacy of Jedwabne* uses Walerstein's recollections to allow the viewer to get closer to historical truth and to access the domain of historical reality in a way that echoes Carlo Ginzburg's claim that even the voice of one single witness can be effective for this purpose (1992: 82–96).[19] The film epitomises the idea of loss while giving the task of bearing witness to the few individuals who can provide either a direct or a transgenerational connection with the events, and thus populate with memories and images the incongruous landscape of present-day Jedwabne.

Polish violence against the Jews continued after the war, aimed at those who returned from the concentration and the death camps or who emerged from hiding. Persecution was not limited to individual episodes such as the killing investigated in *Birthplace*; it included infamous pogroms, such as that which took place in Kielce in 1946 and became the subject of the investigation presented in Łoziński's *Witnesses*. Like *The Legacy of Jedwabne*, this documentary opens with a news report, in this case archival footage from *Polska Kronica Filmowa* ('Polish Film Chronicles', 1946). This newsreel condemns unequivocally the events which took place in Kielce and emphasises the status of the victims as survivors of the concentration camps, now butchered at the hands of Poles. And yet, despite this early admission of responsibility, the mosaic of testimonies gathered by Łoziński in the 1980s demonstrates that the town's memory of the Jews and of their murder remained controversial for decades. The newsreel footage is followed by a panoramic view of the city in 1987 accompanied by the sound of church bells. Łoziński introduces Kielce with street scenes filmed during a busy weekday, showing car traffic and pedestrians in the central district of the city; one of these shots is taken from the *rynek* looking towards the Cathedral Basilica of the Assumption of the Blessed Virgin Mary. As in *The Legacy of Jedwabne*, the sound of the bells and the image of the cathedral are used as narrative tropes to indicate that Kielce has become a fully Christian city with only a few surviving traces of its Jewish heritage. These scattered remains include the house at 7/9 Planty Street, where over one hundred Jews who survived the Holocaust, including the forty-two victims of the pogrom, found shelter soon after the war. Several shots of this building, filmed by Łoziński from different

Figure 1.4 *Świadkowie* (*Witnesses*, Marcel Łoziński, 1986).

angles, punctuate the film and inscribe in the present-day built environment of the city the accounts provided by the witnesses interviewed by the filmmaker (Fig. 1.4).

Witnesses uses a number of talking-head interviews with local attestants of the pogrom, including a teacher, a nurse, a shop owner, an artist, an engineer, a Polish photographer who survived Auschwitz I and a factory worker. Łoziński does not appear on film; his voice and questions are not heard, and yet his editing follows what Nichols describes as an interactive mode of documentary inasmuch as it maintains continuity between various viewpoints whose logic 'shifts to the relationship between the more fragmentary statements of the subjects in interviews' (1991: 45). On this basis, the relationship between the various testimonies recorded by Łoziński reveals different and at times discordant memories of the Jews of Planty Street, who are either remembered for wearing dark clothes, for being very rich or incredibly poor, for their envied positions in the public sector or for their being unemployed, depending on who is narrating the story. Several witnesses explain that indeed many Poles believed the Jews were using children's blood for their *matzah*. The worker also acknowledges the presence of anti-Semitism in interwar Poland, while the photographer evokes the cityscape of the 1930s and its multiculturalism as he explains that Henryk Sienkiewicz Street, which runs from the railway station to the centre of Kielce, had Jews living on one side of the street and Poles living on the other. A philologist remembers that the Jews were wealthier than the Poles and, while condemning their murderers, admits she did not like the Jews and suggests the Poles benefited from their annihilation. These testimonies are accompanied by recurring shots of the house in Planty Street, partly derelict at the time of filming, and by footage of the graves at the neglected Jewish cemetery in Kielce, with its numerous broken gravestones piled up on the ground. The juxtaposition between these images and the oral accounts of the pogroms emphasises the absence of the Jews of Kielce, their final destruction at the hands of Poles after they had survived the Nazi Holocaust. In the absence of real environments of memory, the house in Planty Street, even more so than the cemetery where Jews found a dignified resting place before the war, becomes a site of memory and, like the film itself, reveals more about the perpetual lingering of the past in the present than about the precise chronicles of the events surrounding the pogrom. Like *Birthplace*, *Witnesses* thus inscribes into specific locations the astounding horror of the murder of those who had survived the Holocaust and hints at a present where such events are not yet comprehended and absorbed in a shared history, and still contribute to raising difficult questions about the ramifications of the genocide and its aftermath in the present.

The killings in Kielce were immediately attributed to Poles acting with the support of Soviet occupation forces. Consequently, and unlike the events of Jedwabne, the local population had time to come to terms with the idea of Polish responsibility and the pogrom challenged the narrative of Polish martyrdom which was dominant after the war. However, while the testimonies included in *Witnesses* do not deny Polish responsibilities, they reveal dormant elements of anti-Semitism in Poland in the 1980s, expressed for example by the aforementioned comments of the philologist interviewed by Łoziński. In this regard, it is worth noting that in 1983, three years before the release of *Witnesses*, Józef Orlicki wrote an anti-Semitic book in which he claimed that Zionist agents caused the pogrom in order to make a case for the creation of the State of Israel, on the basis of the continuing violence against the Jews in Eastern Europe.[20] The only truth in this anti-Semitic fantasy is that more than any other event in the immediate post-war years, the pogrom in Kielce contributed to the eradication of the surviving Jewry of Poland and led to mass emigration to Israel and America. In doing so, the Kielce pogrom defies that common and complacent tendency in Holocaust narratives which has been criticised by Omer Bartov and which implies a view of the destruction of the Jews 'as a well-ordered plot, in which anti-Semitism led to Nazism, Nazism practised genocide, and both were destroyed in a spectacular, "happy" ending' (1996: 53). On the contrary, this post-war pogrom and its memorialisation redefine the Holocaust as an evolving phenomenon whose aftermath pervaded the historical consciousness of Poland in the second half of the twentieth century. Between the time of the massacre in Jedwabne and the day of pogrom in Kielce, Polish Jewry was destroyed by the Nazis and their collaborators: what remains are memories, often lost and at times regained. Documentary accounts of the events which took place in the Mazovian countryside, in the *shtetl* Jedwabne, and in the city of Kielce confront what these places had wished to do away with; they acknowledge the void left by the Holocaust and give the Poles the task of bearing witness and the duty of engaging with their own responsibility in the annihilation of the Jews. Film such as *Birthplace*, *The Legacy of Jedwabne* and *Witnesses* can contribute to the rejection of that interpretation of the Holocaust defined by Bartov as 'a well-ordered plot' and, by giving voice to discordant accounts and providing multiple points of view, can record its open-ended ramifications in time and space, its persistence in memory and its inscription in the present-day landscapes of Poland. The following chapter explores these ramifications further and investigates the interplay between the testimonies of survivors, the accounts of the bystanders and the experience of the postgeneration in the context of the *shtetlekh* Gąbin, Suchowola, Brańsk, and Luboml; as we shall see, remnants, leftovers and debris of Jewish life emerge from film archives and from the ground, and populate a cinematic landscape where temporal layers are merged and made to resonate in the process of remembering.

Notes

1. Over half the pre-war population of the *shtetl* Otwock, amounting to about 13,500 people, was Jewish. The Germans occupied the town in September 1939 and established a ghetto in November 1940. The district was fenced in 1941, and in the winter of 1942 several hundred Jews were transported to the death camp in Treblinka. The ghetto was eventually liquidated on 19 August 1942, when as many as 8,000 Jews were deported to Treblinka and to Auschwitz II-Birkenau. See Miron, *The Yad Vashem Encyclopaedia of the Ghettos During the Holocaust*, pp. 564–6.
2. Jonathan Webber's restoration of a Jewish cemetery, for example, is the subject of Simon Target's recent documentary *A Town Called Brzostek* (2014). Webber's grandfather was buried in Brzostek's cemetery before the war, and the film provides a narrative of reconciliation between the local community and the Jews who return to Poland for the consecration of the

cemetery. This film hints at the presence of anti-Semitism in Poland, and at the fact that the memorialisation of the Holocaust in towns like Brzostek has seen prejudice, atonement and nostalgia wrestling one another. It ultimately puts forward a positive vision for the future of Polish–Jewish relations.

3. Hirsch and Spitzer, '"We Would Not Have Come Without You": Generations of Nostalgia'.
4. Shandler, *Shtetl: A Vernacular Intellectual History*.
5. Kirshenblatt-Gimblett, 'Introduction'.
6. Burleigh, *The Third Reich: A New History*.
7. Steinlauf, *Bondage to the Dead*.
8. Nichols, *Representing Reality: Issues and Concepts in Documentary*, pp. 32–75.
9. He was one of over 350 Jews who were murdered by Poles in the seven months that followed the end of the war (Gilbert, *The Holocaust: The Jewish Tragedy*, p. 816).
10. One of the Polish witnesses interviewed in *Birthplace* makes the following statement: 'The Jews were scared of Poles and Germans alike. Because our people, our sons of bitches could be worse than the Germans.' When the film was released, this type of admission of national responsibility had rarely been seen in Polish cinema.
11. Lowenthal, 'Past Time, Present Place: Landscape and Memory'.
12. Levy, *Antisemitism: A Historical Encyclopaedia*. Jedwabne was occupied by the Germans in 1939 and then again in 1941, after Hitler declared war on the Soviet Union. The Jews who survived the pogrom lived in a small ghetto that was liquidated in November 1942, when they were deported to a transit ghetto and from there to Auschwitz II-Birkenau. Of a population of about 1,000 individuals, only seven Jews from Jedwabne survived the war (Miron, *The Yad Vashem Encyclopaedia*, p. 268).
13. On 1 July 1946, nine-year-old Henryk Błaszczyk set out to visit friends of his parents in Bielaki, a village located almost twenty miles from Kielce. The boy returned home after two days and, to avoid punishment, told his parents that he had been abducted by Jews. This story was reported to the police and eventually led to the deadly pogrom (Gilbert, *The Holocaust: The Jewish Tragedy*, p. 819).
14. Pogroms against the Jews had already taken place in Kielce in 1918, 1934 and 1938, and resulted in the death of eighteen Jewish men and women. Just before the war, 21,000, or one-third, of the population of Kielce was Jewish. The number grew to 30,000 in 1941 owing to the influx of Jews from the areas annexed to the Reich. The ghetto was established in March 1941; several hundred Jews from Kielce survived the war, but the great majority were deported and exterminated in Treblinka and Auschwitz II-Birkenau between 1942 and 1944 (Miron, *The Yad Vashem Encyclopaedia*, pp. 307–12).
15. For example, several photographic portraits of the victims of the pogrom are included in the closing sequence of *The Legacy of Jedwabne*.
16. Later in *The Legacy of Jedwabne*, another long shot of the church includes

in the foreground an old wooden barn whose presence and appearance are reminiscent of the site of the massacre.

17. The film is also based on expository interviews with Anna Bikont, a journalist and writer from Jedwabne who has studied the pogrom, and with Jan Gross, the author of *Neighbours*, the book that stirred the debate about the pogrom in the early 2000s (see Gross, *Neighbours*).
18. The elderly Polish couple living at that address fear that the Walersteins might be planning to make a claim to the house. This sequence reveals persisting tensions between Jews and Poles, conveyed by misconceived ideas about the return of the survivors and the imagined claims to what belonged to them or to their families before the war.
19. Ginzburg, 'Just One Witness'.
20. Orlicki, *Szkice z dziejów stosunków polsko-zydowskich*.

CHAPTER 2

Conflicting Memories in the *Shtetlekh* Gąbin, Suchowola, Brańsk and Luboml

'This is the market. This is where my grandmother sold soap in the market.'
—Jack Rubin, *Shtetl*

In his work focusing on Polish–Jewish relationships, Holocaust historian Raul Hilberg has explained that 'in the prevailing Polish view, the Jews could not, despite their protestation of loyalty to the Polish state, share the spirit and longings of the Polish people' (1993: 204).[1] During the war, this particular perspective resulted in a country divided between those who saw the deportation of the Jews as wish fulfilment and those who sensed that the Jews had to be helped. This ambiguity emerges in Holocaust documentaries that address issues of memory and loss in relation to the void left by the murdered Jews in the cultural and physical landscape of post-war Poland. The present chapter investigates the locations of five films where the testimonies given by survivors and those provided by Poles who spent the rest of their lives in the former *shtetlekh* are juxtaposed and articulated in connection to the impact of the past on present-day spaces. In *Shoah*, Claude Lanzmann visits Grabów nad Prosną, a former *shtetl* situated sixty miles south of the killing centre in Chełmno nad Nerem, and interviews local men and women who remember the Jews of Grabów and their deportation to the camp. What emerges from the filmmaker's discussion with Poles who now live in the houses left vacant by the murdered Jews is a display of anti-Semitism, ignorance and at times genuine sorrow for what happened to their neighbours during the war. This ambivalence has also characterised the more recent cinematic investigations of former *shtetlekh* which will be discussed in this chapter. A largely reconciliatory image of the Polish–Jewish relationship emerges from Jolanty Dylewskiej's *Po-lin. Okruchy pamięci* (*Po-lin. Slivers of Memory*, 2008). This documentary is based on an interplay between past and present images in a number of old *shtetlekh*, and is partly set in the town of Gąbin, which is also the location of Minna Packer's *Back to Gombin* (2002). As we shall see, Packer's film presents a more conflicted portrayal of the life shared by Jews and Poles in this *shtetl* before the war. An image of pre-war coexistence that reflects the ambiguity of Polish responses to the persecution of the Jews is also articulated in *Każdy miał swojego Żyda* (*Everyone Had Their Own Jew*, Tomasz Wisniewski, 2014), a documentary based on the memories of three elderly Polish men from Suchowola who lived with the Jews and witnessed their destruction. The fourth case study, *Shtetl* (1996), was directed by Holocaust survivor Marian Marzynski and juxtaposes Polish and Jewish testimonies in order to unlock interwar and wartime memories of Brańsk. Finally, Holocaust survivors provide testimonies, mostly filmed in remote locations outside Poland, illustrated by archival footage and present-day images of the *shtetl* Luboml in Aaron Ziegelman's *Luboml: My Heart Remembers* (2003). The personal points of view emerging from these five documentaries provide diverse reconstructions of the relationship between Poles and Jews, and their investigation aims to articulate a narrative tension between the accounts of those who stayed and the testimonies of those who left, with both overlapping memories and contrasting perspectives on Jewish life in the *shtetl* and its destruction.

According to a Yiddish legend, when the Jews fled persecution in the West and arrived in Eastern Europe in the Middle Ages they heard a voice from heaven saying *po-lin*, which in Hebrew translates as 'lodge here', and thus decided to settle in these regions and to call their new home Poland (cf. Bar-Itzhak, 2012: 167).[2] This legend provides the title of Dylewskiej's documentary *Po-lin. Slivers of Memory*, a film focusing on the testimonies of a group of elderly Poles from a number of villages located in the former regions of the Second Polish Republic.[3] The Jewish communities of the places investigated in this film shared the same fate of annihilation at the hands of the Nazis, and *Po-lin* addresses these sites of memory by juxtaposing pre-war archival footage with contemporary images of the former *shtetlekh*, including fading traces of the lost Jewish world such as gravestones, wooden houses, empty market squares and derelict synagogues. *Po-lin* thus investigates physical environments where, as Shandler has argued, 'absence, not simply of Jewish life but even of traces of its past, looms larger than presence' (2014: 104).

In a series of talking-head interviews, Polish witnesses recall various aspects of Jewish religious rituals, political parties, educational and health organisations, trade and crafts, clothing and cuisine. Additionally, an expository commentary read by Polish actor and singer Piotr Fronczewski, and based on the post-war memorial books known as *yizker-bikher*, establishes thematic links between the oral testimonies and the archival footage included in the film.[4] *Po-lin* thus adopts a polyphony of voices, as opposed to a dominant voice-over narration, which addresses the viewer in that direct way typical of the expository mode of documentary which, as Nichols has suggested, is based on the use of images as illustration in order to advance the film's argument (1991: 34). Dylewskiej's documentary provides a mosaic of testimonies and results in a detailed reconstruction of life in the *shtetlekh*, distant from the myth of a hermetic Jewish world and open to the multicultural complexity of the geographical regions that were irremediably affected by the war and the Holocaust. In this context, the accounts given by the Polish witnesses are characterised by nostalgia and longing for a time when these towns saw the allegedly peaceful coexistence of Jews and Poles, and they even emphasise the practical difficulties encountered by Poles after the war when many professions and trades associated with the Jews disappeared with them.[5]

Po-lin primarily aims to unlock and exhume memories of pre-war Jewish life by means of a consistent use of amateur films made in the 1930s by returning Jewish migrants. Between 1880 and 1924 over two million Jews emigrated from Eastern Europe to the United States and in the decade that preceded the war a number of migrants and second generation American Jews returned to Poland in order to visit the places of their youth or of their elders (Stone, 1996: 95–6).[6] These heritage journeys from the United States to Poland are reminiscent of the postmemory journeys undertaken by the second and third generations after the war and yet, whereas post-Holocaust journeys are part of a process of mourning, grieving and passing on the knowledge of the destruction of Polish Jewry, in the 1930s Polish-American Jews found a lively culture still intact though on the brink of annihilation. Many of them used 16mm cameras to capture everyday life in the *shtetlekh* and thus created what was to become a vast and eerie archive of images of what is now a long-gone world.[7] Often used in traditional expository documentaries about Jewish customs in interwar Eastern Europe such as *Image Before My Eyes* (Joshua Waletzky, 1980) and *A Yiddish World Remembered* (Andrew Goldberg, 2002), in *Po-lin* these amateur films are manipulated and integrated with a plurality of oral and written testimonies in order to compose a complex narrative which is equally concerned with long-gone customs and traditions as with the persistence of the past in the present. Dylewskiej uses these archival films as remnants of Jewish life, edits their contents and presents them in slight slow-motion accompanied by a new soundtrack mimicking the noises of marketplaces, crowded streets or playgrounds. These images and the added soundtrack are then juxtaposed with the silence and emptiness shown in the present-day footage of the sites filmed by Dylewskiej, who purposely captured these locations at quiet hours of the

Figure 2.1 *Po-lin. Okruchy pamięci* (*Po-lin. Slivers of Memory*, Jolanty Dylewskiej, 2008).

day in order to emphasise the absences that define these landscapes. For example, lively archival footage from the town of Kałuszyn filmed in 1936 is presented in opposition to the empty spaces of the town in 2008 and is accompanied by an expository commentary revealing various aspects of everyday life in the *shtetl*, including trade and festivities. Archival footage from Kolbuszowa filmed in 1930 is accompanied by the oral testimonies of Krystyna Godlewska and Mieczysław Godlewska, and shows a local band playing music in the foreground while children play in front of the camera. These images are followed by present-day footage of the old synagogue surrounded by empty streets, a crumbling trace in a landscape where absence looms upon its own representation (Fig. 2.1). In 1932, Jack Weisbord filmed lively street scenes of everyday life in Kurów with particular attention to trade and religious rituals. In *Po-lin*, this footage is combined with Witold Mikołajczyk's oral testimony about Jewish life in Kurów and juxtaposed with contemporary footage of the empty streets of the town. In this sequence, archival images of the market are followed by a panoramic view of present-day Kurów, an empty and silent place where the cawing of the crows is the only sound that can be heard. The image emerging from *Po-lin*, with its old dwellings, empty synagogues, derelict cemeteries and quiet marketplaces, is one characterised by fading debris of Jewish culture inscribed in a built environment where, as the title of the film suggests, only slivers of memory remain.

Despite the absences affecting a given place, the past is always and inevitably present; the landscapes of memory in *Po-lin* become intelligible because of the combination of the oral testimonies, the memoirs read by the narrator and the archival images. In particular, the Polish witnesses interviewed in this documentary engage with the past of their towns in order to cope with the features and the patterns of a present-day landscape that acquires meaning through a shared history. *Po-lin* thus enacts that connection with the past and its inevitability which has been described by Lowenthal as follows: 'Each scene and object is invested with a history of real or imagined involvements; their perceived identities stem from past acts and expectations. Without the past as tangible or remembered evidence we could not function' (1975: 5–6). *Po-lin* is ultimately a film about Poles having had to bear witness to the destruction of the Jews, about their subjective and at times selective reminiscences; the bystanders' nostalgia and hindsight enables the viewer to read those past landscapes by means of testimonies and archival images in ways that contribute to structuring the absences in the present, and the viewer thus becomes Lowenthal's 'new visitor', one who 'is most apt to read the past into the present' (1975: 7).

Gąbin, a small town in central Poland, is both one of the recurring sites addressed in *Po-lin* and the main location of *Back to Gombin*, a documentary filmed by daughter of Holocaust survivors Minna Packer during a postmemory journey to Central Poland.[8] Hirsch and Spitzer have argued that in the context of this type of journey, 'the location authenticates the narrative, embodies it, makes it real to the point where it threatens to re-engulf those who come to tell and to listen' (2003: 92). In Parker's film, the visit to the former *shtetl* Gąbin (Gombin in Yiddish) authenticates the postgeneration's experience of a place where the present is perpetually informed by the past. These two documentaries adopt different strategies in their use of the town as a site of memory: whereas the Gąbin sequence in *Po-lin* relies on the testimony of Polish witness Jan Borysiak, *Back to Gombin* presents a tapestry of interviews with Holocaust survivors from Gąbin, their children and grandchildren. The journey in time and space is conveyed in both films by the inclusion of contemporary images of the town juxtaposed to still photographs and archival footage from the 1930s. At first, the portraits of the town presented in *Po-lin* and *Back to Gombin* are remarkably similar as they both include accounts of the German invasion and are characterised by a sense of profound nostalgia for the lost world of Jewish Gąbin. In both instances the urban fabric of Gąbin, its streets, houses, marketplace and cemetery, are used as sites of memory in order to raise questions on the role of Jewish heritage in the history of the town. These documentaries also address Polish responsibilities in the Holocaust and pre-war tensions between Poles and Jews; but while *Po-lin* emphasises the nostalgic evocation of Jewish Gąbin made by a Polish witness, with minor hints of the widespread religious tensions, *Back to Gombin* addresses the anti-Semitic forces and the conflicts between

Jews and Poles before and during the war, as well as in the present-day landscape.

Like *Po-lin*, *Back to Gombin* uses the amateur film taken in 1937 by Sam Rafel, a Polish-American Jew who founded the New Jersey and New York Gombin Societies after the war. In *Po-lin*, Jan Borysiak's reminiscences of pre-war Gąbin are accompanied by Rafel's amateur footage of Jewish children playing in the streets and other daily activities, including images of the Thursday market and a religious function at the local cemetery. The present-day images of the town include a long shot of Borysiak standing in the middle of a car park and a panning shot from left to right revealing an empty and apparently lifeless town. This is edited with a similar shot which was filmed by Rafel in 1937 and which continues the panning motion from left to right in order to reveal a bustling townscape crowded with Jewish men, women and children. Borysiak discusses the German invasion and the burning of the synagogue, the establishment of the ghetto and its liquidation. In particular, he remembers a Monday afternoon when the last group of Jews was gathered on Kutnowska Street, loaded on large trucks and deported to the death camp in Chełmno. His testimony also establishes a thematic connection between personal memories and archival images when his account of the time he spent playing with Jewish children is juxtaposed with Rafel's footage of young Jewish boys playing on the streets of Gąbin in 1937. These juxtapositions, and more broadly the use of archival footage in both films, aim at reversing the Nazis' attempt to destroy every record that could testify to the existence of the Gąbin community annihilated in the Holocaust.

Minna Packer's film focuses on a group of fifty children of survivors from Gąbin and on their journey to the sites of a labour camp in Konin and the death camp in Chełmno, to Warsaw and finally to the *shtetl* of their parents and its market square (Fig. 2.2). As in *Birthplace*, the marketplace embodies nostalgia for a lost world and harrowing memories of destruction as it is presented as the former core of a Jewish economy, and also as the place where Jews were assembled by the Germans before being sent to the labour and death camps. In *Back to Gombin* the present-day interviews with Holocaust survivors and with members of the second and third generations are here juxtaposed with Rafel's amateur film, an archival contribution which provides a contextual framework and visual referent to the attempt to conjure the memories of the destruction of the *shtetl*. This site-specific connection between past and present is made explicit at the beginning of the film, when one of the survivors explores Gąbin with a hand-drawn map of the town and seeks the location of his family house in Moniuszki Street, previously Garbarska Street. A close-up of

Figure 2.2 *Back to Gombin* (Minna Packer, 2002).

the map briefly fades into a shot filmed by Rafael showing a small group of Jews walking in Moniuszki Street in 1937. This juxtaposition reveals the centrality of the provincial space of Gąbin to the journey portrayed by Packer and to her use of locations according to Hirsch's description of postmemory as a mode of 'questioning, resistance, and contestation' (1997: 7). This mode is articulated in *Back to Gombin* by the use of archival photographs and footage, providing the journey to the *shtetl* with a sense of pastness and thus resisting the annihilation to which even the memory itself of the Jews was meant to succumb.

The survivors interviewed by Parker report nostalgic memories of pre-war Gąbin, with references to the Jewish school, the local library, the beautiful wooden synagogue and the local cinema. And yet, memories of the cultural and ethnic tensions between Jews and Poles are also central to these testimonies. Chana Guyer, a Gąbin survivor who was living in Detroit at the time of filming, remembers that a Jewish girl converted to Christianity in order to marry a Polish man and that local Jews threw stones at her while she was going to church. She also remembers the emergence of anti-Semitism in the interwar years: 'They never liked the Jews. A Jewish girl had a store; a crowd formed shouting "Don't buy from the Jews, they are a cancer." I went closer, where my neighbour stood and said "Yashek, are you right? You have known her for so many years and you say these things!" So he said "Chana, if I don't do this, they will kill me too."' Similarly, Geoffrey Greenwood, a descendant of a Jewish family from Gąbin, expresses his concern regarding anti-Semitism in Poland and claims that the 'good Poles' were a minority and that the Polish responsibilities in the persecution of the Jews were very significant. This is confirmed by George Zolna, a Gąbin survivor who was interviewed by Packer in New Jersey and claimed that the Poles actively contributed to the destruction of the Jewish cemetery during the war. Anti-Semitism is also presented by Packer as a problem affecting present-day Gąbin in a sequence where Holocaust survivor Itzhak Zielonka identifies the house that belonged to his family and visits the yard, where he is met by the current occupiers and their neighbours' aggressive anti-Semitic comments. Nevertheless, the film suggests that anti-Semitism and fears over property claims are only the expression of a small proportion of the inhabitants of the town. This view is supported by Zbigniew Lukaszewski, the president of a local history association, who leads the visit to the streets of Gąbin and, while he acknowledges the increased tensions between Jews and Poles in the interwar period, explains that his association has always recognised the importance of Jewish heritage in the history of the town. Ultimately, *Back to Gombin* articulates that particular sense of ambivalence in Holocaust documentaries characterised by the contrasting roles of saviours, bystanders or perpetrators played by Poles, and by the persistence of racial and religious tensions into the present; the film thus reveals ramifications of the events of the 1940s beyond their temporal and spatial boundaries, with unresolved narratives still affecting the present and the lives of a postgeneration for whom the *shtetl* is a foreign country.

The history of Gąbin is pervaded by the problematic stance of the Poles towards the persecution of their Jewish neighbours, and defined by their response to anti-Semitic violence. The complexities of Polish–Jewish relationships are also exemplified by the events which took place in Suchowola, a town in north-eastern Poland, during the Polish–Soviet War (1919–21).[9] In September 1920, riots against the Jews erupted on the eve of Yom Kippur and resulted in looting, physical assaults and the killing of three Jews at the hands of Polish soldiers and civilians. On this occasion many Poles helped the Jews and were deeply shocked to hear about the murder of their neighbours (cf. Khevin Goldberg, 1959: 160).[10] The reaction to the Yom Kippur pogrom anticipated the local response to the captivity and the extermination of the Jewish community of the town during the Second World War, when a number of Poles contributed to the Nazis' effort to capture and kill the Jews of Suchowola, while others helped their neighbours to hide in the surrounding fields or to survive in the ghetto. These events are accounted for in *Everyone Had Their Own Jew*, a documentary directed by Tomasz Wisniewski and based on the testimonies of Edward Turel, Jan Guzowski and Edward Szkilondz, three Poles from Suchowola who witnessed the events that took place there during the war. In the opening sequence of the film, a map of the region introduces their testimonies and illustrates Suchowola's location thirty miles north of Białystok and thirty-five miles west of Grodno, two cities with large Jewish communities where ghettos were established by the Nazis in 1941. Reminiscent of Claude Lanzmann's investigation of the void left in the town of Grabów by the Jews murdered in Chełmno, *Everyone Had Their Own Jew* is a site-specific exploration of a former *shtetl* carried out by Poles, with no survivors or members of the postgeneration returning to Suchowola; its focus is nevertheless on the Jews of this town, on their fate and their absence, and is articulated by those who spent the rest of their lives in this irremediably altered place.

In its use of site-specific testimonies according to that culturally enabling aspect called by Andreas Huyssen 'a potential antidote to the freezing of memory into the one traumatic image' (1993: 258),[11] *Everyone Had Their Own Jew* provides a narrative of loss by means of a series of documentary practices. Wisniewski avoids the use of voice-over narration and attempts to revive memory by means of archival photographs of interwar Suchowola and surviving documents, including census records and German public orders. The archival images of the town before the war are included in the film for the purpose of remembrance and commemoration, and in the attempt to fill absences in a present-day landscape where only the faintest traces of Jewish life are extant. In *Everyone Had Their Own Jew*, this archival material is juxtaposed with present-day footage of the town in a series of visual and temporal associations that recall those seen in *Po-lin* and *Back to Gombin*. For example, when the witnesses recall that only Jews owned trucks, archival photographs of the town's Jews and their vehicles are juxtaposed with present-day footage of light traffic in Suchowola; this thematic association thus provides a visual referent to the emptiness which followed the annihilation of the Jewish community. As the three men talk about a time of peaceful co-existence between Jews and Poles and provide a vibrant picture of Jewish life in the market square of Suchowola, which before the war was almost entirely Jewish, Wisniewski's camera explores this site, now empty and deprived of remnants of Jewish life.[12]

Beside the sense of loss articulated by these juxtapositions, the film also addresses the ways in which the past pervades the present and is still vivid in the eyes of witnesses whose testimonies contribute to bridging the chronological gap between the war and the time of filming. Accordingly, the testimonies of Turel, Guzowski and Szkilondz contribute to sustaining what, in relation to the monumentalisation of the sites of the

Holocaust, Huyssen defines as a 'tension between the numbing totality of the Holocaust and the stories of individual victims, families, communities' (1993: 260). In a series of expository interviews, these witnesses provide a lively map of the town in the interwar period and recall the precise locations and the names of the Jewish families that lived near the church, the marketplace and surrounding streets. The witnesses' accounts are provoked by direct questions typical of the participatory mode of documentary, and yet Wisniewski's voice is not heard and the testimonies appear to emerge spontaneously as the film shifts back and forward from present-day interviews to archival photographs.

Everyone Had Their Own Jew pays particular attention to the built environment of Suchowola, with a significant number of old photographs of Jewish synagogues and schools juxtaposed with present-day shots of sites where these buildings were either demolished, converted into private homes or left to stand derelict. Images of Jewish men, women and schoolchildren punctuate the film, emphasising the void by providing an answer to what Huyssen has discussed as the necessity of making the Holocaust 'palpable not just by focusing on the sites of extermination but on the life-worlds of those murdered in the camps' (1993: 259). In the absence of survivors, these images do not serve the purpose of establishing a familial connection with those who provide the testimonies; on the contrary, they are visual referents of what was erased during the Holocaust. In this context, Turel, Guzowski and Szkilondz recall with affection their Jewish neighbours and friends while they also acknowledge the role played by other Poles in the Holocaust, and the extent to which anti-Semitism affected everyday life in the town. The witnesses remember the arrival of an anti-Semitic priest in 1937 and the boycott of Jewish shops that took place in the following year, accompanied by aggression against Jews and acts of vandalism towards their properties at the hands of Polish youth. Anti-Semitic newspapers were also distributed, and gave credit to the claims that all Polish problems were caused by the Jews. During the war, as the three witnesses recall, the Polish auxiliary police, the *Schutzmannschaft*, which was made up of just five Poles, helped the Germans to establish the local ghetto and actively contributed to the deportations and killings. A particularly violent episode of Polish collaborationism, echoing the events which took place in Jedwabne, saw the murder of a number of Jews in a local barn set ablaze. While several Poles participated in this pogrom, others smuggled food into the ghetto for the starving Jews and put their own lives at risk in order to save their neighbours.

The quest for remnants of Jewish life takes Turel, Guzowski and Szkilondz to the site of the old wooden synagogue, which was taken apart

Figure 2.3 *Każdy miał swojego Żyda* (*Everyone Had Their Own Jew*, Tomasz Wisniewski, 2014).

by the Jews under German orders in 1941. Its absence from present-day Suchowola is one of the most conspicuous voids in the built environment of the town. A series of photographs of the synagogue in the 1930s is followed by footage filmed by Wisniewski on the same site: the building is gone, while Saint Peter and Saint Paul's Church can still be seen in the background (Fig. 2.3). This juxtaposition effectively provides a visual referent to the destruction of the Jews of Suchowola and the places they inhabited, while emphasising the Christian identity of the present-day town. The itinerary followed by the witnesses continues to the stone building of a Jewish prayer house which was used as a gym after the war and, although derelict, is still standing; a comparison with an old photograph reveals the disappearance of the Star of David from the building. Archival photographs are thus called on to integrate the landscape emerging from present-day filming and to reveal and identify the disappearing traces of Jewish Suchowola. Although the viewer does not see the camps nor the immediate aftermath of the war, images of *before* are here intrinsically connected with mental images *during* and *after* the event; in this and in the other documentaries investigated here, archival images cannot be insulated from the anonymous images of the persecution, the camps and the mass graves.

In this absence of archival referents of the killings, the exploration of Suchowola continues to the sites where the destruction took place. Guzowski walks over the bridge on the Olszanka River, where many Jews were drowned, and leads the filmmaker to the site of the ghetto between Augustowska Street, Sadowa Street, Sportowa Street and Switokrzyska Street. Guzowski remembers a ghetto overcrowded with Jews from the town and several other villages in the district, and shows the sites of the main gate to the ghetto and the house of the ghetto commissioner, which is still standing as a community centre. The present-day location is juxtaposed with archival images of the ghetto and of German posters threatening persecution for anyone prepared to provide help, food or shelter to the Jews. During this time, the Jews were also forced to destroy their cemetery and use the gravestones to pave the road to Grodno; *Everyone Had Their Own Jew* reveals fragments of gravestones with inscriptions in Hebrew as part of the cobbled pavement, another faint trace of the life that was destroyed during the Holocaust. Turel explains that before the war, fearful of ghosts, Poles did not visit the Jewish cemetery. Today, Suchowola is populated by the ghosts of its past, and *Everyone Had Their Own Jew* reveals the emptiness left behind by the Jews who were murdered at Treblinka and portrays another landscape made of absences and scattered remains, a few wooden houses and derelict brick buildings. In the closing sequences of the film, present-day footage of children playing in a local park is juxtaposed with Guzowski's account of children playing in the mud in the poorest district of the town near the bridge on the Olszanka River, and with an archival photograph of the Jewish children who were destined to die in Treblinka. The final scene of film takes us from Suchowola to the site of this death camp, and includes a medium shot of the Suchowola memorial stone. This is the place where most of the Jews of Suchowola met their deaths, having witnessed the betrayal of many of their neighbours as well as the destruction of their cemetery, their synagogue, their homes and their world.

Like *Everyone Had Their Own Jew*, Marian Marzynski's *Shtetl* reveals Polish attitudes towards the Jews which, as Raul Hilberg suggests, are 'embedded in a constellation of pre-war sentiments that ranged from tolerance to animosity' (1993: 203). However, whereas *Everyone Had Their Own Jew* relies on Polish witnesses, *Shtetl* is based on the accounts provided by two Jews on a visit to Brańsk, their ancestral *shtetl* located about one hundred miles south of Suchowola. Unlike Wisniewski, Marzynski is more concerned with the ways in which past relationships between Poles and Jews still inform the present than with a detailed reconstruction of the events which took place in the *shtetl*. The filmmaker himself is a Holocaust survivor, and most members of his family were deported from the Warsaw Ghetto and the *shtetl* Łęczyca, eighty-two miles west of the capital, to the death camps. He returned to Łęczyca in 1969 but could not pursue his investigation into a familial past: 'When I started asking questions about those in my family who were killed and those who betrayed them, I couldn't take it. I decided never to return to my *shtetl*. I left for America with the image of *shtetl* life frozen in time. It smelled of death.' And yet, Marzynski returned to Łęczyca in 1981 during the filming of his documentary *Return to Poland* (which will be discussed in Chapter Four), and *Shtetl* opens with the footage from this earlier documentary, which shows Marynski walking on the streets of the village followed by a hand-held camera. According to the filmmaker, that visit failed to establish a more intimate connection between past and present. The expedition to Brańsk can thus be seen as an attempt to enter the haunted world of Marzynski's ancestors by vicariously living the exploration carried out by American-born Nathan Kaplan, whose parents moved from Brańsk to the United States before the war, and Jack Rubin, a Holocaust survivor from Brańsk who was based in Baltimore at the time of filming.[13] Marzynski confirms this reading of the film in his voice-over commentary: 'I couldn't face the memories of my own family's *shtetl*. I have adopted Kaplan's Brańsk as my own.' For the filmmaker, the recovery of memories bound to pre-war Jewish life is no longer a familial errand, and in *Shtetl* it becomes a shared experience where a specific town is called to stand in for all the *shtetlekh* annihilated by the Nazis.

In the course of two visits to Brańsk, Marzynski, Kaplan and Rubin seek those elderly Poles who gave shelter to the Jews as well as those who reported them to the Germans. They are guided by Zbigniew Romaniuk, a young local historian who devotes his time to the study of Brańsk's Jewish heritage. Travelling in time and space is a theme made explicit in the opening sequence of *Shtetl*, which includes a series of scenes filmed on the train and on the bus bringing Marzynski and Kaplan to Brańsk; the investigation begins in these scenes, during which Marzynski's questions about the Jews of Brańsk addressed to other passengers are met with reticence. In the former *shtetl*, Marzynski discovers a site of intrigue, doubt, unresolved narratives, lies and half-truths regarding the Polish involvement in the persecution of the Jews, hiding beneath the quiet surface of the town's small community. *Shtetl* also focuses on the hostility experienced by Romaniuk for his interest in the local history of the Jews: anti-Semitic tensions emerge from the comments made by witnesses who resent the wealth of many Jews, claiming they were responsible for their own plight because they lived in segregated communities and owned all businesses in the town. From this ambivalent context emerges a place that for Kaplan and Rubin, as Jeffrey Shandler suggests, becomes 'the locus of the destruction of their fathers' cultural world' (2014: 112); but the film also reveals that trades and businesses in the marketplace were often entirely run by Jewish women, and Brańsk is thus the locus of the destruction of their mothers', as well as their fathers', cultural world. Within this cultural context, Rubin's quest is for the memories of the *shtetl* of his childhood, while Kaplan, who was born in the United States, is chasing memories of a place that has until then only existed in the stories he heard from his parents as a small boy in Chicago. As they visit Brańsk on their individual trips these men can observe that several pre-war wooden houses are still intact, but the five synagogues that stood there before the war, the bathhouse or *mikvah*, and other buildings associated with the Jewish community of the town were demolished during and after the war. For Kaplan and Rubin, the challenge is thus given by the ways in which Brańsk changed in the course of fifty years, by its absences, by the almost total lack of traces of the town's Jewish past. And yet, as Kaplan notes in his journal, the location authenticates the processes of memory: 'Brańsk is no longer a hidden world to me. I am touching the places my parents touched. I walk on the ground they walked on.'

Of primary importance amongst the locations explored by Kaplan is Brańsk's marketplace. The use of the market square as a defining site of memory – which has already been discussed with a focus on films such as *Birthplace* and *Back to Gombin*, and to which I will return in the next chapter – is a powerful recurring trope in Holocaust travel documentaries. In Marzynski's *Shtetl*, the marketplace in Brańsk emerges from memory as a locus closely connected with the erased Jewish community of the town; here, echoing the accounts provided by Suchowola's witnesses in *Everyone Had Their Own Jew*, Marzynski's Polish guide explains that 'in the market square, all the houses belonged to the Jews. In those houses, Jewish tailors, shoemakers, bakers, and sellers of fancy goods had their shops.' Kaplan walks in the marketplace and connects the childhood stories he heard from his relatives with his present-day experience of the site: 'This is the market. This is where my grandmother sold soap in the market. This is the market where my grandmother sold soap' (Fig. 2.4). Rubin's family had a goose farm and they sold their animals at the market. Marzynski explains that the Monday morning market was the only place where Jews interacted with Poles, and he takes Rubin to see the place. Unlike Suchowola's marketplace, Brańsk's is bustling with activity and livestock is still traded here. Rubin's memories are also bound to the marketplace, to the place where he started working at the age of sixteen; after forty-five years he returns to the *rynek* and immediately runs into Polish acquaintances, including a farmer who used to work for his father's business. In Brańsk's marketplace, memory is seized by history and has

Figure 2.4 *Shtetl* (Marian Marzynski, 1996).

crystallised at the moment of the goose boy's return to the *shtetl*. This encounter is defined by the experience of an alien present, and yet, as Jeffrey Shandler suggests, the visit to Brańsk is ultimately articulated as an exploration of 'the emblematic locus of a personal quest, whether mourning the loss of family and community, addressing crimes of the past, reconciling with one's elders, or providing one's children with moral edification' (2014: 111).

Like Rubin, Kaplan and Marzynski, other survivors and members of the postgeneration engaged with personal quests and with a mythical memory of the *shtetl* which, in the process of the exploration of the present-day sites, is grounded in the alien reality of those spaces that used to be the core of Eastern European Jewish life. Documentary films have addressed the investigations made by survivors in the former *shtetlekh* in relation to spaces where the history and memory of the Jews is inscribed in a built environment deprived of visible traces. Among these spaces, as we have seen, the marketplace emerges as the core of the *shtetlekh* and as one of the key sites where the negotiation between memory and history takes shape. Like Marzynski's *Shtetl*, *Luboml: My Heart Remembers* juxtaposes the past and the present of a market square in the context of a return journey to a small town whose Jewish community was annihilated during the war. This documentary was directed by Aaron Ziegelman, a former resident of the *shtetl* Luboml, a town now located in western Ukraine, who migrated to the United States with his mother and sister in 1938. It is composed of interviews with survivors, archival photographs and amateur films. [14] As it aims at conjuring an image of Jewish life in pre-war Luboml (or Libivne in Yiddish), *Luboml: My Heart Remembers* opens and closes with two sequences filmed at the site where 4,000 Jews from Luboml and other villages were executed in 1942. Here, standing by the memorial erected after the war, Ziegelman and Abe Getman, another former resident, pray for those who were killed and buried there. Between these two scenes, the film uses interviews in an expository mode in order to introduce the viewer to various cultural, religious, familial and social aspects of pre-war life in the *shtetl* Luboml. As Ziegelman's camera captures old wooden houses, empty squares and the town's cobbled streets, the voices of the witnesses provide testimonies remotely from their homes in the USA and are interspersed with a narration that connects distant site-specific memories of a world on the brink of annihilation.

The empty spaces of the *shtetl* Luboml are populated in Ziegelman's documentary by the inclusion of photographs of the Jews of the town taken in the 1920s and the 1930s. Accompanied by voice-over testimonies, these images of familial life and private spaces were taken to the United States by those who had the chance to migrate before the beginning of the Second World War. The photographs are framed by a familial gaze in a way that, as Hirsch suggests, 'situates human subjects in the ideology, the mythology, of the family as institution and projects a screen of familial myths between camera and subject' (1997: 11). The resulting juxtaposition of past images and present-day sites such as the marketplace thus defines the processes of memorialisation of family life in the *shtetl*, and has the potential to inform the transmission of knowledge to the postgeneration. In particular, the opposition between memories and present-day reality is channelled by the filmmaker in a sequence evoking Marzynski and Kaplan's exploration of the marketplace in Brańsk, which shows Ziegelman and Getman on a visit to the site of the *shtetl*'s market square. The place is introduced by archival photographs from the 1920s representing a busy market square in all its bustling activity, its traders, peasants, produce and livestock. As in Brańsk, the marketplace consisted mostly of Jewish businesses, and the association of the area with the local Jewish community was also exemplified by the presence of the Great Synagogue facing the square. As the camera pans on details from these photographs, the archival images fade into a map of Luboml which provides the exact location of the marketplace. These inserts are accompanied by the voice-over testimonies of Lillian Chanales, Moshe Shalev and

Victor Gershengorn, three survivors living in the USA. They recall that all the streets in the town ran into the marketplace, where the *shtetl*'s life was organised, and that every Monday a great number of farmers and traders from the region gathered in Luboml. On these days, the survivors explain, the square was incredibly crowded and the noise of vendors and livestock could be deafening. Archival footage of the place reinforces the idea of the marketplace as the centre of life in the town and shows stores, workshops and even a cinema located on a site characterised by intense activity taking place every day of the week except for Saturday. The alien reality of the present-day space is articulated in the sequence where Ziegelman, accompanied by Getman, walks on the site of the marketplace while holding in his hands an old photograph of it taken in the 1920s (Fig. 2.5). This juxtaposition reveals a place that has changed beyond recognition, where emptiness and silence have replaced the hustle and bustle of the image of the market projected by the survivors' memories. *Luboml: My Heart Remembers* thus uses testimony and archival material to convey the importance of the marketplace and then cuts abruptly to a present perpetually affected by the devastating impact that the Holocaust has had on the places once inhabited by the Jews. Past and present wrestle

Figure 2.5 *Luboml: My Heart Remembers* (Aaron Ziegelman, 2003).

one another in Luboml, as well as in Gąbin, Suchowola and Brańsk, four former *shtetlekh* whose cinematic exploration has revealed the lingering of the Holocaust in those present-day landscapes that once saw everyday Jewish life and its final destruction.

In the following chapter, the interplay between past and present in the cinematic images of the *shtetlekh* Eishyshok, Delatyn, Opatów, Zdunska Wola, Urzejowice and Pińczów will be articulated, with a particular focus on a theme and a space already introduced in this and the previous chapter: the workings of postmemory and the significance of the marketplace.

Notes

1. Hilberg, *Perpetrators Victims Bystanders.*
2. See Bar-Itzhak, 'A Materialised Settlement'.
3. These towns are now within the borders of Poland (Gąbin, Kałuszyn, Kock, Kolbuszowa, Kozienice, Kurów, Raniżów, Sędziszów Małopolski, Sejny, Skierniewice, Sokołów Małopolski, Tykocin, Tyszowce, Zaręby Kościelne, the Kazimierz district in Kraków and the Bałuty district in Łódź), Belarus (Borysław/Boryslav, Nowogródek/Navahrudak, Skidel/Skidzyel and Słonim/Slonim), and Ukraine (Bolechów/Bolekhiv and Gródek Jagielloński/Horodok). These notes include past and present names of places now located in Ukraine or Belarus.
4. The memoirs used in *Po-lin. Slivers of Memory* include the following titles: Jack Ziklin (ed.), *Gombin: dos lebn un umkum fun a yidisch shtetl in Polyn* ('Gombin: The Life and Destruction of a Jewish Town in Poland'), New York: Gombin Society, 1969; Szalom Chmiel and Załman Drezner (eds), *Księga Żydów Ostrołęckich* ('The book of the Jews of Ostrolenka'), Tel Aviv: Oficyna Art & Archeology, 2004; Z. N. Dorfman, N. Lawa, Z. Rumianek and Moshe Shtarkman (eds), *Le-zikaron olam; die Zaromber yidn voszayen umgekumen al kidesh-hashem* ('For Eternal Remembrance: The Jews of Zaręby Kościelne'), New York: United Zaromber Relief, 1947; *Ostrovtse; geheylikt dem ondenk . . . fun Ostrovtse* ('Ostrovtse; dedicated to the memory of Ostrovtse'), Buenos Aires: Former Residents of Ostrovtse and Vicinity in Argentina, 1949; I. M. Biderman (ed.), *Pinkas Kolbishov* ('Kolbuszowa Memorial Book'), New York: United Kolbushover, 1971; Alexander Harkavy (ed.), *Pinkas Navaredok* ('Nowogródek Memorial Book'), Tel Aviv: Navaredker Committee in Israel, 1963; Kalman Lichtenstein (ed.), *Pinaks Slonim* ('Słonim Memorial Book'), Former Residents of Slonim: Tel Aviv: 1962–79; Y. Zipper (ed.), *Pinkas Tishovits* ('Tyszowce Memorial Book'), Tel Aviv: Association of Former Residents of Tiszowic in Israel, 1970; Daniyel Leybl (ed.), *Sefer Dembits* ('Book of Debica'), Tel Aviv: Irgun yots'e Dembits be-Yiśra'el, 1960; A. Shamri and Sh. Soroka (eds), *Sefer Kaluszyn: geheylikt der khorev gevorener kehile* ('The Memorial Book of Kaluszyn'), Tel Aviv: Former Residents of

Kaluszyn in Israel, 1961; J. Perlow (ed.), *Sefer Skierniewice* ('The Book of Skierniewice'), Tel Aviv: Former Residents of Skierniewice in Israel, 1955; Moshe Grossman (ed.), *Yisker-bukh Koriv; sefer yizkor, matsevet zikaron la-ayaratenu Koriv* ('Yiskor Book in Memoriam of Our Hometown Kurow', Tel Aviv: Former Residents of Kurów in Israel, 1955; Shimon Kanc (ed.), *Yisker-bukh tsum fareybikn dem ondenk fun der khorev-gevorner yidisher kehile Ryki* ('A Memorial to the Community of Ryki, Poland'), Tel Aviv: Ryki Society in Israel, 1973; Sh. Tsesler (ed.), *Zabludow yisker-bukh* ('Yiskor Book in Memoriam of Zabłudów'), Buenos Aires: Zabludowo Book Committee, 1961.

5. Polish witnesses include Józefa Dąbrowska (Tykocin), Jerzy Srzednicki, Helena Warakomska (Sejny), Władysław Pożarowszczyk (Kock), Jan Borysiak (Gąbin), Krystyna Godlewska, Mieczysław Godlewska (Kolbuszowa), Witold Mikołajczyk (Kurów), Zofia Grudzińska (Nowogródek), Franciszek Partyka (Raniżów), Weronika Jagoda, Teresa Jasińska (Sędziszów Małopolski), Michał Darocha, Teresa Drapała, Janina Nowak, Bronisława Piersiak (Sokołów Małopolski), Leonard Dębkowski, Zdzisław Żebrowski (Zaręby Kościelne).
6. Stone, 'Jewish Immigration from Poland Before World War Two'.
7. Several films have survived and are preserved at the National Centre for Jewish Film (Waltham, MA), YIVO Institute for Jewish Research (New York), Slonim Jews' Association (Tel Aviv), and Yad Vashem (Jerusalem), among other archives. Footage used in *Po-lin* includes amateur films taken in Bolechów (1935), Borysław (Josef Waldman, 1933), Gąbin (Sam Rafel, 1937), Gródek Jagielloński (David Shapiro, 1933), Kałuszyn (1936), Kraków – Kazimierz (Moshe Eisner, 1935), Kolbuszowa (1930), Kurów (Jack Weisbord, 1932), Łódź – Bałuty (1930), Nowogródek (Aleksander Harkavi, 1931), Raniżów (1930), Sędziszów Małopolski (Sidney Herbst, 1935), Skidel (1930), Skierniewice (1930), Słonim (Lewady, 1929), Sokołów Małopolski (1930), Tyszowce (1933), and Zaręby Kościelne (1930).
8. Before the war, half of Gąbin's population, about 2,300 people, were Jewish. The town was occupied by the Germans in September 1939; a ghetto was established early in 1940 and liquidated in May 1942. Almost the entire Jewish population of Gąbin perished in Chełmno, Auschwitz II-Birkenau and local labour camps (Miron, *The Yad Vashem Encyclopaedia*, pp. 203–4).
9. Over 1,500 Jews lived in Suchowola before the war – about half of the overall population of the town. The Germans occupied Suchowola in June 1941 and established a ghetto at the end of that year. Along with more than 3,500 Jews from local villages who had been brought to the ghetto, the Jews of Suchowola were deported to Treblinka in November 1942 and murdered by the Nazis (Miron, *The Yad Vashem Encyclopaedia*, pp. 773–4).
10. Goldberg, 'The Riots of the Eve of Yom Kippur', p. 159.
11. Huyssen, 'Monument and Memory in a Postmodern Age'.
12. Additionally, archival photographs from the 1930s show the marketplace

and its Jewish traders in order to convey the absences which pervade the cinematic images of the old *shtetl*.

13. Before the war, over two-thirds of the population of Brańsk was Jewish – about 2,200 people – and the town had institutions such as a Tarbut Hebrew School, a Talmud Torah and Batei Midrash. The ghetto was established by the Nazis in July 1941 and liquidated in November 1942. While a number of Jews managed to hide in the local forest, the remaining Jewish population of the town was transferred to Białystok and deported to the death camp in Treblinka. After the liquidation, about seventy Jews who had managed to hide in the ghetto were shot in Brańsk's Jewish cemetery (Miron, *The Yad Vashem Encyclopaedia*, pp. 72–3).
14. Before the war, ninety per cent of the population of Luboml was Jewish (c. 3,500 people). The Germans occupied the town in September 1939 and again in June 1941. The ghetto was established in December 1941 and liquidated in October 1942. Almost all the Jews of Luboml were murdered in the forests near the town by the Germans and their Ukrainian collaborators (Miron, *The Yad Vashem Encyclopaedia*, pp. 426–7).

CHAPTER 3

The Marketplaces of Postmemory in the *Shtetlekh* Eishyshok, Delatyn, Opatów, Zdunska Wola, Urzejowice and Pińczów

> 'For as long as I can remember I have had nightmares and relived things that happened before I was born in a place I had never seen.'
>
> — Debbie Goodstein, *Voices from the Attic*

The acquisition of knowledge and the exhumation of memories by means of site-specific explorations is central to the documentaries discussed in the previous chapters. In Packer's *Back to Gombin*, this transmission is articulated in terms of postmemory, with survivors and members of the postgeneration engaged in a visit to the ancestral *shtetl* aimed at unlocking painful memories of the Holocaust. In the present chapter, this process will be investigated in the context of a series of travel documentaries that use spaces such as market squares, cemeteries and synagogues in former *shtetlekh* as sites of postmemory. This chapter is divided into two parts, the first of which discusses *There Once Was a Town* (Jeffrey Bieber, 2000), *Paint What You Remember* (Slawomir Grünberg, 2009) and *Return to My Shtetl Delatyn* (Willy Lindwer, 1992) in relation to processes of postmemory; in particular, it addresses the historical importance of the marketplace as the place of the encounter between Poles and Jews and, in continuity with the argument introduced in the previous chapter, it focuses on the juxtaposition between archival images of the bustling marketplaces of the past and present-day footage of these locations.

The second half of the chapter is concerned with the intertwining of postmemory and individual and familial responses to the righteous actions of the Poles during the Holocaust. The memories of the pogroms in Jedwabne and Kielce, as well the persistence of anti-Semitism in post-war Poland, are a reminder of the active participation of Poles in the destruction of the Jews. As we already know, films such as *Birthplace*, *Witnesses*, *The Legacy of Jedwabne* and *Shtetl* have addressed such questions in connection with a series of site-specific events and their aftermath. Documentary cinema has also recorded return journeys to the *shtetl* where survivors and members of the postgenerations aim at expressing their gratitude to those Polish peasants who risked their own lives to save the Jews. This particular role played by Poles as saviours of their Jewish neighbours during the Holocaust will be investigated with a focus on three key case studies: *So Many Miracles* (Katherine Smalley and Vic Sarin, 1987), *Voices from the Attic* (Debbie Goodstein, 1988) and *Hiding and Seeking: Faith and Tolerance after the Holocaust* (Menachem Daum and Oren Rudavsky, 2002). These documentaries provide three accounts of cinematic journeys to ancestral villages where members of the second and third generations are called to question the place of Poland in their own heritage, and to recognise the debts of their families towards those Poles to whom their parents and grandparents owe their survival. These postmemory journeys will take us from the *shtetl* to the most remote countryside, to the farms and barns where Jews found shelter during the war and from which they emerged after the conflict in an irremediably altered post-war landscape.

Postmemory, according to Marianne Hirsch, connects past and present in a way that is mediated by imagination and not by recall (2008: 108–9). Film can record this process as it emerges from family journeys to the sites where Jews went into hiding, and can thus be discussed as a powerful tool for the negotiations of memory and trauma from the generation that recalls to the one that imagines. The processes of postmemory in these journeys allow nostalgia for the old Jewish *shtetlekh* to be experienced vicariously by those who were not there, by that postgeneration for whom the ideal of the *shtetl* is mediated by the act of remembrance of their parents and their grandparents. Equally mediated, the memory of the destruction of that Jewish world is also at the centre of an understanding of postmemory as an act of transmission and acquisition of knowledge. As Eva Hoffman has argued, several layers of mediation are required by those who did not live through the Holocaust in order to receive its knowledge; as she reflects in writing on her own second-generation identity, Hoffman has thus suggested that 'the memories – not memories but emanations – of wartime experiences kept erupting in flashes of imagery; in abrupt but broken refrains' (2004: 9).[1] These images, she continues, are being passed on to the postgeneration and, in particular, to the second generation by those who were there, the survivors of the Nazis' attempt to eradicate Jewry from Europe (2004: 178–87). Images of a long-lost life in the *shtetlekh* and horrific chronicles of death in the camps and the forests of Eastern Europe constitute an inner landscape that, according to Hoffman, belongs to the second generation's 'primary geography and location in the world' (2004: 194). This inner landscape is given a physical referent by the postgeneration's exploration of the sites of the Final Solution. Hoffman, herself the daughter of Holocaust survivors, visited her ancestral village of Załośce in today's Ukraine and explained that such visits can serve the purpose of anchoring the mediated postmemories of one's childhood into the physical evidence emerging from places that have acquired a mythical status in the personal histories of the survivors. Her journey to Załośce allowed Hoffman to memorialise and pass on to the reader a fragment of a broader history shaped by a series of 'incursions of the past into the present' (2004: 203–20). As we shall see, the documentaries investigated in this chapter have the power to record the processes of postmemory articulated by Hirsch and described by Hoffman, and thus provide evidence of the ways in which the mediated memories of the mythical *shtetl* in Eastern Europe can be anchored to the present-day experience of the built environment.

Jeffrey Shandler has argued that the post-Holocaust memorialisation of the *shtetl* is deprived of an ongoing actuality and a referent, and its experience is characterised by a shift from memory to 'an archetype in the mode of postmemory' (2014: 44–5). For the postgeneration, the journey to the *shtetl* answers the need to achieve a higher proximity with the experiences of their parents and grandparents. The cinematic image of the provincial urban spaces of the former *shtetlekh*, as it emerges from documentary films, speaks differently to the survivors, the postgeneration and the viewer; in all instances this is a representation that summons nostalgia for a vanished world by means of the juxtaposition of irremediably altered sites in the present day, archival images and oral histories narrated by the survivors. As it addresses the transactions of memory inherent to this process in spatial terms, documentary cinema can thus facilitate the mediation of knowledge by combining the physical exploration of the sites with what Hirsch has discussed as the traditional reliance on archival photography as a privileged medium for the transmission of trauma (2008: 103).

The documentaries investigated in the previous chapters are pervaded by a sense of loss, and all use the post-war *shtetl* paradigm according to what Shandler, in his study of scholarly writing on the concept of *shtetl*, defines as a cultural matrix for the understanding of the life and annihilation of the Jews in Eastern Europe (2014: 72–3). The same focus can be found in the documentaries investigated in this chapter inasmuch as they use the *shtetl* as a cultural matrix for transgenerational transmission of knowledge. The journey of Yaffa Eliach, a historian who was also interviewed by Marzynski in *Shtetl*, and three other Holocaust survivors to the ancestral town of Eishyshok (Eišiškės) in today's Lithuania is chronicled in *There Once Was a Town*, a documentary whose narrative is led by Eliach's expository voice-over commentary. 'In order to understand the soul of a people, one must walk on their land and visit their *shtetl*', reads the incipit of a film whose narrative is built on the visit to Eishyshok undertaken by survivors, their children and grandchildren. *There Once Was a Town* focuses on four personal quests; Reuvan Paikowsky identifies his father's grave and finds it empty; Abe Asner tries to no avail to find the Torah that he hid in a house in the small ghetto of Radun, in today's Belarus; Zvi Michaeli seeks and finds the farmers who saved his life; Yaffa Eliach looks for and discovers the names of the Polish murderers, now deceased, who shot her mother when the war had already ended. Michaeli and Eliach's quests for Polish saviours and executioners thus embody the two ways in which the role of the Poles is integrated in Holocaust narrative in terms that require reassessment through time and investigation in space.[2]

There Once Was a Town relies on present-day images of the journey to the sites of Jewish life and death in Eishyshok and on archival footage and photographs of the place. These images are combined with interviews with the survivors and their families in order to illustrate the transition of memory into postmemory and to memorialise Eishyshok as a landscape made of absences and populated by few fading traces of the past. As in Marzynski's *Shtetl*, this emptiness is the main challenge encountered by the survivors; as Eliach leads the group through the streets of the town, she observes that there are no Jews left in Eishyshok and that the cobbled streets, typical of Eastern European *shtetlekh*, and the Star of David on the old mill building are amongst the very few remnants of Jewish life. Hence only the survivors' oral testimonies and the family photographs she has taken with her can provide a more comprehensive image of Jewish Eishyshok and fill the voids on the map of the town. In particular, the site of the market square in Turgaus Street emerges as a pivotal site of postmemory as Eliach takes her children and grandchildren to this place and describes in great detail the frenetic trading that used to take place there. On the market square she identifies the site of her grandmother's house and explains that it was also a pharmacy, a bakery and a photographic studio (Fig. 3.1). Echoing the claims made by Rubin in *Shtetl*, she talks to her grandchildren about her own grandmother and emphasises the ways in which the affairs of daily life were very often run by women. Eliach's testimony transfers her own memories by means of a spatial experience of family history while, on the site of one of her fondest childhood memories, she recalls the photographic session that took place on the third floor of the building on market days, when thousands of photographs of Jewish men and women who would soon perish in the Holocaust were taken.[3]

As in Brańsk and Luboml, the market square in Eishyshok saw the meeting of Poles and Jews, when every Thursday hundreds of farmers

Figure 3.1 *There Once Was a Town* (Jeffrey Bieber, 2000).

from miles around came to the town to trade and bargain while performances took place on the cobbled pavement of the square:

> Market day began Thursday at dawn. From a distance the earth could be heard rumbling as if an army were on the march – an army of merchants from the countryside [. . . .] From each of the *shtetl* streets, wagons overflowing with fowl, fruit, grain, and other produce were streaming toward market square, their iron-rimmed wooden wheels making a huge racket as they rolled over granite cobblestones. There was also the click-clack of horseshoes and the chatter of the peasants. The animals contributed their sounds to the market symphony. (Eliach, 1998: 317)[4]

Eliach's memories of the market, the pulsing heart and the centre of the economy of the *shtetl*, are contrasted with the image of the site in 2000, empty and almost lifeless. During the visit to this site and in the attempt to fill the void, Eliach encourages her family's identification with her experiences by means of archival photographs of everyday life in Eishyshok from the 1930s, the type of photographs that Hirsch has defined as 'the fragmentary remnants that shape the cultural work of postmemory' (2008: 116). As they reveal familial aspects of postmemory and are combined with the visit to the sites, these images serve the purpose of reducing the distance between past and present and aim to accelerate the process of memorialisation of the ancestral town. Photographs of the market square are here presented as the visual referents of a pre-modern world paradoxically captured, as Shandler suggests, by the quintessential modern medium (2014: 84). The nostalgic view of the marketplace provided in *There Once Was a Town* is challenged by Eliach's darkest memories, which also belong to this site. As the film shows again the empty streets around the market square, Eliach recalls the arrival of the Nazis on tanks and motorcycles, taking over what had been the vital centre of Jewish Eishyshok.[5] In September 1941, on the evening of Rosh Hashanah, one of the SS mobile killing squads, known as the *Einsatzgruppen*, and Lithuanian auxiliaries imprisoned more than 4,000 Jews from Eishyshok and the neighbouring villages in three synagogues and then took them in groups of 250 to the old Jewish cemetery, where they were shot (cf. Barmatz, 2013: 75).[6] Before reaching their final destination, hundreds of Jews were also forced to stand in the marketplace for more than twenty-four hours (Gilbert, 1986: 200).[7] In a way that is reminiscent of the marketplace evoked by Henryk Grynberg in *Birthplace*, the market square of Eishyshok ambivalently reappropriates memories both of pre-war life in the *shtetl* and of the destruction of its Jewish community. It thus fulfils a fundamental requirement for the transmission of knowledge from the witnesses to the second and third generations – that is, the understanding of the ways in which life, atrocity, pain and nostalgia can coexist in a specific site of memory.

In *There Once Was a Town*, the survivors offer their children and grandchildren another spatial experience of their history when the group visits the derelict building of the former *yeshiva*, where the Jews were incarcerated by the Nazis before being taken to the site of the executions on the outskirts of town. On this location the postgeneration hears the testimony of Zvi Michaeli, whose brother and father were killed while he survived hiding in the bushes. This is followed by a visit to the abandoned synagogue, a wrecked building which was used as a sport hall after the war and which is juxtaposed in *There Once Was a Town* with old photographs of this location taken in the first half of the twentieth century. Reuvan Paikowsky enters the place, stands in the rubble in the middle of a large room and recalls through his memories the look of the synagogue; he then identifies the locations of the ark, the women's section, as well as the exact spots where the cantor and the rabbi would stand. Paikowsky's testimony is filled with nostalgia for the old world of the *shtetl* and articulated by the trauma of the loss of a familial world and a community. It reaches his niece, who, by means of the workings of postmemory, has acquired knowledge and understanding of the ultimate paradox of the survivor's journey to the old *shtetl*: 'He will never find the thing that he is looking for,' Paikowsky's niece explains. 'He is not looking for a grave. I think he is looking for his family. I think each time he goes back he is convinced that when he will come to Eishyshok, past the bridge, his family will come to him.'

The spatial experience of history articulated in *There Once Was a Town* relies on the support of archival photographs to facilitate the process of postmemory initiated by the journey itself. Grünberg's *Paint What You Remember* aims at unfolding a similar process by means of the use of contemporary art. In this short documentary, the naïve paintings of the *shtetl* Opatów in south-eastern Poland, made in the present by one of the town's survivors, Mayer Kirshenblatt, are used for the purpose of reducing the distance between past and present and to transmit the memory of Opatów to the postgeneration.[8] *Paint What You Remember* is also an account of Kirshenblatt's return to Opatów, which he left in 1934 and whose Jews were then murdered in Treblinka in 1942. Apart from a few gravestones, hardly any trace of 500 years of Jewish life in this town remains.[9] As Shandler has argued, Kirshenblatt's paintings recall Jewish life in Opatów as a childhood experience and provide a referent to his process of remembering all details, including those that appear trivial (2014: 102–3); the transmission of knowledge is thus implicit in the use of Kirshenblatt's images inasmuch as they were made over half a century after the events and belong to a personal, private and creative process of recollection aimed at a shift from memory to postmemory.

Years before the German occupation, tensions between Jews and Poles had already characterised life in Opatów: in 1936, two years after Kirshenblatt moved to Canada, a pogrom carried out by inhabitants of the town and local farmers left thirty Jews injured and several stores damaged (Miron, 2010: 547). And yet, except for the testimony of an old Polish woman regarding a Jewish family hidden by Poles and then handed to the Germans, no other reference to the darker side of Polish–Jewish relationships in interwar Poland is made in *Paint What You Remember*. Kirshenblatt had left before the war; his memories and paintings of the *shtetl* are idealised, and reflect a narrative of peaceful coexistence between Poles and Jews. In particular, the marketplace in Opatów emerges from two scenes painted by Kirshenblatt as a key site of memory portrayed with a focus on the stores, their signs and the lively square where Jews and Poles traded, walked and discussed in small groups. Kirshenblatt explains that each store was named after the surname of its owner and recalls a list of businesses: Kaplanski's clothing store, Shucht's barber shop, Bochinski's restaurant, Blumenfeld's tailor workshop, Urbinder's bookstore, Wiess's tobacconist and Kandel's hardware store. This pictorial recreation of the marketplace is then reinforced by another spatial experience of history;

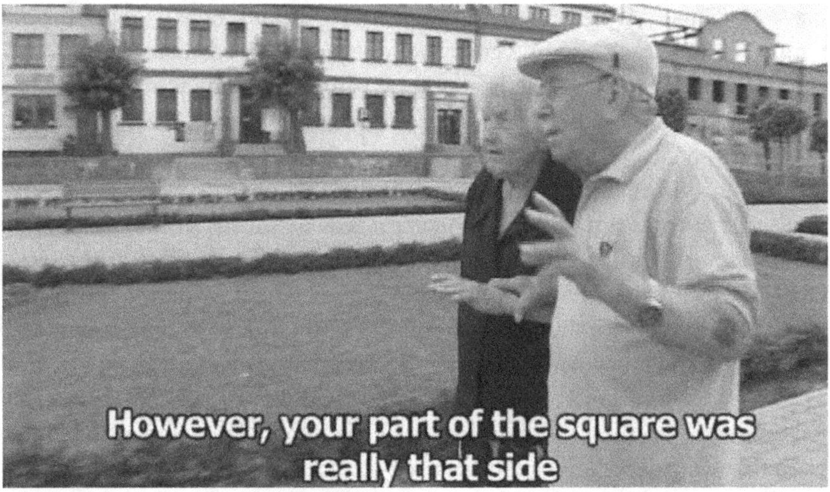

Figure 3.2 *Paint What You Remember* (Slawomir Grünberg, 2009).

during a visit to Opatów accompanied by his daughter and his niece on the occasion of an exhibition of his paintings, Kirshenblatt visits the site of the marketplace in Obrońców Pokoju Square and is accompanied by two elderly Poles, a woman and a man (Fig. 3.2). According to their account, the shops and restaurants on one side of the square were mostly Polish while on the other side there were wooden houses with mostly Jewish businesses: as in Eishyshok, Luboml and Brańsk, the market square was thus the site of the encounter between Jews and Poles which defined the *shtetl* as a multicultural complex space rather than a hermetic Jewish world.

As he walks the streets of his old town, Kirshenblatt summons familial memories of Jewish Opatów and tries to let the past re-emerge by identifying buildings and streets. A visit to the scene of one of his paintings, the building that housed his father's leather shop in Waska Street, near the marketplace, brings the past particularly close to the present. Kirshenblatt is here allowed to experience that particular transition of the past into the present described by Lowenthal in these terms: 'if the character of the place is gone in reality, it remains preserved in the mind's eye of the visitor, formed by historical imagination, untarnished by rude social facts. The enduring streets and buildings persuade him that past is present' (1975: 7). Kirshenblatt, for whom the traumatic memories of annihilation belong to those who stayed in Poland, is thus a vehicle for the transmission of knowledge; as his mind's eye sees the character of the place and allows him to experience history spatially, his creative process contributes to the transmission of his memories of the old *shtetl* to his daughter and niece.

Informed by a topographical approach to their subject, the documentaries investigated in this chapter are site-specific and reject the concept of *shtetl* as an abstracted site transcending the topographical specificity of each Jewish village. Only this precision can allow the workings of postmemory to contribute effectively to the transmission of knowledge regarding the individual communities that were erased during the Holocaust. A multigenerational example of a cinematic process of postmemory is provided by *Return to My Shtetl Delatyn*, a film directed by Willy Lindwer, the son of Holocaust survivor Berl Nuchim Lindwer, and articulated in relation to a mechanism of transmission of knowledge from the first to the third generation mediated by the work of a member of the second generation who is standing behind the camera. In this documentary, the filmmaker remains offscreen and travels with his father and his daughter Michal to Delatyn, in today's Ukraine, to trace their family history en route to the old *shtetl*. This cinematic journey provides a mediation from the survivor's memories to his son and his granddaughter and, despite the occasional mediation of archival photographs and footage, it primarily uses the scattered remains of Jewish life in Poland and Ukraine to authenticate the process of postmemory, an aim which is made explicit in the film's incipit: 'In fond regard for my father. He wanted to pass the story on to his granddaughter Michal.'

Berl Nuchim and his wife moved to Amsterdam before the war and survived there in hiding, while the rest of the family was killed in the forests near Delatyn. The journey to the old *shtetl* aims at finding spatial referents to Berl Nuchim's memories in order to facilitate the transmission of knowledge. Przemysl, in the south-east of Poland, and the *shtetl* Delatyn are the two main locations associated with the familial history of the Lindwers. Their arrival in Przemysl, the birthplace of Berl Nuchim's wife, is introduced by seven archival photographs representing Na Bramie Square (formerly Fiakrów Square), Zionist groups posing for the camera and the filmmaker's parents in the second half of the 1920s, when they lived in the city.[10] The reliance on photography is limited and the spatial experience of familial history allows an effective transmission of knowledge when Berl Nuchim identifies the house where he lived between 1924 and 1929. At the arrival to this location, he points at a significant remnant of Jewish culture inscribed in the building: the now empty space for the *mezuzah*, a parchment with verses from the Torah that used to be kept in the old doorway. The apartment is now occupied by a Roma woman who survived Auschwitz II-Birkenau, where she was taken at the age of eleven and used for medical experiments, and by her children. This location thus becomes the site of an encounter between two families affected by the Nazi extermination plans, and results in a mutual and transgenerational transmission of knowledge. The visit to Przemysl continues on to the ground which used to be occupied by the Hirt Synagogue, where only a section of the women's prayer house has survived the war, to the sites of the Old Synagogue, the former New Synagogue, which is now a public library, the abandoned Zasanie Synagogue, and the ruins of a *mikvah*. The Lindwers' exploration continues to a more familial site of memory, Franciszkańska Street, where many Jews, including Berl Nuchim's mother-in-law, plied their trades. Here the communal memories of Jewish Przemysl embodied by the synagogues are replaced by a more familial engagement with a past that anticipates the visit to the *shtetl* Delatyn.

After three stops in Lviv, Stryj and Bolekhiv, the Lyndwers arrive in Delatyn on a quest for the family home where Berl Nuchim grew up.[11] The house is still there and is now occupied by a Ukrainian family; an old photograph representing Berl Nuchim's family standing outside the porch of the house is used as an insert, revealing that the building has hardly changed since the 1930s. The Lindwers are invited to the sitting room, and here Berl Nuchim explains that his mother, grandmother and sisters were shot by the Germans in the Wilchowets forest, the main execution site in the area. Like Mayer Kirshenblatt in *Paint What You Remember*, in the following sequence Berl Nuchim returns to the site of the marketplace in what used to be the Jewish district of the town and lists the Jewish businesses which were based in the area (Fig. 3.3); however, unlike Opatów, Delatyn appears to have changed beyond recognition, and the only traces of Jewish life are a few bricks from the house inhabited by Rabbi Naftali Ehrlich and the *mezuzah* on the doorway of one of the very few formerly Jewish houses that are still standing. Berl Nuchim finally visits the derelict cemetery where his father was buried before the war, and then the Wilchowets forest where the rest of his family was executed and buried. He is not accompanied to this place by his granddaughter. Berl Nuchim accomplished the transmission of knowledge related to Jewish life in the *shtetl*; the visit to the last stage of his family's destruction is shared only with his son standing silently behind the camera. As they reach this final destination, the actor/survivor and the member of the postgeneration/filmmaker address and use the camera as a tool in a process of postmemory that is anchored to what is left of their family history in Eastern Europe, and to the attempt to find closure amid the disappearance of traces.

The process of anchoring memory to a physical environment is mediated by the interaction with those who occupy these locations in the present and their connection to the events which took place during the war. At times

Figure 3.3 *Return to My Shtetl Delatyn* (Willy Lindwer, 1992).

this connection is articulated in film in relation to themes of betrayal and guilt, while at other times it embodies ideas of righteousness and heroism. For example, *Chutor Konne*, a short film directed by Michał Nekanda-Trepka in 2007, is an account of a postmemory journey to Konne, near Białystok, undertaken by members of three generations of Israeli Jews who visit a woman who brought food to one of their relatives who was hiding in a barn, and then in a forest near Konne, during the Holocaust.[12] An increasing number of documentaries are addressing this debt felt by survivors and members of the postgeneration towards the Poles who sheltered and saved the lives of their Jewish neighbours. Another example is provided by *Diamonds in the Snow* (Mira Reym Binford, 1994), the story of three Jewish children from Będzin (Bendin) who were rescued by Poles and survived the Holocaust. The plots of *Chutor Konne* and *Diamonds in the Snow*, reminiscent of Zvi Michaeli's quest in *There Once Was a Town*, reveal a challenge to the postgeneration and invite an open engagement with Jewish fears, prejudices and knowledge about Poland. This is a theme developed more extensively in Smalley and Sarin's *So Many Miracles*, Goodstein's *Voices from* the *Attic* and Daum and Rudavsky's *Hiding and Seeking: Faith and Tolerance after the Holocaust*. These films focus on postmemory journeys to the former *shtetlekh*, and to the farms of Polish peasants who decided to save their neighbours from assassination. As Janet Walker has argued, this type of documentary is never 'a mere record of an autonomous itinerary', but rather a narrative where 'words and gestures are brought into being, and place itself is enacted' (2012: 270). As they raise questions on the role played by those Poles who helped the Jews, these documentaries make active use of the provincial locations filmed on the way to those remote rural sites which were used as hiding places during the war. In these instances, the visit to the streets, houses and ruins of the old *shtetlekh* are included to reduce the distance between past and present in the memories by recall of the postgeneration while their cinematic image emphasises the sense of absence which characterises the experience of all landscapes of postmemory.

For both survivors and postgeneration, Poland is a destination of family histories, memories, myths, prejudices and quests. As Hirsch and Spitzer have argued, 'in the act of recall, traumatic events are inevitably linked to the place of their occurrence, and thus physical return can facilitate the process of working through' (2003: 84). Accordingly, *So Many Miracles* is a cinematic account of a journey to Pińczów, a small village between Krakow and Warsaw, where the investigation of a family's ancestral home, of the trauma suffered here and of a debt to local Polish peasants is facilitated by the spatial experience of the places where the events occurred. In 1942, most of the Jews of this *shtetl* were deported to Treblinka and exterminated; however, several Jews were saved by their Polish neighbours, who kept them in hiding.[13] Among these Poles, Zofia and Ludwig Banya, with the help of their young son Maniek, sheltered Israel and Frania Rubinek for twenty-eight months in their small farmhouse. Zofia helped the Rubineks because of genuine affection for the couple, and in particular for Frania; Ludwig was interested in the money given to them by the Rubineks, and often contemplated asking them to leave. *So Many Miracles* follows Israel and Frania's return journey to Poland forty years after the end of the war with their son Saul, who was born in 1948 in a displaced persons' camp before the family emigrated to Canada. In 1986, Zofia wrote a letter to Israel and Frania and asked them to visit her in Poland, as she wanted to see them again before her death.[14] The film uses contemporary images of Pińczów in combination with archival material and occasional dramatic recreations of the events, accompanied by a voice-over narration provided by Saul and his parents. The journey to the derelict one-room house where Israel and Frania lived during the war is also defined by Saul's quest for his Jewish identity by means of a first-hand experience of the places where his parents lived, fell in love and escaped deportation and death.

Pińczów is introduced as a provincial town, where horse-drawn carts carrying local produce can still be seen on the streets. Derelict buildings once inhabited by Jews can also be observed throughout the film, which includes a scene where Israel looks at a street from a hole in the wall similar to that from which he saw other Jews being deported by the Nazis. Two of Pińczów's three synagogues were demolished by the Germans, and the oral account of their destruction is juxtaposed in the film with the recurring presence of the Church of St John the Evangelist in present-day footage, archival photographs and postcards of the town. The church is filmed from the hills around Pińczów, where Israel and Frania view the city from what used to be one of their favourite spots, and from Freedom Square (Plac Wolności), the place where the Rubineks lived before the war and which is also shown in a photograph from the 1930s. As in *The Legacy of Jedwabne* and *Witnesses*, recurring shots of the local church emphasise the fact that the once multi-religion *shtetl* is now exclusively Christian. In Pińczów, the church is also directly associated with a specific event which took place in the course of the destruction of the local Jewish community. At the beginning of the Nazi occupation a German soldier was killed by a sniper near the church, and in order to retaliate, the Nazis burnt to the ground most of the buildings which stood on the main square. The archival images of the square in the 1930s are followed by photographs of the place in ruins after the German retaliation, and subsequently by present-day images accompanied by Frania's account of the events.[15] The Jews were gathered in the square and forced to the front yard of St John's; the Germans machine-gunned their captives in front of the church, and Frania's family survived by standing near the wall, protected by the bodies of those who had been killed. St John's is thus presented as a site of Jewish martyrdom in a way that is reminiscent of Lanzmann's use of the Church of the Nativity of the Virgin Mary in Chełmno in *Shoah*, where the director interviewed bystanders who remembered when the Jews were trapped in the church waiting for the gas vans that would take them to their graves in the Rzuchowski forest.

Like other films investigated in this chapter, *So Many Miracles* juxtaposes archival photographs and contemporary footage of the sites; for example, a photograph of the sixteenth-century synagogue taken in the 1930s is followed by contemporary images of the building, eerily empty and derelict. This juxtaposition anticipates Israel's visit to the site, where he stands silently as he tries to come to terms with the painful memories associated with the place. Back on the streets of Pińczów, Israel and Frania are recognised and welcomed by several Polish men and women in their age group, but despite the warm welcome, Israel remembers the presence

Figure 3.4 *So Many Miracles* (Katherine Smalley and Vic Sarin, 1987).

of anti-Semitism in pre-war Poland; however, he suggests that, despite some tensions, Poles and Jews mostly lived peacefully. Before the war Israel and Frania ran a small store near the main square, and the memories of their business are juxtaposed, as in *Paint What You Remember* and *There Once Was a Town*, with present-day footage of the marketplace, crowded with local farmers and their customers (Fig. 3.4). This exploration of Pińczów in time and space ends with the arrival at the farm and the encounter with Zofia. *So Many Miracles* is less about the account of Israel and Frania's time in hiding, and more about their rediscovery of the world they left behind and their experience of those sites of memory that allow the past to inform the present, amidst the voids and absences inscribed in the built environment of the *shtetl*. The film thus articulates a process of postmemory facilitated by the physical experience of the sites and, as the camera indulges his expressions and responses to the information gained during the visit, the Rubineks' son Saul can connect by imagination the memories that populated his childhood to the built environment of Pińczów, to a past evoked by means of testimonies, archive and staging in the context of the act of journeying.

One hundred miles south-east of Pińczów lies the small village of

Urzejowice, in Przeworsk County. In *Voices from* the *Attic*, Debbie Goodstein, her aunt Sally and five of her cousins travel from New York to this *shtetl* and visit a local farm where sixteen members of their family were sheltered during the Holocaust in a cramped attic for over two years.[16] The film opens with present-day footage of the attic where Goodstein's family hid during the war, accompanied by the voice-over of the director providing an account of the events. As she sits in the attic, Goodstein tries to imagine what it would be like to spend years in a such a small space in the company of many others and in the constant fear of being caught. The narration shifts from third to first person as Goodstein makes her aunt's words her own, thus giving shape to a postmemory account of the suffering of her family. Her physical presence in the location that witnessed the events allows Goodstein to articulate a response to her memories by imagination, rather than by recall, which she describes as follows: 'My mother would never talk about this experience but I always knew it must have shaped her life; I also felt it shaping mine. For as long as I can remember I have had nightmares and relived things that happened before I was born in a place I had never seen. I was haunted by stories I had never heard.' As Goodstein establishes this connection with the past, more details of the events are provided by her aunt in a series of talking-head interviews and thus, as Annette Insdorf suggests, in *Voices from the Attic*, 'the survivors provide the facts, the members of the second generation offer the necessary questions and connections' (1989: 219). On this basis, as Goodstein's words make explicit, the idea of postmemory is here articulated before Hirsch gave a name to it and introduced the concept in the early 1990s.

Goodstein and her relatives arrive at their destination on board a coach and, after a long journey from Warsaw to Urzejowice, they stop in front of the Parish Church of St Nicholas, the only recognisable landmark of the town which appears both in the archival images included by the filmmaker, and largely unchanged in the present-day footage. A trope of Holocaust documentaries of return, images of churches are a reminder of the fact that the old *shtetlekh* have now become Christian villages. Footage of Urzejowice in the interwar period introduces the small village, where no more than fifty Jews lived before the war. The archival material used in the film is not always site-specific and, in an attempt to place Urzejowice in the broader context of the Holocaust, the film also includes photographs of the ghetto in Warsaw, Nazi rallies and concentration camps in Germany. In 1988, when Goodstein filmed *Voices from the Attic*, Przeworsk County was still a provincial and rural area, with old wooden houses, barns and horse-drawn carts (Fig. 3.5). The film uses this landscape to address the

Figure 3.5 *Voices from the Attic* (Debbie Goodstein, 1988).

relationship between Poles and Jews in ambivalent terms that hint at past and present anti-Semitic tensions. The family is welcomed by the locals, and their encounter with Marią Grocholską, one of the peasants who helped Goodstein's mother and her family, evokes a peaceful coexistence between the two groups. However, as a local child shouts 'Heil Hitler' to the group, the postgeneration is reminded of the anti-Semitic tensions that affected Polish society before the war and still haunted Poland in the 1980s.

An attic, just like a marketplace or a cemetery, can be used in Holocaust documentaries as a site of memory aimed at retrieving familial histories of life and death, to make what was unspeakable ultimately expressible. As Hirsch and Spitzer have argued, 'in reconnecting with both the *positive* and the *negative* in the past at the site, journeys of return require a renegotiation of the conflicting memories that constitute the returnees' ideas of "home"' (2003: 84). *Voices from the Attic* enacts this type of negotiation and expresses the process of transmission of knowledge from the survivors to the second generation as it is articulated by Goodstein's voice-over narration and by the direct testimony of her aunt Sally. Towards the end of the film, Goodstein and her cousins join Sally and Marią Grocholską in the attic; here members of the postgeneration, the survivor and the saviour live a transmission of knowledge based on the site-specific experience of the attic, the one place where such exchange can effectively provide answers to the cousins' desire to understand their family history.

In *So Many Miracles* and *Voices from* the *Attic*, members of the postgeneration are introduced to the landscapes of destruction in Poland by relatives who survived the Holocaust. In more recent years, as survivors grow older and die, the second generation has been called to take the role of guardian of memory and to pass on knowledge and memories to younger members of their families. This process is recorded in Daum and Rudavsky's *Hiding and Seeking*, a documentary where second-generation Menachem Daum takes his wife Rifka and his sons, Talmud students Tzvi Dovid and Akiva, from Israel and Boston to southern Poland. From a traditional Jewish background, the Daums are going to Eastern Europe to face their own preconceived ideas about the Poles, and *Hiding and Seeking* thus addresses a transaction of memory from the second to the third generation, here represented by Tzvi Dovid and Akiva, two young men with right-wing orthodox views and mistrustful opinions of the Poles. As Janet Walker has argued, *Hiding and Seeking* is anti-redemptive in its narrative and characterised by a significant degree of Jewish anger, uncommon in most documentaries of return (2012: 278–84). Walker has also explained that 'the film is open to an alternate architectonics where knowledge circulates semi-autonomously from the physical proximity of people who "were there" at the time of the original events and place' (2012: 282). Indeed, as his father and father-in-law remain in the United States, Daum appoints himself as the guardian of memory, responsible for the transmission of knowledge by means of the processes of postmemory. Daum has made his father and father-in-law's memories his own postmemories and, like Goodstein in *Voices from the Attic*, he has figuratively experienced events that happened before he was born in a place he had never seen.

The journey's final destination is the small hamlet of Bronów, where they identify the farm in which Rifka's father, Chaim Federman, and his brothers were sheltered by a Polish family. The Daums' visit to the sites of familial memory anticipates the encounter with Honorata and serves the purpose of establishing a connection between the present and the familial past on a location hitherto known only from the oral accounts of the survivors. On their way to Bronów, the family visits Zduńska Wola and Działoszyce, where they seek familial traces inscribed in the built environment of these towns.[17] In the course of this process, personal pre-war stories of Zduńska Wola are anchored to the site-specific filmic exploration of this town in a quest for remnants of Jewish life. Daum's father, Menachem, used to live in Zduńska Wola at 7 Steszycka Street, now renamed Jewish Ghetto Street (ul. Getta Zydowskiego). The Daums arrive at 7 Steszycka Street, presently occupied by a pharmacy, and can observe that all the Jewish dwellings, often made of wood, were dismantled after the war and replaced by stone buildings; Steszycka Street thus presents no traces of its Jewish heritage and reveals yet another townscape made of absences. In the following sequence, the Daums are guided by local historian Kamila Klauzińska to the site of Zduńska Wola's synagogue, now an empty space, a car park where a lorry can be seen delivering goods to a local store. Inspired by the Hasidic practice of *kvitel*, Menachem leaves a prayer note with the names of family members who died during the Holocaust next to a lamp post at the site of the synagogue. The journey continues to the area of the old ghetto, between Getta Zydowskiego Street, Ogrodowa Street and Sieradzka Street, and to the site where the Germans set up the gallows and executed twenty Jews during Purim and Shavuot in 1942 (Fig. 3.6). Martin Gilbert has reported the testimony of eyewitness Dora Rosenboim, a survivor who saw what happened in Zduńska Wola during the Purim festival:

> The Gestapo ordered the Jewish police to bring the ten Jews to a place where gallows had already been prepared and the Jewish police had to hang the ten Jews with their own hands. To add to this horrible, unheard-of crime, the Gestapo drove all the Jews out of the houses to the hanging-place, so that all the Jews should witness the great catastrophe. Many women fainted seeing the terrible and horrible sight, how

Figure 3.6 *Hiding and Seeking: Faith and Tolerance after the Holocaust* (Menachem Daum and Oren Rudavsky, 2002)

> ten of our brothers were writhing on the gallows. Our faces were ashamed and our hearts ached, but we could not help ourselves. (in Gilbert, 1986: 299)

In *Hiding and Seeking*, this story is not reported by a survivor but by second-generation Menachem Daum, the guardian of the postmemories of the extermination of the Jews of Zduńska Wola, who relies on his memories by imagination of the events of Purim and Shavuot. Entitled by the previous acquisition of knowledge and the direct experience of the location, Daum tells his children the story of the gallows of Zduńska Wola as he thus turns his father's testimony into his own words, in a process that is reminiscent of the ways in which Goodstein made her elders' words her own in *Voices from the Attic*.

Hiding and Seeking makes very sporadic use of archival inserts and yet, in the sequence filmed on the site of the killings, it accompanies Daum's testimony with footage of the execution showing the Jews of Zduńska Wola standing in front of the gallows on a snowy day, with the Star of David on their coats. Most of the Jewish men and women seen in this footage would have died in Chełmno before the end of the summer of that year. They left a physical and cultural void in this town and, as the film demonstrates, there are no traces of the ghetto and no Jews left in Zduńska Wola today; this is a town where time has never ceased to pass, and yet the past informs the visitor's reading of its spaces, its oldest buildings and unassuming sites of memory. From the site of the gallows, Klauzińska guides the family to the local Jewish cemetery, where they identify the gravestone of Menachem's great-grandmother Purya Yiska, who died in 1907. In the following sequence, the Daums drive to Działoszyce and visit the site of the synagogue in Krasickiego Street; the building is now in ruins and largely overgrown with weeds.[18] However, the inscription 'Congregation Tfilas Adas Yisrael' can still be read on the façade of the building. This visit anticipates their arrival in Bronów, where the Daums meet Honorata Mucha, the daughter of the farmers who risked their lives to shelter Chaim. Gratitude, curiosity and resentment emerge from the meeting between the two families, with questions about the specific motives behind the actions of Honorata's family and Chaim's silence after the war, as well as a broader inquiry into what made some Poles risk their lives for the Jews while others sent them to their deaths. Anchored to the built environment of Zduńska Wola, Działoszyce and Bronów, the Daums' investigation of their family history aimed to unearth what was hidden; in doing so, they assessed the role played by Poles in the context of the Holocaust and found a conflicting answer exemplified in the response given by the two orthodox Talmud students to the visit to

Bronów and to the encounter with Honorata. Tzvi Dovid reveals how his understanding has changed as he refers to the Polish farmers as being 'of blessed memory', a definition normally reserved for ancestors or rabbis; Akiva, on the other hand, remarks that the rescuers were just an exception to the rule, and maintains his view of Poland as a deeply anti-Semitic country. While not mutually exclusive, these views reflect the ambivalent stance of Poland in the context of the Holocaust, with its complex interplay between collaborationism and indigenous anti-Semitism on the one hand, and righteousness and sacrifice on the other. This ambiguity is still reflected in the locations of the documentaries investigated in this chapter, in their observational approach to the former *shtetlekh* of Poland, in their narratives articulating the process and the result of having to come to terms with one's memory by recall or one's memories by imagination, and with that proximity to the past achieved by means of a spatial experience of history.

Polish witnesses and testimonial performances on the one hand, and the return journey of the survivors and the postgeneration on the other, are fundamental to the ways in which documentaries filmed in the former *shtetlekh* articulate the memorialisation of the lost world of Polish Jewry. A significant number of films with these characteristics has been made after the fall of the Iron Curtain, in anticipation of the time when there will no longer be first-hand witnesses. A much earlier example of documentary of return to the *shtetl* was made outside Poland just over twenty years after the end of the war: Harold Becker's *Sighet, Sighet* (1967) focuses on Elie Wiesel's return to his *shtetl* in Romania, and is likely to have been the first documentary of this kind. However, in the first two post-war decades, the history of the *shtetl* had already been the subject of memoirs which were written by survivors and were often characterised by grand-scale narratives of pre-war Jewish life in Eastern Europe (cf. Kirshenblatt-Gimblett, 2001).[19] The abstractions of this type of memoir, often written in English, significantly differs from the geographical specificity of Yiddish *yizker-bikher*, the most conspicuous body of post-Holocaust writing about life in the *shtetl* and a resource used in films such as Dylewskiej's *Po-lin*. As Jack Kugelmass and Jonathan Boyarin explain, *yizker-bikher* are spontaneous and indigenous responses to the Holocaust in the form of hundreds of localised memoirs written by Jews who lived in the *shtetlekh*, and they focus on individual towns erased during the Holocaust and aim at the preservation of living memories of these places (1998: 5–11).[20] The site-specificity of the documentary films investigated in this chapter also allows the transmission of knowledge to the postgeneration and contributes to projecting visually and verbally what had been erased from the original locus; like the compilers of these memoirs, documentary filmmakers have used the built environment of the former *shtetlekh* to provide a structure for their accounts of pre-war Jewish institutions, rituals and practices. Both written and cinematic memoirs of the *shtetl* thus become part of those modern archival indicators of memory that are assiduously collected, as Nora suggests, as if they were 'to be called upon to furnish some proof to who knows what tribunal of history' (1989: 13–14). In what Nora calls a 'hopelessly forgetful modern society' (1989: 8), the documentaries studied in these three chapters are cinematic localised memoirs addressing the sites of the old *shtetlekh* and their voids, absences and ambivalence in memory and history; they are highly personal journeys, at times filmed by Holocaust survivors and other times by their children, inspired by the autobiographical paintings or by written narratives created by survivors, and always apt to exhume and unlock memories and to pass them on to the postgeneration and to the audience.

Notes

1. Hoffman, *After Such Knowledge.*
2. Eliach's family history is reminiscent of that of Henryk Grynberg, whose return journey to Poland was explored in Paweł Łoziński's *Birthplace*, and those of many other Jewish families such has those affected by the events in Kielce, which were discussed in Chapter One in relation to Marcel Łoziński's *Witnesses.*
3. Eliach also used 1,500 of these photographs to create the installation 'Tower of Life', on display at the Holocaust Museum in Washington, DC.
4. Eliach, *There Once Was a World.*
5. Before the war, eighty per cent of the population of the town was Jewish, for a total of over 3,000 people (cf. Barmatz, *Heroism in the Forest*, p. 75).
6. Barmatz, *Heroism in the Forest.*
7. Gilbert, *The Holocaust: The Jewish Tragedy.*
8. Kirshenblatt, who died just before the release of the film in 2009, was urged in his old age by his daughter, Barbara Kirshenblatt-Gimblett, to paint images of his childhood memories in the *shtetl.*
9. Before the war, two-thirds of Opatów's population – about 5,500 individuals – were Jewish. The ghetto established in April 1941 was overcrowded with the Jews from Opatów as well as Jewish refugees from Warsaw, Vienna and Łódź. Particularly active in the partisan resistance against the Nazis, the Jews of the ghetto in Opatów were deported to Treblinka in October 1942 (Miron, *The Yad Vashem Encyclopaedia*, pp. 547–8).
10. Przemysl had a pre-war population of 17,300 Jews, one-third of the town's inhabitants. The ghetto was set up in July 1942 and the murder operations began at the end of that month and resulted in mass deportation to Auschwitz

II-Birkenau and Bełżec, and executions in the nearby Grochowce forest (Miron, *The Yad Vashem Encyclopaedia*, pp. 617–20).

11. Over 2,000 Jews, or 35 per cent of the overall population of the town, lived in Delatyn before the war. The Germans arrived in June 1941, and in October of the same year almost the entire Jewish population of Delatyn was murdered in the Wilchowets forest and buried in three mass graves (Spector and Wigoder, *The Encyclopaedia of Jewish Life Before and During the Holocaust: A-J*, p. 300). The pogrom was carried out by the Nazis with the support of local Ukrainians, led by music teacher Slawko Waszczuk (Gilbert, *The Holocaust: The Jewish Tragedy*, p. 174).
12. This film uses Jack Weisbord's street scenes, filmed in 1932 in Kurów, which were also used in *Po-lin*, and archival photographs to introduce the history of the Jews of this part of Poland.
13. In the interwar period Pińczów was a small town of about 8,000 people, half of them Jews. With its three synagogues, Pińczów was one of the major rabbinical centres in the region. The Germans established a ghetto in Pińczów in 1941 and one year later deported 3,300 Jews to Sandomierz and then to Treblinka. Up to 200 Jews from Pińczów survived the war in hiding places or thanks to false Polish papers (Miron, *The Yad Vashem Encyclopaedia*, pp. 587–8).
14. Zofia's husband, Ludwig, had already died at the time of filming.
15. The square was mostly made of Jewish stores and homes, including the family home of the Rubineks; the house inhabited by Frania's family, on the contrary, survived the war and is identified during the visit to Pińczów.
16. Goodstein's mother and her sister could not or did not want to face Poland, and remained in the USA during the making of the film.
17. Over 10,000 Jews lived in Zduńska Wola before the war, about one-third of the total population of the town in south-western Poland. The ghetto was established in spring 1940 and sealed in the autumn of that year. The liquidation began in August 1942 and, after the Jews had been kept in the local cemetery for two days without food or water, 8,954 of them were sent to the death camp in Chełmno and 1,169 to the ghetto in Łódź (Miron, *The Yad Vashem Encyclopaedia*, pp. 973–4). Almost 6,000 Jews lived in Działoszyce before the war, a community consisting of over eighty per cent of the town's population; the Jews of Działoszyce were murdered in Chełmno (Michman, *The Emergence of Jewish Ghettos During the Holocaust*, p. 87).
18. A group of Polish youths laughs at the sight of Tzvi Dovid and Akiva's traditional clothing and their *kippah*, while on the ground of the synagogue Rifka reads a prayer and lights a candle. This instance of anti-Semitism is reminiscent of earlier episodes of Polish violence against Holocaust survivors that took place in the town of Działoszyce. On 20 May 1945, twenty-five surivors, including Jews who had been saved by Oscar Schindler in Kraków, returned to their hometown to find their homes occupied by Poles. Within a week, four of them were murdered, and eventually the remaining twenty-one

left Poland and moved to other countries (Gilbert, *The Holocaust: The Jewish Tragedy*, p. 812).

19. Kirshenblatt-Gimblett, 'The Popular Arts of American Jewish Ethnography'.
20. Kugelmass and Boyarin, 'Introduction'.

CHAPTER 4

A Tale of Two Cities: Warsaw and Kraków

'I feel a little like an archaeologist, walking through bits and pieces of the past.'
— Marian Marzynski, *Return to Poland*

On 1 August 1940, almost a third of the Jews of Kraków were taken to Warsaw (Gilbert, 1986: 123). This deportation was part of a large number of actions taken by the Nazis across a vast chequerboard of ghettos, labour camps and killing centres. As *Shoah* reveals, the complexity of the forced resettlements even saw the Jews of Oświęcim being deported from their town to labour camps and eventually taken back to Auschwitz II-Birkenau for extermination. The intricacies of the topography of the Holocaust have also affected its cinematic landscape, with particular neighbourhoods called on to play the role of other districts which were more extensively devastated during the war. This spatial interplay can be observed in two of the most successful and widely debated Holocaust dramas of the past twenty-five years and their connection to the wartime histories and memories of the cities of Warsaw and Kraków. Roman Polanski's *The Pianist* (2002) was filmed on location on the streets of the Polish capital city and at the Babelsberg studios in Potsdam, Germany; however, Polanski used districts of the city which survived the war and were not originally part of the Jewish ghetto. Similarly, Steven Spielberg used the topography of Kraków creatively in *Schindler's List* (1993), a film which was set and filmed in and around Kraków and, as we shall see, whose success had significant and multilayered implications in the memorialisation of the Holocaust in this city.

The annihilation of the Jews of Warsaw and Kraków presents common traits and considerable differences which are reflected in the documentaries filmed on these locations. Before the war, the Jewish communities of both cities were largely concentrated in two districts: Praga in Warsaw, and Kazimierz in Kraków. When the Germans occupied Warsaw and Kraków, thousands of Jews were resettled from these neighbourhoods to the ghettos established on the opposite bank of the Vistula, respectively in the Warsaw districts of Muranów, Powązki, Nowolipki, Śródmieście Północne and Mirów, and in the Kraków district of Podgórze. In both Warsaw and Kraków, the ghettos were established in areas that had a significant pre-war Jewish population. Men, women and children from smaller communities were also taken to these larger ghettos and eventually, along with the Jews of these cities, to labour and extermination camps, primarily Treblinka, Auschwitz II-Birkenau and Bełżec. The Jewish Combat Organization (Żydowska Organizacja Bojowa) contributed to the resistance against the Nazis in both cities but, while the ghetto in Kraków was liquidated before a general insurrection could be staged, the Warsaw Ghetto Uprising of 1943 resulted in hundreds of casualties among the invaders. Both cities experienced physical destruction, but while Kazimierz and Podgórze survived the war largely intact, Warsaw was almost entirely destroyed, with the exception of the Praga district. The parallel histories of these two cities during the German occupation have been addressed in a series of documentaries investigating the different issues encountered in the memorialisation of the Jewish communities that were annihilated. In particular, the physical destruction of Warsaw and the abundance of traces of the past in Kraków have defined the documentary image of these cities. In Warsaw, filmmakers and survivors have struggled to inscribe personal and collective histories in the urban fabric of a city whose built environment has changed beyond recognition, whereas in Kraków they have had to come to terms with the popularisation of its sites of memory and with the impact of mass tourism on these places. This chapter aims at a site-specific investigation of the Holocaust in Warsaw and Kraków by means of a study of recent documentaries and their engagement with the processes of recalling the murdered Jews.

Warsaw

In the final sequences of *Shoah*, testimonies about life in the Warsaw ghetto and the uprising of 19 April 1943 are provided by resistance fighters Jan Karski, Simcha Rotem and Yitzhak Zuckerman, as well as by Franz Grassler, a former assistant to Nazi ghetto commissioner Heinz Auerswald. Their accounts accompany present-day street scenes filmed on various locations, including the area of the ghetto, the Jewish cemetery, the site of the headquarters of the Jewish Combat Organization at 18 Miła Street and the Monument to the Ghetto Heroes in Zamenhofa Street. After *Shoah*, these places returned in a number of documentaries focusing on the history of the Warsaw ghetto, the uprising and the memorialisation of the city's sites of the Holocaust. For example, Michał Nekanda-Trepka's *Campo di Fiori* (2012) is a short documentary about life in the ghetto based on archival footage and interviews with survivors.[1] In particular, the film addresses the 1943 insurrection, which anticipated the Warsaw Uprising of the following year and resulted in the liquidation of the ghetto by means of mass deportations to Treblinka in the months which followed.[2] The title of this documentary originates from a reference to Czesław Miłosz's *Campo dei Fiori*, a poem that juxtaposes two sites of martyrdom, the Warsaw ghetto and Campo dei Fiori in Rome, the square where philosopher Giordano Bruno was burned at the stake on 17 February 1600. Nekanda-Trepka's film is punctuated by scenes in which Miłosz reads his poem; these are edited with interviews, archival images of the ghetto and a few present-day shots filmed on location in Warsaw, including images of the building that had previously been the Berson and Bauman Families Children's Hospital, at 60 Sienna Street; the devotion chapels built by Poles at 12 Waliców Street and 3 Ciepła Street, in the courtyard of two Jewish tenements that have survived the war; and a medium shot of survivor Feliks Tych standing by the section of the ghetto wall at 55 Sienna Street. *Campo dei Fiori* reveals that a few fragments of that wall and a small number of buildings are all that is left of what the Germans called Jüdischer Wohnbezirk (the Jewish residential district), while archival photographs and film footage of everyday life in the Warsaw ghetto abound. And yet these images are problematic inasmuch as they were largely captured by the perpetrators, Nazi officers who used their cameras for propaganda or private purposes.[3] The scarcity and the unreliability of remnants of the ghetto, in the built environment of Warsaw and at the archive, have thus challenged the process of transmission of knowledge inherent to the cinematic return journeys to the city made by survivors and by members of the postgeneration. Stella Bruzzi has described travel documentaries as ambling and chaotic narratives that 'can seem to have marginalized purposefulness, although their coherence tends to be cerebral, political or emotional rather than formal, as they frequently conclude ambiguously or their journeys left unresolved' (2006: 119). Accordingly, largely unresolved cinematic journeys with a profoundly emotional coherence emerge from Ilan Ziv's *Tango of Slaves* (1994), Marian Marzynski's *Return to Poland* (1981) and *Never Forget to Lie* (2013), three travel documentaries which will be investigated in this section of the chapter in relation to their exploration of the cityscape of the Holocaust in Warsaw, and to their attempt to reassess the experience of the ghetto while carrying out quests for a truth often frustrated by the disappearance of traces. These three films address Holocaust survivors' return journeys to Poland amidst a landscape that has changed irremediably and the survival of an unreliable photographic archive which was taken by the Nazis. As we shall see, only in the 1990s did documentaries begin to reflect on the nature of images which had been used widely in earlier films about the Warsaw ghetto, and to articulate a critical discourse on the ways in which this material had long been unceremoniously repurposed from its original propaganda function into a testimonial performance.

Arguably the best-known Nazi propaganda film that uses images of ghettos in Poland for political purposes, Fritz Hippler's documentary *Der ewige Jude* (*The Eternal Jew*, 1940) was based on a book published in 1937 by Zentralverlag der NSDAP, the Nazi party's publishing house. The film presented the Jews living in captivity in the ghettos as uncivilised and parasitic people, often engaged in what are described as barbaric religious rituals and ceremonies; its message was exemplified in the opening statement of the film:

> The civilized Jews that we know in Germany give us only an incomplete picture of their racial character. This film shows genuine shots of the Polish ghettos. It shows the Jews as they really are, before they conceal themselves behind the mask of the civilized European. (in Taylor, 1998: 175)[4]

This commentary introduced the viewer to the narrow alleys of various neighbourhoods overcrowded with Jews who, despite what the film refers to as their wealth, are poorly dressed and appear unwell. As Robert Reimer suggests, the film was effectively showing the result of Nazi rule while claiming to display the natural depravity of the Jews (2000: 135).[5] During the occupation of Poland, German cameramen repeatedly filmed scenes of everyday life in the ghettos staged for propaganda purposes that echoed the devious message of *The Eternal Jew*. And yet, after the war footage of the ghettos taken by the Nazis was used, among other films, in Erwin Leiser's *Mein Kampf* (1960), Frédéric Rossif's *Le Temps du ghetto* (*The Time of* the *Ghetto*, 1961), *The Warsaw Ghetto* (1968), and Dieter Hildebrandt's *Der Gelbe* (*The Yellow Star: The Persecution of the Jews in Europe 1933–45*, 1980), a group of documentaries that does not engage with the ambiguity of the inclusion of street scenes filmed by perpetrators and does not acknowledge the extensive staging involved in this archival footage.

More recently, Israeli documentary *A Film Unfinished*, directed by Yael Hersonski in 2010, has critically addressed the nature and the fictitiousness of the footage of the Warsaw ghetto filmed in 1942 by Nazi cameraman Willy Wist. The ambiguity of these archival images and the ways in which Hersonski exposes their lack of authenticity has been investigated by Brad

Prager, who has argued that 'one must simultaneously maintain that the footage is genuine – it is "real" insofar as it depicts the faces, the objects, and some aspects of daily existence that constituted life in the ghetto – but it is also very much staged' (2015: 190). *A Film Unfinished* juxtaposed this footage, which re-emerged in 1954 in Berlin, with voice-over excerpts from ghetto diaries, a re-enactment of the testimony given by Wist in the 1970s and present-day interviews with survivors of the ghetto, which were filmed in a cinema screening Wist's footage for the purpose of reviving their memories. Hersonski's film provides a reflection on the ways in which footage from the ghetto should be contextualised within the Nazi propaganda efforts and, like *The Eternal Jew*, it should be taken as a largely unreliable record. As it reveals the ways in which scenes were staged for the camera, *A Film Unfinished* exposes the challenge of relying on visual evidence that, as Prager suggests, comes from footage taken by the Nazis as part of their genocidal project: 'The film is a distorted performance of life; yet it also remains a source of information about those lives, unlike any other. What we see is connected to the truth, but it is false; it is at once a genuine document and a counterfeit one' (2015: 190).

In 1994, well before Hersonski's film attracted considerable attention from critics, scholars and festival audiences, the issues related to the use of film footage taken by the Nazis were addressed by Ilan Ziv in *Tango of Slaves*, another Israeli documentary that articulates this preoccupation while addressing at the same time the consequences of the physical destruction of the ghetto in relation to the act of bearing witness. Developed as a cinematic account of a postmemory journey from Israel to Warsaw, *Tango of Slaves* addresses the ways in which the transmission of knowledge from a survivor to the postgeneration unfolds both in regard to the use of archival material and in the context of a visit to the sites of memory. This documentary, which is titled after the pre-war Yiddish street song *Niewolnicze Tango*, was made by Ziv for his two daughters in the attempt to provide a personal and familial image of the Holocaust that could be juxtaposed with the impersonal and distant image created by fictional accounts of the events. Ziv's father, whose name is never mentioned in the film, joined the Jewish Combat Organization (Żydowska Organizacja Bojowa) in 1943 and survived the German occupation. He left Poland soon after the end of the war and, in *Tango of Slaves*, he returns to Warsaw for the first time on a journey through the city of the 1990s that becomes a narrative inquiry into history, memory and the traces of a past inscribed into the built environment of the city and its archival image. This site-specific investigation is based on the juxtaposition of archival footage and photographs, present-day location shooting and dreamlike sequences inspired by the family stories heard by Ziv since childhood.

In the opening sequence of the film, Ziv's voice-over narration provides a reflection on the ways in which photographs from pre-war Warsaw can contribute to the postgeneration's knowledge and understanding of the Holocaust. In particular, a recently found photograph from the 1930s, which shows Ziv's father lying on the grass with his grandmother sitting on a chair behind him and his parents standing behind her, ignites the filmmaker's quest for his family history. Private photographs can facilitate the processes of postmemory and, as Marianne Hirsch has argued, have the power to establish personal connections with the past and 'to diminish distance, bridge separation, and facilitate identification and affiliation' (2008: 116). In *Tango of Slaves*, the photograph of Ziv's father and his family contributes to building this connection and to the unfolding of the most familial aspects of postmemory in relation to the filmmaker's attempt to come to terms with a past he never experienced and with events he did not witness. Ziv's voice-over narration articulates the primary aim of the film as it explains that the postgeneration has inherited memories but never the imagery, and that when he was a child he could only think of the ghetto as a plastic model at the museum. This cinematic journey thus aims at making real and personal what had belonged to the fictional and the public spheres, and the filmmaker uses the photograph of his family – of which his father is the only survivor – to diminish the transgenerational separation and to contribute to establishing an intimate connection based on a cinematic attempt to visualise the past. The photograph of Ziv's family punctuates this documentary and, in the opening sequence of the film, is shown in the course of its processing in a darkroom from a latent image into a visible one. In the same sequence, as the filmmaker reflects on the importance of this image in the attempt to facilitate identification with the experiences of his father, the photograph appears on a television screen placed in the background of expressionist drawings reflecting the experience of the ghetto. This self-reflexive use of a photograph accentuates the power of photography and reflects Hirsch's claim that 'when we look at photographic images from a lost past world, especially one that has been annihilated by force, we look not only for information or confirmation, but also for an intimate material and affective connection' (2008: 116). The only family photograph in Ziv's possession contributes to the process of bridging the gap between past and present evoked by Hirsch as it introduces the story of Ziv's family and the account of their move from Praga to the ghetto across the Vistula. And yet one photograph is not sufficient to guarantee a successful transmission of knowledge and affiliation, and the documentary's negotiation with the past as well as its attempt to visualise a familial history continues with a present-day exploration of the sites of persecution in Warsaw, opening with a panning shot of the river followed by a tracking shot filmed from a car crossing the Śląsko-Dąbrowski Bridge. [6]

Tango of Slaves introduces the visit to Warsaw with personal and public forms of archival material including a number of photographs of the ghetto district in ruins, taken just after the war by Ziv's father, and sequences from a newsreel entitled *A Day in Warsaw* (Yitzhak Goskin, 1939), which contains street scenes filmed in the commercial and shopping district of the Jewish quarter in Muranów. This is one of the districts where the ghetto would later be established, and Goskin's newsreel includes scenes filmed at Nalewki Street, now Ghetto Heroes Street (ul. Bohaterów Getta), and Dzika Street. This documentary compares lively images of Jewish life in the 1930s with the scenes of annihilation and destruction that followed the Warsaw Uprising of 1944, and thus provides temporal and spatial context to the alien cityscape experienced by Ziv's father on his journey to Poland. In the following sequences the survivor visits sites of family life in Praga and, on the other side of the river, the places in the district where the ghetto was established and where the disappearance of traces inhibits his evocation of distant memories, as well as Ziv's attempt to acquire knowledge and visualise the events which took place here in the 1940s. In the first sequence filmed on location in Warsaw, a taxi takes the two men from the Central Station to the Praga district, where the survivor tries to identify the building that hosted his uncle's meat-packing plant in the 1930s. He walks to a courtyard and talks with local workers who were born after the war and cannot provide any information about the place; the site of the plant remains unidentified. As *Tango of Slaves* reflects Lowenthal's suggestion that the remembered past can be 'a more emphatic landscape than that experienced today' (1975: 28), the memories of the survivor travel to a more resounding past incited by a lethargic present populated by the faint inscription of traces on the cityscape. Past and present conflate in the survivor's mind and revive old wounds as he successfully locates the site of the family home in Praga, now a crumbling building in the process of being gutted for renovation, and reflects upon the challenge of binding his memories of the people who lived there to the empty space he is now visiting.

The survivor's journey to his sites of memory continues on the other bank of the Vistula to the former area of the ghetto. Ziv's father visits the memorial located on a mound made of rubble at the site of the headquarters of the Jewish Combat Organization at 18 Miła Street, the location of the family house at 8 Pawia Street near Mieczysław Apfelbaum Square, and finally the site of the *Umschlagplatz*, the collection point in Stawki Street from where Jews were deported to Treblinka via Warszawa Gdańska station.[7] A sequence filmed at the Pomnik Bohaterów Getta (Ghetto Heroes Monument), located in the square between Lewartowskiego Street, Karmelicka Street, Anielewicza Street and Zamenhofa Street, shows the estranged reaction of Ziv's father to the enormous changes that have affected the area. Lowenthal has argued that 'we retain traces of our past to be sure of our enduring identity' (1975: 9), a claim illustrated by the scene where Ziv's father stands on Lewartowskiego Street and holds in his hands a photograph which he took on the same spot just after the war. The juxtaposition between the old photograph and the present-day cityscape is problematic for the survivor because of the lack of any resemblance between the two; and yet, the photograph is a trace of a long-gone past which can assure the survivor of his enduring identity. Warsaw was destroyed and rebuilt, and the events which took place on its soil have been concealed by empty spaces and new buildings, as well as by the monumentalisation of sections of the former ghetto. As the survivor struggles to recognise the place as one of his own sites of memory, the transmission of knowledge to the postgeneration is inhibited by the difficulties posed by the radical changes in the urban fabric of the city. The destruction of Warsaw and its present-day appearance challenge both the attempt to visualise everyday life in the ghetto and the processes of memorialisation of the lively pre-war Jewish community of the district. In order fill this void, *Tango of Slaves* resorts to archival footage from Alexander Ford's Yiddish documentary *Mir kumen on* (*Children Must Laugh*, 1936), with a sequence filmed during Sabbath at Krashinsky Park, where children and adults can be seen playing and talking in small groups, and scenes from *A Day in Warsaw* filmed in Nalewki Street and Franciszkańska Street. The film also uses the photographs of the ghetto and its liquidation, taken by Joe Heidecker for the photographic unit of the SS. While all these images aim at filling the gap left by the destruction of the city, Ziv's commentary reflects on the absences in the archival repertoire of Warsaw: most of the footage from the 1920s and 1930s is now lost, images of the ghetto were taken by the Nazis, and post-war films portrayed the Jews merely as victims rather than as a significant part of the cultural, economic and public life of the Polish capital. The issue of the origin of archival images of life in the ghetto is also addressed in a long sequence in which father and son visit a film archive to watch the footage filmed by Willy Wist, which is also investigated in *A Film Unfinished*. This includes scenes showing Adam Czerniaków, the head of the Warsaw Ghetto's *Judenrat* (the Jewish Council), in his office; Hasidic Jews on the streets of Warsaw; and images revealing a deliberately staged contrast between the poor starving on the streets of the ghetto and the rich dining at an expensive restaurant. The survivor is more impressed and touched by this footage than by the present-day experience of the places, notwithstanding the implications of watching footage staged and filmed by the perpetrators. His memories and his knowledge can discern the falsity, the staging and the propaganda elements of these images from their actual value as images of places and people that are long gone. An emphatic past still exists in the survivor's mind, and yet, curbed by the limitations inherent to the visit to the sites and to the use of spurious archival images, it ultimately struggles to emerge from the film and to facilitate Ziv's attempt to gain postmemory knowledge of the events for himself and for his daughters.

Several locations explored in *Tango of Slaves* are also visited by Marian Marzynski in his documentaries *Return to Poland* and *Never Forget to Lie*. Filmed thirty-two years apart, these two cinematic journeys to Warsaw are built upon the exploration of present-day sites and make a limited use of archival images. Marzynski was born in 1937 and survived the Holocaust sheltered by Poles in the Christian district of Warsaw; unlike Ziv's father, who left Poland soon after the war, the filmmaker remained in the country with his family until 1969, when he fled to Denmark and then to the USA following a wave of anti-Semitism waged by the Minister of Interior Mieczysław Moczar. At this time Jews were removed from jobs in public service, including government, schools and universities, and the overall Jewish population of Poland decreased from 90,000 in 1947 to a number between 5,000 to 10,000 by the end of the 1960s (cf. Steinlauf, 1997: 75–88). Marzynski's documentaries provide a contemplation on life and survival in the occupied city, as well as a reflection on the relationship between Poles and Jews during and after the war. Like Marzynski, Jewish-Polish historian Emanuel Ringelblum found shelter in the Aryan side of Warsaw, but he was discovered by the Gestapo and executed, along with his family and with those who hid him, in the Pawiak Prison on 7 March 1944. In his writing, Ringelblum articulated an ambivalence towards the Poles and their role in the Holocaust, considering both the heroism of 'those who saved thousands of human beings from destruction in the fight against the greatest enemy of the human race' and the fact that overall 'Polish Fascism and its ally, anti-Semitism, have conquered the majority of the Polish people' (cf. Gilbert, 1986: 660–1). This ambivalence mirrors Marzynski's own view of the Poles, balanced between profound gratitude for a limited number of individuals who saved him and many others from certain death, and the indifference and hostility of the majority. *Return to Poland* and *Never Forget to Lie* investigate remnants of the city of Marzynski's childhood and youth, and use specific locations in the area of the former ghetto and other districts in order to articulate a personal and private discourse on the destruction of the city's Jewish community. In particular, the surviving courtyards of the former ghetto emerge as the most significant sites of memory in two documentaries where the act of entering these spaces from the busy thoroughfares of present-day Warsaw serves to establish a connection between past and present, and to inscribe personal and collective histories on the surviving buildings of the ghetto. Empty, derelict or at times refurbished, these courtyards and their physical exploration define the absences left behind by the destruction of the filmmaker's familial world and reveal autobiographical connections to specific sites. The events which took place on these locations are thus not articulated as fixed moments in the past, but rather as part of a persisting process of coming to terms with the Holocaust in the present.

Filmed in 1981, *Return to Poland* is an account of the filmmaker's return journey to Warsaw and to the family *shtetl* Łęczyca, eighty-two miles west of the Polish capital. In this documentary, an autobiographical narrative provides the context for an investigation of Jewish captivity in the ghetto during the war, the anti-Semitic campaign of the 1960s and the changes affecting Polish society in the early 1980s during the rise of Solidarność. The trauma of the Holocaust pervades the present in a film that is about contemporary Poland and the ways in which survivors and bystanders experience a city where different temporal layers coexist and contribute to articulating a discourse on present-day political developments. Within this context, the act of bearing witness to the destruction of the Jews of Warsaw emerges as the main challenge encountered by the filmmaker in the production of the film, as the traces of the world of his youth are scarce in a built environment largely reconstructed after the war on the rubble of the ghetto. In attempting to fill this void Marzynski avoids the use of archival footage and provides a personal account intertwined with the voices of his former neighbours and his old friends, creating a narrative of wartime Warsaw that emerges from the disappearance of the actual environments of memory.

Like *Tango of Slaves*, Marzynski's film can be seen as a travel documentary whose coherence lies primarily in the emotional engagement with its destinations rather than in its historical argument. *Return to Poland* makes the theme of journeying explicit in its title and in its opening scene, filmed on board a train directed to Warsaw, and to a present informed by the past and defined by the necessity to unbury distant memories.[8] This journey takes the filmmaker to the site of a house in a residential area of the city he left in 1969. Here, Marzynski explains his intention to find remnants of what has been destroyed during and after the war: 'I feel a little like an archaeologist, walking through bits and pieces of the past.' Marzynski thus tries to overcome the obstacles posed by the destruction of the sites, and his journey reflects Lowenthal's belief that 'physical residues of all events may yield potentially unlimited access to the past' and that, given the right methodology, no historical record can elude retrieval (1985: 19).[9] The devices employed by Marzynski include the use of a hand-held camera which follows the survivor in his exploration of this neighbourhood, while the filmmaker's voice-over commentary articulates his thoughts about the return to the place where he lived with his mother and then his wife. The visit reveals that the wooden building, one of ninety houses built after the war to accommodate the men and women who were working on the reconstruction of the city, has disappeared, just like other earlier sites associated with the filmmaker's family history. Marzynski walks near the surviving houses and stands on the flat-topped stone used as a doorstep to his old house, all that is left of the original building (Fig. 4.1). During this visit he talks to his former neighbours and recalls his youth in this district of Warsaw as he explores a site ultimately associated with his failed attempt to build a life in Poland after the Holocaust, and with his exile to a foreign land.

Marzynski's most painful memories of Warsaw are related to the districts of the former ghetto and are articulated in the sequence where, like Ziv's father in *Tango of Slaves*, he visits the Ghetto Heroes Monument. Here the filmmaker encounters a small group of children who are compil-

Figure 4.1 *Return to Poland* (Marian Marzynski, 1981).

ing a list of sites of historical interest for a school project; the pupils demonstrate little knowledge of the history of the Jews of Warsaw, who are described as having 'a different look in the eyes' but 'no religious difference' when compared to the Poles. The dialogue with local school pupils establishes childhood as a thematic link with the filmmaker's past, which is explored in the following sequences. In 1942, Marzynski was smuggled out of the ghetto on a horse-drawn carriage; in *Return to Poland*, a similar carriage takes him along the streets of Warsaw as his voice-over narration provides an account of his survival in the Aryan district of the city, where he stayed with sixteen different Polish families who helped him either in exchange for money, or to fulfil a moral obligation. While Marzynski explains that his hideouts were Warsaw's courtyards, the camera enters one of these spaces and a tracking point-of-view shot reveals a group of Polish children playing on a site where Jewish children in hiding played during the war. A tilting shot shows the windows of the apartments looking onto the courtyard and turns into a circular camera movement taken from Marzynski's point of view. This scene is accompanied by the sound of the horse's steps, which establishes a thematic connection between Marzynski's escape on a horse-drawn carriage and his present-day exploration of the city.[10] In the former Christian district of Warsaw, the filmmaker also identifies two surviving locations with a significant connection to his personal history: the top floor of a building at 59 Mokotowska Street, where his mother had briefly contemplated jumping from the window with her child in her arms, and the courtyard of a building hosting a Catholic charity organisation, where she resolved to leave Marzynski in the hope he would be sent to an orphanage. The camera follows the filmmaker in these places as his voice-over narration provides a detailed account of the events. Marzynski's memories are specific to the sites visited in this journey, and are given strength by his present-day experience of these places. The past is embodied in the fading traces of the city of his childhood, in the ways in which absences and presences wrestle one another along a personal and private itinerary, and on a map drawn by the filmmaker by means of a persisting voice-over. This narration renders Marzynski's thoughts as he expresses his need to recall and pass on the knowledge of the events despite the alienation experienced in the present, and the impossibility of deciphering the full meaning of the Holocaust in the traces inscribed in the cityscape.

Marzynski is not seeking specific answers, nor is he solving riddles related to his family history in order to obtain closure; rather, he is trying to reintroduce his individual memories to the sphere of collective history. This process continues on Marzynski's second cinematic journey to

Warsaw in 2013, and with his return to the sites visited in his earlier documentary. *Never Forget to Lie* opens with a scene showing Marzynski sitting on an electric tram taking him to the site of the ghetto. Again, a means of transport is employed in the opening sequences of the film in order to emphasise the importance of the act of journeying. As Stella Bruzzi suggests, a travel documentary does not need to provide narrative coherence structured around a precise argument, and can rather be seen as 'a chronicle of events linked by location, personality and theme' (2006: 83). Accordingly, *Never Forget to Lie* is a collection of fragments linked by Warsaw locations, Marzynski's personal history and the theme of survival in the Nazi-occupied city. In this documentary the filmmaker returns to the subject of his own childhood while chronicling the experiences of other children who were smuggled out of the ghetto and sheltered by Poles in the Christian district of the city. Here, in order to survive, they were warned to tell everyone that they were indeed Polish Catholics, and thus instructed 'to never forget to lie'. Marzynski's reflections on his survival and his childhood, as they had already emerged from *Return to Poland*, are reassessed in *Never Forget to Lie* as a collective experience shared by other survivors who, like the filmmaker, witnessed the annihilation of their people and a personal fight to stay alive in the hell of occupied Warsaw.

Never Forget to Lie was shot on location in Warsaw, Kraków, Katowice and Treblinka, and uses footage from *Return to Poland* and family photographs from the 1930s, accompanied by the filmmaker's voice-over account of his survival. At the beginning of the film, Marzynski's mother, who also survived the war, and his father, who was killed by the Nazis, are shown walking on a Warsaw street in a black-and-white photograph from the 1930s. This image has a similar function to the family photograph used by Ziv in *Tango of Slaves* and is used both to diminish distance between the present and a lost world forcefully destroyed by the Nazis, and to establish that abovementioned 'intimate material and affective connection' with the past evoked by Hirsch (2008: 116).[11] *Never Forget to Lie* also uses archival images physically inscribed in the built environment of the former ghetto district. Marzynski stands in Grzybowski Square and films the few surviving buildings of the ghetto at 14 Próżna Street, now uninhabited and partly covered with large photographs portraying members of the annihilated Jewish community of the city. These dilapidated tenement houses, also chosen as a location for the closing scenes of the film, date from the end of the nineteenth century and were selected in 2008 for *I ciągle widzę ich twarze* ('I Can Still See Their Faces'), an outdoor exhibition built on images from the collection of Polish actress Gołda Tencer to commemorate the 65th anniversary of the Ghetto Uprising. This installation is reminiscent of other ways in which photographic remnants have been used in the attempt to fill the void. In her discussion of the 'Tower of Faces' installation at the United States Holocaust Memorial Museum in Washington, Hirsch argues that the tower situates the visitor right inside a family album that becomes a site of remembrance (1997: 250–2). Similarly, 'I Can Still See Their Faces' places the visitor inside a family album located in the urban fabric of the city and uses this space to erase the passing of time and to preserve memory. These archival photographs eerily occupy the façades of buildings that are now empty and, while making space for identification, they emphasise the void that Marzynski and the other survivors have to face during their visits to Warsaw.

The derelict courtyards are used as spaces that allow the survivors to engage with site-specific memories in locations that evoke their youth and establish connections with a past inscribed in the physical remains of the city of their childhood. As in *Return to Poland*, Marzynski enters the courtyard of one of the few surviving buildings in Próżna Street; filmed from Marzynski's point of view, a tilting shot of the windows overlooking the courtyards makes a circular movement, reminiscent of a similar shot in *Return to Poland*. Here, he recalls fragmented memories of life in the ghetto amidst fading traces of Jewish life, as he stands still and allows the shadows of the past to catch up with him (Fig. 4.2). Marzynski also visits the apartment where he believes he might have stayed with his family for a few months in 1941, and speaks with the elderly Polish woman who lives there. This exploration evolves from a personal to a collective dimension

Figure 4.2 *Never Forget to Lie* (Marian Marzynski, 2013).

in the sequences which show Marzynski joining survivors Celina Jaffe and Sophia Schulman on a visit to derelict courtyards near Próżna Street. In one of these old courtyards Sophia's mother died of typhoid fever, and the survivor tries to establish a connection with the past by contemplating the scenery while the camera reveals the broken or walled-up windows overlooking the place; the point of view is inverted when they move inside the building and observe the courtyard from one of the windows on the upper floors. 'The place is dead,' explains Schulman as she remembers the people who lived there during the war and, like Ziv's father in *Tango of Slaves*, observes that the emptiness of the place emphasises a very private sense of loss and destruction.

In *Never Forget to Lie*, Marzynski also returns to the same locations explored during the filming of *Return to Poland* in 1981, including the house at 59 Mokotowska Street and the courtyard of the charity organisation where the building's janitor kept him in hiding. The return to these places indicates the passing of time, not only from the 1940s to the present time but also from the early 1980s to today. The country moved on from communist rule to democracy when, following the 1989 general election, a Solidarity-led coalition government was formed and, in the following year, Lech Wałęsa was elected President of Poland. After this seismic change in Polish history, many Warsaw buildings were demolished, while others are now derelict or have been refurbished; thus the attempt to establish a connection by means of a space-specific inquiry is more difficult than it was in 1981. The most significant disappearance that occurred before the making of *Never Forget to Lie* is deeply personal. In *Return to Poland* Marzynski met Krysia Baranowa, a Polish woman who contributed to saving his life and that of his mother by sheltering them in her apartment. Baranowa died soon after this encounter and, in *Never Forget to Lie*, the filmmaker remains on the street outside her building and looks up at yet another private space in Warsaw which is rich in personal memories, and from which he is now excluded. This progressive rejection from spaces whose experience belongs to the personal memories of the survivors characterises the films studied in this section. The Warsaw documentaries directed by Ilan Ziv and Marian Marzysnki face the challenges brought about by the destruction of the sites, and yet function as mnemonic devices in the context of the memorialisation of a lost Jewish city. In the case of Kraków, as we shall see, an abundance of traces and the preservation of historical locations embodies different challenges to site-specific processes of Holocaust remembrance.

Kraków

Kuba Karys and Natalia Schmidt's short documentary *Miasteczko Kroke* (*The Little Town of Kroke*, 2008) uses the testimonies of Holocaust survivors to tell the story of interwar Kraków and builds on oral accounts of those years in order to reveal the striking oppositions between nostalgic and fond memories from the 1930s on the one hand, and the devastation of places, lives and personal relationships following the German occupation of the city on the other. The opening sequence of this film includes three establishing shots of Kraków, taken from a helicopter. They are views of Stare Miasto (Old City) – the monumental and central part of Kraków, which is historically the Polish Catholic area – and the two districts where the history of Jewish Kraków and its destruction unfolded: Kazimierz, whose north-eastern section was the heart of the pre-war Jewish community of the city and which hosted most of the 120 synagogues built in the city; and, on the other bank of the Vistula, Podgórze, a neighbourhood which was partly Jewish before the war, and where the Germans established the ghetto in the spring of 1941.[12] The opening sequence of The *Little Town of Kroke* thus visualises the two districts that are central to the cinematic image of Kraków in Holocaust cinema; haunted by memories of death and loss, Kazimierz and Podgórze have been caught in the process of looking back by means of that fragmented experience of history provided by the exploration of Holocaust sites in documentary films, and by the investigation of the relationship between places, their past and their archival memory. Non-fiction cinema has explored Kazimierz and Podgórze in an attempt to reinsert individual histories in the urban fabric of the city, and has sought to articulate visually that type of modern memory which, as Pierre Nora suggests, 'depends entirely on the materiality of trace, the immediacy of the recording, the visibility of the image' (1989: 8). Traces, records and images can be found in that interplay between the memorialisation of Kazimierz and Podgórze and its impact on the ways in which documentaries have addressed the life and destruction of the Jews of Kraków.

The films investigated in this section of the chapter have reflected upon the ways in which specific sites of the Holocaust have been monumentalised after the war and, in particular, following the collapse of the communist regime in Poland. At this juncture in the history of the city, Steven Spielberg's *Schindler's List* (1993) was filmed next to the site of the concentration camp in Płaszów, located just over one mile away from Podgórze, and in Kazimierz, where the sequences set in the ghetto were filmed. The popularity of Spielberg's film contributed to the phenomenon of Holocaust tourism in several historical locations of Kraków, a circumstance which is part of the broader context of the present-day popularisation of the Holocaust in media and popular culture. As Andreas Huyssen has argued, 'the problem for Holocaust memory in the 1980s and 1990s is not forgetting, but rather the ubiquitousness, the excess of Holocaust imagery everywhere in our culture', including 'the fascination with fascism in film and fiction' (1993: 256). Documentaries have addressed this ubiquitousness and the impact of popular culture on the visitor's experience of the city in relation to the history and the memory of its occupation. Accordingly, the investigation which follows addresses this process of memorialisation as it emerges from the interplay between history, fiction, present images and retrospective testimonies of the Holocaust in the specific contexts of Kazimierz and Podgórze in relation to, among other documentaries, three main case studies: *The Holocaust Tourist* (Jes Benstock, 2006), *Apteka pod Orłem* (*Under the Eagle Pharmacy*, Krzysztof Miklaszewski, 2006), and a film which has already been discussed in Chapter Three, Lindwer's *Return to My Shtetl Delatyn*.

The unchecked proliferation of Holocaust memorials and tours of Kraków can be seen as a sign of what Huyssen calls the 'traumatic ossification' of the memory of the Holocaust and the risk of 'its remaining locked in a melancholic fixation' (1993: 256). Accordingly, a reflection on the ways in which the tourist's experience of historical locations in Kazimierz has become part of this 'melancholic fixation' with the Holocaust is the theme explored in Benstock's *The Holocaust Tourist*. This short documentary addresses what Huyssen has called an obsession with the memorialisation of a past caught in a process of forgetting and in the realisation 'that the Holocaust has indeed become dispersed and fractured through the very different ways of memorializing it' (1993: 258). Benstock's film is concerned with the impact of the Holocaust on the present, and with the ways in which mass tourism and the monumentalisation of historical sites is experienced by visitors of Kazimierz and of the town of Oświęcim. As a starting point, *The Holocaust Tourist* addresses that conflicting identity which has been called by G. J. Tunbridge and J. E. Ashworth a *dissonant heritage*: Poles are now living in Kazimierz, and the neighbourhood is thus characterised by a temporal and spatial incongruence between the present and a heritage which derives from atrocity (1996).[13] Benstock himself has no claims to the Jewish heritage of the city, and explains at the beginning of the film that his own perspective is that of a tourist: 'I didn't want to make a film about the Holocaust but if you are a filmmaker and you are Jewish then it comes with the job description. What right have I to make a film about the Holocaust? I am not a direct descendant of victims or

Figure 4.3 *The Holocaust Tourist* (Jes Benstock, 2006)

survivors, I am just a tourist.' This statement is given a visual referent in a short animation accompanied by the sound of Klezmer, the musical tradition of the Ashkenazi Jews of Eastern Europe, and representing the tracks and the entrance of Auschwitz II-Birkenau, with a number of coaches on the side and signs with regulations for the tourists visiting the site of the camp (Fig. 4.3). The animation is followed by images of the ceremony for the sixtieth anniversary of the liberation of the camp, when some of the 2,000 survivors who attended the event are shown standing at night in the snow waiting for the coach that will take them back to Kraków. Uncomfortable with this sight and with the sense that those survivors were being neglected, Benstock's voice-over narration explains that from the release of *Schindler's List*, Holocaust tourism in Oświęcim and Kraków has begun to follow a trail dictated by Hollywood. The ceremony in Auschwitz II-Birkenau ignites a reflection on the ways in which the fictional dimension of the Holocaust in Spielberg's film thus appears to have been given priority over the survivors' experience of the sites of their persecution. Edited in order to support this claim, a rapid montage sequence presents places and tropes of Holocaust tourism in Kazimierz and in the area of the former ghetto in Podgórze, including shots of Hanukkah *menorot*, shop signs in Hebrew, posters advertising tours to Oświęcim in combination with visits to the Wieliczka Salt Mine and to Oscar Schindler's factory in Podgórze, souvenirs representing rabbis and fiddlers, Jewish-themed restaurants and groups of tourists walking in Kazimierz and dancing to Klezmer music. As G. J. Ashworth explains:

> The popularisation of Keneally's book by Spielberg's 1993 film [. . .] was the catalyst for rapid tourism development focusing specifically upon Kazimierz. A world-wide notoriety for the district led to a demand for 'Schindler tourism' focused especially on the evocatively photogenic cluster of synagogues, cemeteries and now also Jewish restaurants in the north-east of Kazimierz. (2010: 365)[14]

The following sequence illustrates what Ashworth calls 'Schindler tourism' and shows a guided tour to various locations in Kazimierz, including Szeroka Street and Jósefa Street. This tour privileges Spielberg's fictional world over the real location of the ghetto on the other bank of the Vistula; Szeroka Street and Jósefa Street were also used in *Schindler's List*, although the actual ghetto was located in Podgórze and, during the war, the north-eastern section of Kazimierz was Polish. The juxtaposition of fiction and history continues in the following scene, where a map shows the sites visited by the group and a portion of the screen is occupied by footage of an interview with a waiter from a local Jewish-themed restaurant revealing that the Hebrew letters decorating the place have no meaning and were randomly selected; the fabrication is thus unveiled.

Concerns with this trivialisation of Jewish culture are also articulated by Holocaust survivor Emanuel Elbinger, who is still living in Kraków and designs Jewish souvenirs for tourists. Interviewed by Benstock, Elbinger claims that most of the souvenirs on sale in Kazimierz are made by people who have never even seen a Jew, while he makes accurate sculptures in order to preserve the memory of the Jews of the city. This interview suggests the possibility of a different type of engagement with Holocaust tourism, based on the necessity of an accurate and thoughtful approach to history. This idea also emerges from the sequence filmed at the Galicia Museum, the location of a photographic exhibition focusing on derelict sites associated with the history of the Jews of Poland, including synagogues and cemeteries. The director of the museum, Chris Schwartz, explains that these photographs should be placed alongside images of Auschwitz I and Auschwitz II-Birkenau in order to shift the focus from the actual process of destruction of the Jews to a reminder of the world that was destroyed, and from a fascination with the crimes of the Nazis to a more nuanced engagement with Jewish heritage. This preoccupation is articulated further in the following sequence, where a series of shots portraying the Remuh Synagogue and the New Jewish Cemetery in Kazimierz accompany an interview with Professor Jonathan Webber, who argues that Kraków is a sacred place for the Jews and yet the city risks being experienced merely as a 'beautiful Disneyland' by tourists. Webber's claim is illustrated by a close-up of a postcard representing city landmarks and Jewish figurines, which unfolds into a digital animation including a map of Auschwitz II-Birkenau.

The polyphony of voices emerging from the Kazimierz sequences of *The Holocaust Tourist* and its accompanying visual commentary illustrate those excesses in the memorialisation of the Holocaust that can be defined, according to Huyssen, as the result of that tendency to popularise historical events and their representation which belongs ineradicably to an understanding of Holocaust memory that has become increasingly fractured (1993: 256–7). Kazimierz, its museums and synagogues reveal the importance of this district to the history and memory of the Jews of Eastern Europe; and yet the popularisation of the area tends to ossify this memory in a fixed obsession with the attempt to experience the sites of the Holocaust as if they were a film set. Benstock addresses the ways in which the genocide can be trivialised or misrepresented in the context of Holocaust tourism and, perhaps paradoxically, the filmmaker himself is presented as a tourist who wants to get closer to the Holocaust by means of an in-depth understanding of its spaces. *The Holocaust Tourist* is not an accusation against the exploration of historical sites, but rather an acknowledgement of the difficulties encountered by those who want to get closer to the horror and achieve a full understanding of the events aimed at evolving into more than a fractured and partial reading of the Holocaust. Fabrication and manipulation affect the experience of the city in ways which are thus accounted for in a film that captures the fragmented itinerary in time and space followed by those who want to comprehend.

A comparison between the cinematic image of Kazimierz as it emerges from *The Holocaust Tourist* and from an earlier documentary such as *Return to My Shtetl Delatyn* reveals a shifting type of engagement with the sites of memory in the district. In the Kraków sequence of the film, Berl Nuchim Lindwer, his son and his niece stop in the city on their way from Amsterdam to the *shtetl* Delatyn in Ukraine. This part of the journey contributes to contextualising the destruction of the Jews of Galicia and the dilapidated heritage of what used to be one of the main centres of Jewish life in this region. In 1992, *Return to My Shtetl Delatyn* captured an image of Kazimierz just before the filming of *Schindler's List* and after the relaxation of travel regulations in Eastern Europe, and, with that, the very early days of what was to become the phenomenon of Holocaust tourism in Kraków. Lindwer's film was thus one of the earliest Holocaust travel documentaries including present-day sequences filmed in Kraków and, in particular, in the north-eastern section of Kazimierz. The image that emerges is one in which Jewish culture and heritage pervade the

Figure 4.4 *Return to My Shtetl Delatyn* (Willy Lindwer, 1992).

experience of the district, while the popularisation of the Holocaust in the tourist industry has not yet taken place.

The sequence of *Return to My Shtetl Delatyn* set in Kraków opens with a scene filmed in the main square of the Old City, Rynek Główny, and shows street musicians and artists, horse-drawn carriages and some of the most famous and celebrated landmarks of the city, including the Cloth Hall, the Adam Mickiewicz Monument and St Mary's Church. These images are accompanied by live sound recorded on the square, consisting of the buskers' songs and the voices of the tourists, and they present a lively picture of the area, its visitors and its inhabitants. The film cuts to a shot of Kazimierz taken from the corner of Lewkowa Street and Szeroka Street and looking towards the sixteenth-century Old Synagogue (Fig. 4.4); in contrast with the Old City, Kazimierz is almost empty and silent. The voice-over narration provided by the filmmaker accompanies these images and explains that 'the old Jewish quarter of Kraków lies deserted'. The present-day shot of the synagogue fades into archival footage showing the building in the 1930s and, as the filmmaker tells the history of this district, footage of Kazimierz before the war illustrates the narration in an expository manner. The sense of absence and the void that emerges from the image of the area in 1992 is juxtaposed with the bustling, crowded streets of Kazimierz revealed in the footage: traders, schoolchildren and Hasidic Jews can be seen walking the streets of the district in a series of quotidian images of a world that was soon to be erased. A long shot of the Old Synagogue taken in the 1930s fades back to present-day footage of the site filmed from exactly the same spot on Szeroka Street. Past and present intertwine as the narrative returns to the 1990s and a panning shot follows Berl Nuchim and his niece Michal as they walk to the Remuh Synagogue. The camera follows the pair inside the building, where a custodian tells them the history of the place and how it was almost destroyed by the Germans during the occupation, when the building was used as storage for uniforms while the women's synagogue was converted into a stable. Berl Nuchim and Michal visit the grave of Moses Isserles, a sixteenth-century Ashkenazi rabbi, Talmudist and *posek*, at the Remuh Cemetery, also known as the Old Jewish Cemetery. One of the custodians there explains that the Jewish community of Kraków counts 195 members, all of whom are above the age of sixty-five, as young men and women have left for America or Israel. This revelation is visually juxtaposed with an ancient heritage in order to emphasise the contrast between a rich, lively past and a present made of sparse traces and records, and reiterates the parallel narrative established by the opposition between archival images and present-day footage. The act of looking back by means of temporal juxtapositions continues in the following scene, where an archival film representing Ashkenazi Jews in the 1930s anticipates a shot of the wailing wall in the Remuh Cemetery, which was built with fragments of gravestones smashed by the Nazis during the Second World War and retrieved in the 1950s from several *shtetlekh* in south-western Poland. In their quest for fragments of the Jewish past of Kazimierz, Berl Nuchim and Michal walk back to the Old Synagogue, where they visit the Jewish Museum, and the camera reveals a large number of derelict and dilapidated buildings formerly inhabited by Jews. This eerie image of Kazimierz was destined to change due to the success of Spielberg's film, the opening of the borders, national and foreign funding, and it eventually evolved into that 'beautiful Disneyland' provocatively evoked by Jonathan Webber in *The Holocaust Tourist*.

A comparison between the locations filmed in *Return to My Shtetl Delatyn* and the same locations recorded twenty years later by Marian Marzynski in *Never Forget to Lie* can also reveal the profound changes that affected the experience of this district. Beyond its exploration of Warsaw, this documentary includes a short sequence filmed in Kraków and presents the same preoccupation with the experience of Kazimierz that was articulated in *The Holocaust Tourist*. Marzynski meets two Holocaust survivors from

Katowice and Starachowice at Rynek Główny in the Old City; the square has the same touristic atmosphere it had in 1992, when Lindwer filmed *Return to My Shtetl Delatyn*. In contrast, the environment of Szeroka Street and the square outside the Old Synagogue has changed considerably in the images filmed by Marzynski from a window at the top floor of 30 Szeroka Street: on the square below, thousands of people, including Poles and foreign tourists, are dancing to Klezmer music during 'Shalom in Szeroka Street', the closing concert of the Jewish Culture Festival, an event which is defined by Marzynski as 'a form of atonement.'[15] Whereas *Return to My Shtetl Delatyn* had used Kazimierz as part of a postmemory journey led by a survivor and aimed at a transgenerational transmission of knowledge, *Never Forget to Lie* and *The Holocaust Tourist* thus articulate a discourse on memory and knowledge in relation to the experiences of those who do not have a personal connection with Jewish Kraków, but who want and struggle to understand and memorialise the events amidst the challenges brought about by the popularisation of Holocaust sites and Jewish heritage in Kazimierz.

The long history of Jewish Kazimierz came to an abrupt end during the occupation of Kraków, when the Jews of the area were relocated to the Podgórze district on the other bank of the Vistula, where the ghetto was established and where a number of Jews worked at Oskar Schindler's factory. Many more found their deaths in the Płaszów concentration camp, only one and a half miles south of the ghetto. Along with Kazimierz, Podgórze and Płaszów are defining sites of memory on the map of the city and on the cinematic landscape that emerges from documentary films of the Holocaust in Kraków. Brad Prager has discussed the ways in which Płaszów has been used as a location in Omer Fast's video installation *Spielberg's List* (2003) and James Moll's documentary *Inheritance* (2006), two audiovisual works that respectively build on the information provided by and criticise Steven Spielberg's approach to the past and his use of locations in *Schindler's List*, a film which was partly filmed in a version of the Płaszów camp built next to the actual site (2015: 73–110). Prager has argued that *Inheritance* and *Spielberg's List* 'shared a common point of reference: the extent to which *Schindler's List* shapes twenty-first-century knowledge of the Holocaust' (2015: 109–10). *Spielberg's List*, in particular, aims at challenging the ways in which many viewers encountered *Schindler's List* as reality, whereas film and video must be seen as media and not as experience. Fast's installation consists of a double-channel video display about the experiences of Polish extras who participated in Spielberg's shooting of the film, and includes footage from the set and from the original ground of the Płaszów camp. *Spielberg's List* thus returns to that preoccupation with the ways in which film locations are experienced as actual sites of memory that has been discussed earlier in this chapter. In *The Holocaust Tourist*, as we have already seen, the streets of Kazimierz are explored by visitors because they were the set of the ghetto in *Schindler's List*, whereas the actual ghetto was on the other side of the Vistula. In *Spielberg's List*, accounts of the representation of violence on set replace accounts about the actual experience of the Jews of Kraków.

This interplay between fiction and reality is also central to *Inheritance*, a film that connects the world of Spielberg's film to a documentary narrative focusing on *SS-Hauptsturmführer* Amon Goeth, who was played by Ralph Fiennes in *Schindler's List*. In *Inheritance*, Goeth's daughter Monika Hertwig travels to Płaszów in an attempt to learn more about her father and meets Helen Jonas-Rosenzweig, a Holocaust survivor who was forced to work as a maid for Goeth. The encounter unfolds in Płaszów near the memorial erected in 1964 and at Goeth's former home on the outskirts of the camp. For Monika, whose desire to know more about her father was ignited by the viewing of *Schindler's List* and by Fiennes' performance, the visit to Goeth's house becomes a way to connect with a distant past and allows her to acquire memories by imagination of his actions. Monika thus experiences a process of postmemory from a perspective rarely discussed or seen in documentary film, that of the daughter of a perpetrator for whom the events which preceded her birth have marked her childhood in a way that resembles the experience of children of survivors. Each room, and the history it contains, becomes the tool for the transmission of information from Helen to Monika, in a painful process of acquisition of knowledge mediated by the memories of site-specific events and bound to a place where history is inscribed in its physical reality and reflected in its representation in *Schindler's List*. Monika needs to bridge the gap between the fictional locations of Spielberg's film and the memories revealed by the built environment of the city and, in order to acquire this knowledge, she visits other sites of the Holocaust in Kraków, including the remains of the ghetto wall in Lwowska Street and Schindler's factory in Lipowa Street. *Inheritance* and *Spielberg's List* reveal how, beyond the boundaries of the camp in Płaszów, Spielberg's film has influenced the experience of Jewish heritage in Kraków and, with that, the documentary portrayal of the city. According to Gary Wiesemann, Spielberg has discussed widely the historical accuracy of his film and demonstrated a tendency to tie the authenticity of *Schindler's List* to 'its having been shot at the actual places where the historical events occurred, as if these sites assure the historical accuracy of what was filmed there' (2004: 158–9). As Prager suggests, *Inheritance* and *Spielberg's List* can be read as visual reflections on this assumption and on the locations and the layers of history and memory that belong to Płaszów and Podgórze (2015: 109–10). And yet these films are ultimately less concerned with unveiling a fabrication, and more with the long-lasting impact of the popularisation of the Holocaust on the memorialisation of the locations where the Jews of Kraków lived, were enslaved and died.

The most significant challenge to Spielberg's uses of the past emerges from a well-known and widely debated topic, dissected in most of the critical literature on film, trauma and the Holocaust, and consisting of an assessment of Claude Lanzmann's critique of *Schindler's List* and its fictional dramatisation of the Holocaust.[16] A perspective that has not been explored in this debate is provided by the fact that Lanzmann himself filmed on location in Podgórze, on a visit to a site that was to become a key location in *Schindler's List*: the Apteka Pod Orłem (Under the Eagle Pharmacy), which was located within the borders of the Kraków Ghetto at 18 Plac Bohaterów Getta (Ghetto Heroes Square), formerly Plac Zgody and Mały Rynek. Lanzmann filmed over 350 hours of interviews with survivors, bystanders and perpetrators in the making of *Shoah*, and one of the outtakes from the film is a sixty-minute interview with Tadeusz Pankiewicz, a Pole who ran the pharmacy. Pankiewicz, who had worked at the pharmacy since 1933 when the Nazis established the ghetto in March 1941 and closed off the district, declined the German offer of relocating to the other bank of the Vistula, and continued to operate his business as the only pharmacy in the ghetto.[17] With the support of his staff, he helped the Jews to smuggle various goods into the ghetto, offered shelter to those facing deportation to the concentration and death camps, and fed the Jewish workers from the camp in Płaszów. The conversation between Lanzmann and Pankiewicz took place in the early 1980s in Ghetto Heroes Square, the exact location from which Jews were deported to the camps. Pankiewicz gives a precise account of the organisation of the ghetto into section A (for those still capable of work) and section B (for those to be deported); he recalls the liquidation in 1943, and the network of Polish resistance fighters who helped the Jews during the war. Lanzmann and Pankiewicz are filmed as they sit on a bench, and the background of these shots reveals that most houses are still derelict and probably uninhabited, while the square itself is covered in rubble and is in the process of being redesigned. Various shots of the pharmacy and the civic number above its door bring the building from a past accounted for by a witness into the present: the Under the Eagle Pharmacy existed during the occupation and during the early 1980s, both in its physical state and in the memories of Pankiewicz.

The pharmacist's story, which was not included in the final cut of *Shoah*, was also the subject of a long interview with Pankiewicz filmed in 1981 for public Polish television outside the Under the Eagle Pharmacy, at the time when plans for a museum where put into action. Footage from this interview was used in 2006 by Krzysztof Miklaszewski in *Under the Eagle Pharmacy*, a Polish documentary focusing on Pankiewicz's actions during the war and on the events which took place in and around the pharmacy. In *Inheritance*, one of the locations of *Schindler's List*, Goeth's house in Płaszów, becomes the site of transition of knowledge from one member of the postgeneration to another; in *Under the Eagle Pharmacy*, another location popularised in Spielberg's film ignites a site-specific reflection on the destruction of the Jews of Podgórze. Miklaszewski's film aims at the abolition of all distance between past and present, merging earlier accounts of the history of the pharmacy with present-day images of the site. The film narrative articulates a simultaneity of past and present which can be explained with Huyssen's reflection on the passing of time and the persistence of memory: 'A sense of historical continuity or, for that matter, discontinuity, both of which depend on a before and an after, gives way to the simultaneity of all times and spaces readily accessible in the present. The perception of distance, both spatial and temporal, is being erased' (1993: 253–4). In *Under the Eagle Pharmacy* spatial and temporal distances are diminished by means of the interaction between present-day footage, archival material from 1940s and the 1980s, the commentary from Pankiewicz's memoir *Apteka w getcie krakowskim* (*The Kraków Ghetto Pharmacy*), read by a voice-over narrator,[18] and interviews with witnesses such as Maria Bożek-Nowak, a Polish woman who also helped to feed the Jews in the ghetto, and Jerzy Aleksandrowicz, whose family escaped from the ghetto during the liquidation thanks to Pankiewicz's actions.

Under the Eagle Pharmacy opens with recent images of the pharmacy, which is presently occupied by the Museum of National Remembrance, juxtaposed with extracts from Pankiewicz's memoir. This is followed by scenes from the interview with Pankiewicz recorded for Polish television in 1981 in front of the building in Ghetto Heroes Square, which was occupied by a bar called Nadwiślański between 1967 and the time of the interview, before being transformed into a museum in 1983. Pankiewicz explains that all non-Jews had to leave Podgórze in 1941, and archival footage of the move from this district to the other bank of the river and the subsequent relocation of the Jews from Kazimierz to Podgórze illustrates his narration. An excerpt from Pankiewicz's memoir illustrates the events which took place on those days: 'The move began at dawn and lasted till late evening. People drove platforms, furniture wagons, and handcarts to move their belongings to their new living quarters. There was an incredible rush and there was not much time, and everyone wanted a bearable place to live.' Archival footage shows the scenes recalled by Pankiewicz as they unfolded on Józef Piłsudski Bridge and on the streets of Podgórze, with various shots of Jewish men and women wearing Star of David armbands and carrying their belongings across the bridge to Podgórze while Poles walk in the opposite direction. Miklaszewski uses this material to give a visual referent to the oral accounts included in the film, avoiding the use of staging and dramatic recreations. The images, originally filmed by a German cameraman, are used in *Under the Eagle Pharmacy* to introduce the viewer to the interurban resettlement of the Jews, and yet the use of images taken by the Nazis embodies the selecting and omitting perspective of the German cameramen and the consequent softening of the brutality seen on those days in the streets of the city. This archival footage illustrates Pankiewicz's commentaries from 1947 and 1981 and, despite the distortion of truth that is embodied in the visual records taken by perpetrators, the polyphony of sources used by Miklaszewski contextualises and repurposes this material in order to bridge the chronological gap.

The kind of juxtaposition observed in the opening sequences continues throughout the film for the purpose of diminishing temporal distance; Pankiewicz's account from the television interview fades into the voice-over reading of his memoirs while archival images shift into present-day footage of Podgórze. The result is the creation of a closer proximity to the events by means of merging different layers of time while maintaining the same location.[19] This is also exemplified in the sequence where present-day footage of the fragments of the ghetto wall at the rear of the primary school at 62 Limanowska Street accompany an excerpt from the book, in which Pankiewicz recalls the construction of the wall in the style of Jewish headstones and the barring of all windows looking at the city outside the perimeter of the ghetto. Pankiewicz explains that three gates led into the ghetto and the main entrance was facing the Market Square in Podgórze; a map of the area and two archival photographs of the gate, with its Star of David and a large sign in Hebrew reading 'Jewish District', illustrate the account. This scene is followed by a present-day tracking shot of the district filmed from a car driving along Limanowska Street, providing a visual referent to another excerpt from Pankiewicz's memoirs recalling the trams running along this street. His site-specific memoir also describes the headquarters of the *Judenrat* and of the German police next to the main gate to the ghetto; present-day footage of the place shows the same building, which has now become the New Town Hall of Podgórze in the market square.[20]

Figure 4.5 *Apteka pod Orłem* (*Under the Eagle Pharmacy*, Krzysztof Miklaszewski, 2006).

Lanzmann and Pankiewicz sat on a bench in the middle of Ghetto Heroes Square in the days before its monumentalisation. Today this space is occupied by the Memorial to the Jews from the Kraków Ghetto, created by Piotr Lewicki and Kazimierz Latak in 2005. Towards the end of *Under the Eagle Pharmacy*, a present-day long shot of the square taken from inside the pharmacy shows some of the seventy steel and cast-iron chairs, each representing 1,000 deportees, which compose the memorial (Fig. 4.5). This shot is accompanied by Pankiewicz's account of the deportation from this square extracted from his memoirs, and followed by archival images an*d an extract on the same subject taken from the 1981 interview. Under* the *Eagle Pharmacy* thus includes a sequence filmed at the site of the deportations from the ghetto to Auschwitz II-Birkenau and Bełżec, a place that is now monumentalised and popularised in the heritage tours of the city. In his study of Holocaust monuments such as the memorial in Podgórze, Huyssen has argued that the criteria for the success of such endeavours lies in 'the ways it allows for a crossing of boundaries towards other discourses of the Holocaust, the way it pushes us toward reading other texts, other stories' (1993: 258). Accordingly, Lewicki and Latak's monument crosses the boundaries between personal and collective histories, memories and representations, and so does its image in *Under the Eagle Pharmacy*. This interplay between monumental memorialisation and cinematic image continues in the final sequence of the film, which includes a panoramic view of Podgórze cutting to a long shot of the memorial at the site of the Płaszów camp where Monika Hertwig met Helen Jonas-Rosenzweig in *Inheritance*. As Andrew Charlesworth and Michael

Addis have argued, this site, which had been entirely neglected until the early 1960s, has seen an increased interest from scholars and visitors after the release of *Schindler's List*. And yet, as Charlesworth and Addis suggest, the disappearance of its original buildings has left its post-war monuments to provide a visual referent to the name of Płaszów and to its role in the unfolding of the Holocaust in Kraków (2002: 233–8).[21] In this sequence from *Under the Eagle Pharmacy*, the Płaszów memorial becomes a site of remembrance of the Jews of the ghetto, a place that is inscribed in the Jewish history of the city as part of a process of memorialisation of the events where, as Huyssen argues, 'in the absence of tombstones to the victims, the monument can function as a substitute site of mourning and remembrance' (1993: 258).

The memorials in Płaszów and at the Ghetto Heroes Square, as well as their cinematic image in *The Eagle Pharmacy*, stand for the destruction of a city which left Pankiewicz wandering the deserted streets of Podgórze, as narrated in the final excerpt from his memoirs used in the film: 'It seemed to me that after two and a half years in the ghetto, I had been sent to a land of the dead, a city devoid of inhabitants. I walked the empty streets of this dead city, listening to the sound of my own steps.'[22] Both Warsaw and Kraków were indeed eerie landscapes of death by the end of the war, and yet their memorialisation evolved differently in the following decades, largely because of the disappearance of traces in Warsaw and the abundance of remnants in Kraków. Fictional versions of these cities have complicated further the challenge of memorialising a past which is still inscribed in their built environment and which requires a negotiation between the mutability of space and the passing of time. A full understanding of these locations should thus be based on an investigation chiselled in the process of engaging the visitor or the audience with a heritage that speaks of surviving atrocity, and attempts to fight both forgetfulness and its opposite, the saturation of popularised images of the sites. As we shall see in the following chapter, an equally dynamic interplay between past and present, fiction and reality, space and place also emerges from the documentary cityscapes of Lviv and Łódź, the cities where the other major ghettos were established by the Nazis and where slivers of memory remain, fade and re-emerge in film.

Notes

1. On the eve of Yom Kippur, on 12 October 1940, the Nazis ordered the establishment of the Warsaw ghetto, which was fenced on the 16 November. Over 380,000 Jews, thirty per cent of the population of the city, were

concentrated into a territory covering less than three per cent of Warsaw. Thousands had already died when the deportations to Treblinka began in 1942; from 22 July to 21 September of that year, more than 265,000 Jews were deported from the ghetto to Treblinka (Miron, *The Yad Vashem Encyclopaedia*, pp. 897–921).

2. Other documentaries about the Warsaw ghetto, largely based on archival photographs and talking-heads interviews, include *A Day in the Warsaw Ghetto: A Birthday Trip in Hell* (Jack Kuper, 1991) and *Karuzela* (*Carousel*, Michał Nekanda-Trepka, 1993). The Warsaw Uprising is described in *The Jews in the Warsaw Rising* (Anna Ferens and Anna Kowalewska-Onaszkiewicz, 2004) and *Zejść na ziemię* (*Down to Earth*, Michał Nekanda-Trepka, 2012). Irena Sendler, a woman who contributed to smuggling more than 2,500 children out of the ghetto, is the subject of *In the Name of Their Mothers: The Story of Irena Sendler* (Mary Skinner, 2011) and *Łyżeczka życia* (*Spoon of Life*, Michał Nekanda-Trepka, 2003). The story of Magdalena Grodzka-Guzkowska, a woman who joined the Polish Underground at the age of fifteen, is told in *Magda* (Slawomir Grünberg and Katka Reszke, 2013).
3. For example, expository documentary accounts of wartime Warsaw have included photographs from the report on the liquidation of the ghetto compiled by *SS- und Polizeiführer* Jürgen Stroop for Heinrich Himmler.
4. Taylor, *Film Propaganda: Soviet Russia and Nazi Germany*.
5. Reimer, *Cultural History through a National Socialist Lens*.
6. The motivation for this journey is also articulated in Ziv's interview with Marcel Ophüls, director of the landmark documentary on the German occupation of France, *Le Chagrin et la Pitié* (*The Sorrow and the Pity*, 1969), who explains that survivors and witnesses are getting older and are dying, and filmmakers are responsible for capturing documentary accounts of their experience. This reminder from Ophüls applies to a significant number of documentaries investigated in this book and implicitly gives the postgeneration, along with the filmmakers, the task of keeping memories alive and contributing to the process of transmission of knowledge started by the survivors.
7. Mieczysław Apfelbaum Square was named after a man who has been said to have led the Jewish Military Union (Żydowski Związek Wojskowy), but whose actual existence is still disputed.
8. A trope of Holocaust documentaries, the image of the train, as Annette Insdorf has argued, is also conveyed when Marzynski 'describes how his father cut a hole in the floor of the transport bearing him to a concentration camp, and jumped out to join the partisans' (Insdorf, *Indelible Shadows*, pp. 202–3).
9. Lowenthal, *The Past Is a Foreign Country*.
10. Marzynski's voice-over narration also reveals that, while he was playing in a similar courtyard, a neighbour threatened to reveal his identity to the Nazis and consequently the child had to leave the place and seek help elsewhere.

11. *Never Forget to Lie* avoids the use of photographs taken by the perpetrators, with only one specific exception: in the sequence where Marzynski visits one of the few existing buildings of the ghetto with Lilian Boraks-Nemetz, a survivor who explains how her father was in the Jewish Police and saved her from deportation. In this sequence, the filmmaker holds an archival photograph representing the ghetto wall and a small number of Jews standing on the street. This image is used to establish a topographical link between past and present in the specific location where Boraks-Nemetz gives her account.
12. Before the war, one quarter of the population of Kraków was Jewish – about 56,000 people. All Jewish political organisations were present in the city, which was also a centre of cultural, academic and religious activity. The Nazis occupied the city in September 1939 and established the ghetto two years later. Mass deportations to Bełżec began soon after the sealing of the ghetto. The majority of the Jews of the ghetto were relocated to the concentration camp in Płaszów by the end of 1942. The ghetto was finally liquidated on 13–14 March 1943 (Miron, *The Yad Vashem Encyclopaedia*, pp. 121–8).
13. Ashworth and Tunbridge, *Dissonant Heritage*. See also Ashworth and Tunbridge, 'Old Cities, New Pasts'.
14. Ashworth, 'Holocaust Tourism'.
15. The first Jewish Culture Festival in Kraków took place in 1988, before the filming of *Return to My Shtetl Delatyn*. However, it only became a major cultural event in the late 1990s.
16. See, for example, Hansen, '*Schindler's List* Is Not *Shoah*'.
17. *Shoah* outtake, 'Tadeusz Pankiewicz – Kraców'; story RG-60.5014; film ID: 3220, Steven Spielberg Film and Video Archive, United States Holocaust Memorial Museum.
18. Pankiewicz, *Apteka w getcie krakowskim*.
19. Other examples of this process include a sequence in which the reading of excerpts from Pankiewicz's book recalls the events of 20 March 1941, when the ghetto was sealed and Pankiewicz spent the night on his own at the pharmacy, and accompanies a black-and-white photograph of him standing at the counter followed by a present-day shot filmed from the opening of the pharmacy's door, looking towards the square.
20. The other gate was at the intersection between Limanowska and Lwowska streets; in a short sequence, an archival image of the gate fades to present-day footage of the place and its surviving section of the ghetto wall. The third gate was across the pharmacy and led from what was known as Zgody Square to the bridge over the Vistula, which was known as Most Krakusa and was replaced in 1968 by the Silesian Insurgents Bridge. Present-day footage of this location is juxtaposed with archival images of destitute Jews, accompanied by Pankiewicz's description of poverty in the ghetto provided by the voice-over narrator.
21. Charlesworth and Addis, 'Memorialization and the Ecological Landscapes of Holocaust Sites'.

22. The Jews of Kraków who survived the camps returned to their city and often had to face the hostility of its Polish inhabitants. On 20 August 1945, for example, large-scale riots against the Jews spread across the city (Gilbert, *The Holocaust: The Jewish Tragedy*, p. 816).

CHAPTER 5

Another Tale of Two Cities: Lviv and Łódź

'The return to my native city is painful.'

— Mira Hamermesh, *Loving the Dead*

The cinematic topography of the Holocaust, as discussed in the previous chapter, saw certain neighbourhoods playing the role of other districts of the same city. Holocaust cinema has also seen particular cities being used as sets for events that happened elsewhere, and often in places with their own specific war narratives. Agnieszka Holland's Holocaust drama *W ciemności* (*In Darkness*, 2011) is based on the true story of Leopold Socha, a sewer worker in the then Polish city of Lwów (now the Ukrainian city of Lviv) who used his knowledge of the urban sewer system to shelter a group of Jews who escaped from the local ghetto.[1] *In Darkness* is entirely set in Lviv and filmed in Warsaw, Berlin, Leipzig and, in particular, in and around the city of Łódź. By setting the film in Lviv and filming in Łódź and other places, Holland adopted an approach to location shooting that has been described by François Penz and Andong Lu in terms of 'creative geography' – a distinct way of reading cinematic urban geographies in films that 'reorganize the city spaces into narrative geographies where urban fragments are collaged into spatial episodes' (2011: 14).[2] Documentaries, on the other hand, are traditionally characterised by a topographically coherent approach to their locations, and as such they can be seen as privileged tools in the process of anchoring the memories of the extermination to the landscapes where it occurred. This chapter investigates the ways in which cinematic images of the city where *In Darkness* is set, Lviv, and that of one of the actual locations of Holland's film, Łódź, have been articulated in documentary films about the destruction of their Jewish communities. Before the war, both Lviv and Łódź were important cultural, religious and political centres of European Jewry. During the occupation, both cities saw the establishment of ghettos and the deportation of their Jewish populations to the death camps, with primarily Bełżec as a final destination for the Jews of Lviv and Chełmno and Auschwitz II-Birkenau for the Jews of Łódź. Since the war, small Jewish communities have continued to exist in both cities, and scattered signs of Jewish life have remained inscribed in their built environment. Documentary filmmakers have searched for these remnants and, by means of return journeys to both cities, they have narrated collective and personal stories of the annihilation of the Jews of Lviv and Łódź. The case studies investigated in this chapter are based on that type of juxtaposition of past and present where contemporary footage is used to integrate archival images and the testimonies of the survivors. These space-specific narratives focus on distant events as much as on the ways in which the past still informs the present of Lviv and Łódź; and yet, as in the case of Warsaw and Kraków, the cinematic image of these cities is characterised by profound absences, and by the ongoing attempt of gathering site-specific fragments of the past in response to the impossibility of providing a totalising narrative of the Holocaust.

Lviv

The exhibition *Holocaust in Lviv: 1941–1944* opened in 2006 at the Historical Museum of the city and was accompanied by the production of *Два танго* (*Two to Tango*), a short documentary made by the local Jewish charity Hesed Arieh. This film uses archival photographs from the 1940s showing Lviv under German occupation, and includes images of iconic buildings such as the Opera House decorated with swastikas and juxtaposed with present-day images of the sites.[3] *Two to Tango* also addresses Ukrainian collaborationism, and includes images of women in local costume welcoming the Nazis in 1941. As a result of the film's attempt to address national responsibilities in the Holocaust, Hesed Arieh was accused of anti-Ukrainian activities by members of Svoboda and other nationalist political groups, and the film was banned from public screenings in the schools of the city. These events reveal that the Holocaust in Lviv is a theme that has struggled to emerge in public debates and to inform film narratives.[4] Only two documentaries have consistently used present-day locations in Lviv in order to articulate a discourse on history, memory and the scarcity of traces: Willy Lindwer's *Return to My Shtetl Delatyn*, a film already discussed in earlier chapters in relation to its exploration of Delatyn, Przemysl and Kraków; and Yiddish-language film *Boris Dorfman a Mentsh* (Gabriela and Uwe von Seltmann, 2014).

Return to My Shtetl Delatyn includes a sequence filmed in Lviv, one of the destinations on the journey of the Lindwers to the *shtetl* Delatyn. These scenes are not closely related to the familial history of Berl Nuchim, and their narrative function aims at contextualising this postmemory journey in connection with Jewish culture in the eastern territories of the Second Polish Republic and with the history of the largest community in the area. This site-specific exploration reveals how the past is still inscribed in today's Lviv, and remnants of the ancestral world of the Jewish city are identified throughout this sequence in the present-day built environment. In the opening scene, the filmmaker's voice-over narration summarises the history of the Jews of Lviv and accompanies a long shot of the Bernardine church and monastery taken from Halytska Square. The following street scenes introduce the viewer to a city whose Jewish community has almost been erased. They include images of the Old Town showing pedestrians, street performers, cars of Soviet manufacture and trams, and various shots of iconic buildings such as the Church of St Archangel Michael, the Opera House and, filmed from the Market Square, the Latin Cathedral. The pre-war Jewish community of Lviv is evoked in the next scene as the present-day images fade into archival footage from the 1930s showing the Reform Tempel Synagogue in the Market Square, which was destroyed by the Nazis in July 1941, and members of the Jewish community walking on the streets near the synagogue. This footage ends with a long shot of the Jewish Hospital at 6 Yakova Rappoporta Street, a building decorated with the Star of David, which has survived the German occupation and is today the Third Municipal Clinical Hospital of Lviv; this archival image then fades into a present-day shot of the hospital, taken from the same location on Leontovycha Street. The following shots reveal other remnants of Jewish Lviv, including the remains of the Golden Rose Synagogue at Ivana Fedorova Street (Fig. 5.1), the derelict Jakub Glanzer synagogue in Vuhilna Street, the former Chasidim Synagogue at 3 Ugolnaya Street and Beis Aharon V'Yisrael Synagogue at 4 Brativ Mikhnovskykh Street, the only functioning synagogue in the city.[5] These places, along with the former Jewish Hospital, are amongst the very few surviving buildings associated with the Jewish community of the city. Smaller traces of the past are also identifiable in the built environment of Lviv; for example, in a scene filmed in a narrow alley in the Old Town, where the camera pans left to reveal the space for a *mezuzah* on the jamb of a former Jewish home. According to Henri Lefebvre, history is spatialised by the impact of the events that take place at a particular location and is given a geographical dimension by the inscription of such occurrences into space. And yet space is always a present space, whole and complete, at once product and part of the production process of historical events; any place, continues Lefebvre, is thus continuously elaborated through

Figure 5.1 *Return to My Shtetl Delatyn* (Willy Lindwer, 1992).

the connection between past events and their actuality (1991: 37).[6] As past and present intertwine during this walk through the city, *Return to My Shtetl Delatyn* articulates the spatialisation of history evoked by Lefebvre by tracing a familiar topography consisting of remnants of Polish–Jewish Lwów in the Ukrainian city of Lviv, thus unveiling a collective history inscribed in its buildings and emerging from the archive; the Holocaust is thus given a geographical dimension inasmuch as the present-day city is framed as its product and, at once, its production force.

The exploration of the historical heritage of Lviv and the consequent spatialisation of the Holocaust, processed through that connection between past events and their ongoing actuality articulated by Lefebvre, is also at the core of Gabriela and Uwe von Seltmann's *Boris Dorfman a Mentsh*, a documentary shot entirely in Yiddish language which follows Boris Dorfman to the city's sites of Jewish life and death. Dorfman acts as a guardian of Jewish traditions and of the language of Eastern European Jews, of which he is one of the last speakers in Lviv. He was born in 1923 in the *shtetl* Kagul in Bessarabia and he survived the Second World War in Siberia, where he worked as a coal miner in Kiselevsk,[7] only settling in Lviv in 1950. Dorfman did not witness the persecution of the Jews in the 1940s, but from the 1950s onwards he gathered knowledge and documents on the Jews of Lviv and explored the places where they lived, prayed, worked and died. As it follows Dorfman's activities and rejects the use of archival inserts,[8] *Boris Dorfman a Mentsh* traces a map of what is left of the Jewish city and locates the narration firmly in a present rooted in a distant past that risks being forgotten. Rather than as a witness, Dorfman acts as a historian in the traditional definition articulated by Pierre Nora as 'the spokesman of the past and the herald of the future' – but also as a new type of historian, 'who prevents history from becoming merely history' and who has become, as a result of memory being engulfed by history, 'no longer a memory-individual but, in himself, a *lieu de memoir*' (1989: 18).

Boris Dorfman a Mentsh opens with a series of statements about Dorfman's cultural activism and his scholarship of Jewish traditions, given, among others, by his wife, daughter and grandchild. Dorfman himself sings a religious song in Yiddish while his wife sets the Shabbat table, with the two candles representing the dual commandments to remember and observe the festivities.[9] These beliefs are also the guiding principles of Dorfman's activity, the aims of a life spent remembering the Jews of Lviv and observing the cultural and physical remnants of that community. The scenes which follow the introduction to this *mentsh* – 'human being' in Yiddish – serve the purpose of establishing Lviv as the main location of the film by means of a focus on recognisable landmarks, largely related to the Christian identity of the city. Three establishing shots of the Old Town include views of the Church of Saints Olha and Elizabeth, St George's Cathedral and the Transfiguration Church, filmed at dusk on a Friday at the beginning of Shabbat. These establishing shots are followed by images of a semi-deserted street in the Old Town, accompanied by the sound of church bells. An elliptical cut leads to a medium shot of the street in the early morning, and the daylight later reveals an almost invisible remnant of Jewish Lviv in a close-up of the empty space for a *mezuzah* outside one of the buildings. This shot is followed by early morning scenes filmed at the market square, looking towards Krakivska Street.

Boris Dorfman wakes up in his apartment and is then followed by the filmmakers to three sites associated with the celebration of Shabbat in Lviv, the remnants of the forty-eight pre-war synagogues of the city. He joins the prayers at the Beis Aharon V'Yisrael Synagogue before visiting the remains of the Golden Rose Synagogue. Here, as Dorfman walks around the ruins of the building, the Shabbat hymns recited at Beis Aharon V'Yisrael are juxtaposed with images of the derelict synagogue, which was desecrated in 1941, and evoke the voices of those who have been murdered by the Nazis (Fig. 5.2). Dorfman leaves this site behind and walks on the streets of the Old Town, in the market square; he approaches the Jakub

Figure 5.2 *Boris Dorfman a Mentsh* (Gabriela and Uwe von Seltmann, 2014).

Glanzer synagogue, which was used as a sports centre during the Soviet era and was returned to the small Jewish community of the city in 1989. As Dorfman enters the dilapidated synagogue, prays and tells the story of the building, *Boris Dorfman a Mentsh* ultimately articulates a discourse on space and its continuous processing through the connection between past and present. This sequence illustrates the voids left by the Holocaust at a particularly significant time in the Jewish week, on Shabbat – a choice that emphasises the emotional connection with the erased past and the importance of the attempt to preserve memory in a cityscape irremediably changed.

The second part of his exploration takes Dorfman from the sites of Jewish life to the places associated with the death of the Jews of Lviv, including the monument commemorating the victims of the Lviv ghetto in Viacheslava Chornovola Avenue;[10] the Lviv-Holovnyi railway station, from which, during the Soviet occupation in 1940, thousands of Jews were deported to Siberia;[11] the suburban station of Kleparov, where Jews were packed in cattle trains and taken to the death camp in Bełżec;[12] the site of the Janowska concentration camp, on the outskirts of the city in the Shevchenkivs'kyi district, where Dorfman visits the memorial to victims and walks near the river and the sand and gravel pits into which Jews were thrown by the Nazis; and the Yanivsky Cemetery, where his own mother was buried in 1963. In a manner that resembles the strategy adopted by Lanzmann in *Shoah*, the deportations are evoked in these sequences by means of repeated shots of the railway tracks and the freight trains that punctuate an itinerary characterised by the disappearances of traces, and by the difficulty of inscribing the fate of the Jews of Lviv into a landscape defined by absences. The final location of Dorfman's exploration takes him to the forest near Rudno, the place where the Nazis murdered the last surviving Jews from the Lviv ghetto in June 1943 and where a small memorial was built in 2008. Here, in a sequence that superimposes the sound of prayers recorded at the Beis Aharon V'Yisrael Synagogue onto the image of the memorial, Dorfman prays for the Jews who were killed and, in a direct address to viewers, asks the world to remember the Jews of Lviv. In the absence of traces and to paraphrase Pierre Nora's aforementioned words, Dorfman is no longer a memory-individual but is himself a site of memory. The memorialisation of the Holocaust in Lviv is integrated into the consciousness of a *mentsh* who does not have direct experience of the events, but whose engagement with the traumatic past of the city has made him a guardian of memories by imagination rather than by recall, in a way which resembles the processes of postmemory. As a site of memory, Dorfman can ultimately decipher both the Jewish heritage of the city, its lost language, and the destruction of its people.

Łódź

Born in Łódź in 1925, filmmaker Mira Hamermesh escaped into Soviet-occupied territory during the war, fled to Palestine and then moved to London; her mother died in the Łódź ghetto and her father was murdered in Auschwitz II-Birkenau. In her memoir, *The River of Angry Dogs*, Hamermesh remembers a rainy evening in 1959 when she went to the Academy Cinema in Oxford Street, London, to watch Andrzej Wajda's *Pokolenie* (*A Generation*, 1955), a film about the German occupation of Warsaw set in the working-class district of Wola. As the film's credits revealed, *A Generation* was processed and printed in Hamermesh's native city, whose name 'appeared in large letters that jumped out of the screen like mythical winged horses' (2004: 3). This encounter with the past in the comfort of a cinema on Oxford Street triggered a transformative reflection on her life, her family and the Holocaust. It also ignited Hamermesh's thoughts on the power of cinema: 'With film everything is possible. Even the dead can be resurrected,' and accordingly 'the Academy Cinema had opened a door to ghosts' (2004: 3–7).[13] Many years later, Hamermesh faced these ghosts again in her documentary *Loving the Dead* (1991), a cinematic journey to the sites of memory of the exterminated Jews in Łódź, Warsaw, Auschwitz II-Birkenau and the *shtetlekh* Sobienie-Jeziory and Tykocin. Punctuated by the ghostly apparition of Hamermesh's parents, this film is at once a quest for traces of Jewish culture in 1990s Poland and an exploration of a family's history and its destruction in the Holocaust. In a brief sequence at the beginning of the film, the filmmaker is on the back seat of a car in a foggy Polish landscape; her mother and father, played by two actors, approach the car as Hamermesh recalls a dream where she is driven by a chauffeur along the streets of the Łódź ghetto and sees her parents standing on the pavements. The apparition of Hamermesh's parents in her dreams and in the film, the return of the dead, is the result of what Slavoj Žižek has discussed in terms of a disturbance with one's obsequies and as that ambivalent desire of the living to keep the dead amongst them and to stop them from returning to our world and interrupt normality (1992: 22–3; 2003: 100).[14] In *The River of Angry Dogs*, Hamermesh explains that her own family vanished from her life without obsequies and that this is the void she had long been afraid to be sucked into. In its attempt to fill this emptiness, *Loving the Dead* is Hamermesh's quest for her parent's burial sites, for their unmarked graves in the Łódź Jewish Cemetery and in the killing grounds of Auschwitz II-Birkenau. This film is thus part of a process of grieving and mourning, an attempt to come to terms with the consequences of the disturbances in her parents' burials and, by doing so, to stop the dead from coming back.

In her *Eurydice Series* of compositions about trauma and the transmission of knowledge, artist Bracha Lichtenberg Ettinger uses a street photograph of her parents taken in Łódź in 1937 juxtaposed with two other images: a photograph from her own childhood, and a photograph of a group of Jewish women executed by *Einsatzgruppen* in Eastern Poland. Marianne Hirsch has argued that as objects returning from the past these images activate fears of a repetition of violence and Ettinger's work thus 'absorbs some of the embodied practices of that past moment, enacting a kind of return journey in photographic mode' (2012b: 211).[15] As in Ettinger's work, in *Loving the Dead* memories of the dead are also triggered by familial images; here, photographs of Hamermesh's parents in the 1930s are used as that type of photographic evidence which, as Hirsch suggests, points 'both to the power of the familial mythos in the face of external threat and to the powerlessness of the family as institution to act in any way as a protection' (1997: 36). The combination of Hamermesh's own return journey in photographic mode and her physical journey to Łódź is fundamental to the process of unlocking memories and healing open wounds: 'The return to my native city is painful,' Hamermesh claims on her arrival in Łódź. Here, she identifies the house where she lived with her parents in the centre of the city, and reflects on the painful fact that the building survived while her parents did not. Hamermesh stands outside the house and observes the balcony from which she used to watch city life. The gaze has been inverted and she is now excluded from the place of her childhood; the security of a city viewed from a window is replaced by the uncertainty of a home now inaccessible and observed from the street. During her visit to Łódź, Hamermesh acquires knowledge about her parents' lives in the ghetto by means of the exploration of locations bound to her familial history and thanks to the study of the photographs taken by Mendel Grossman and Henryk Ross, two professional photographers who worked for the *Judenrat* in the creation of a sanctioned archive and who also took clandestine photographs of the ghetto which were discovered after the war. Hamermesh observes their work at a local archive and uses these images to punctuate the sequences of the film shot in Łódź.[16] She also visits the other family house, a small building in the former ghetto located at 7 Zawiszy Street, where her parents lived during the occupation. This is a cramped and derelict building in a rundown part of town, profoundly different from the wealthier family house in the city centre of Łódź. Hamermesh visits this location for the first time as she did not experience the horrors of the ghetto and the deportations but, in a way that is reminiscent of the processes of postmemory, she made her parents' suffering her own: 'I was not there but the horror of their lives has cast a shadow over mine wherever I am.'

In *Shoah*, Auschwitz II-Birkenau survivor Paula Biren gives her testimony from Cincinnati and explains that she could not face a journey to Łódź, the city where she was born, for fear of what she would find there. In particular, Biren heard rumours concerning the demolition of the Jewish cemetery of Łódź, the place where her grandparents were buried and the subject of a long shot juxtaposed by Lanzmann with her testimony. The cemetery was never demolished and, in *Loving the Dead*, Hamermesh visits the section where those who died in the ghetto were buried in unmarked graves. Here she identifies a gravestone placed after the war by surviving relatives and lights a candle in memory of her mother. The discovery of this particular location does not provide closure, but it contributes to that ongoing process of mourning that ambivalently claims the dead back while hoping they will not return. As this action unfolds on the screen, *Loving the Dead* deals with recurring themes, places and tropes which, as we shall see, regularly characterise the documentary image of Jewish Łódź. The use of archival and family photographs, the visit to familial locations and public spaces, the return journey of a survivor and the attempt to come to terms with profound losses will be addressed in what follows in relation to a group of documentaries of Łódź and their engagement with personal stories of the living, and with what can be discussed as the act of loving the dead. In particular, the transition between past and present by means of the juxtaposition of archival images and present-day footage will be tackled in relation to a series of documentaries addressing Jewish life in the city during and after the war, and revealing a continuity between past and present inscribed in the spatialisation of testimonies, physical remnants and archival material.

Before the war Łódź had a Jewish population of approximately 230,000 people, one-third of its overall number of inhabitants. The persecution of the Jews began immediately after the Germans occupied the city on 8 September 1939 and renamed it Litzmannstadt. In November the largest synagogues were torched, and deportations to other cities in the General Government began one month later. The ghetto was established in February 1940 in the Bałuty district and sealed at the beginning of May, while the controversial insurance agent Mordechai Chaim Rumkowski was appointed by the Germans as head of the Council of Elders, the *Judenrat*. In the following years, Jews and Gypsies from other lands in occupied Europe were taken to the ghetto in the Bałuty district of the city, where they were forced to work as slave labour for the Germans along with the Jews of Łódź, and from where they were eventually deported to the sites of extermination in Chełmno and Auschwitz II-Birkenau. Of the 204,800 Jews who lived in the ghetto over four years, fewer than 10,000 survived (cf. Miron, 2010: 403–12). These survivors included Szymon Srebrnik, a Jewish boy who was deported at the age of thirteen to Chełmno, the extermination camp located fifty miles north-west of the city, where he was forced to help the Nazis in their attempt to dispose of all evidence of the mass murder. His father had been killed in front of his eyes in the ghetto, and his mother died in a gas van in Chełmno. In Claude Lanzmann's *Shoah*, Srebrnik gives an account of his arrival at Chełmno and the indifference with which he observed the annihilation of hundreds of thousands, explaining that this attitude was born out of his experience in the ghetto:

> I'd never seen anything else. In the ghetto, I saw . . . in the ghetto in Łódź, that as soon as anyone took a step, he fell dead. I thought that's the way things had to be, it was normal. I'd walk the streets of Łódź, maybe one hundred yards, and there would be two hundred bodies. People were hungry. They went into the street and they fell, they fell. . . . Sons took their fathers' bread, fathers took their sons' bread, everyone wanted to stay alive. So when I came here, to Chełmno, I was already . . . I did not care about anything. I thought: if I survive, I just want one thing: loaves of bread. To eat. That's all. That's what I thought. But I dreamed, too, that if I survive, I'll be the only one left in the world, not another soul. Just me. One. Only me left in the world, if I get out of here.

Srebrnik's reminiscences of Łódź outline a devastating image of persecution and provide an account of the abysmal living conditions in the ghetto. His testimony thus inscribes the place in a landscape of destruction that had its dark heart in the extermination camps and its antechamber in the ghettos. While there is no photographic evidence of the killing centre in Chełmno, the Łódź ghetto was photographed by both Jews and Germans in what eventually resulted in a vast visual archive that has consistently been used in documentaries about the captivity of the Jews of Łódź and their destruction.

Dariusz Jabłoński's *Fotoamator* (*Photographer*, 1998), one of the most widely studied films about the annihilation of the Jews in Łódź, uses colour slides of the ghetto that were discovered in 1987 in a second-hand bookstore in Vienna to illustrate the testimony provided by Holocaust survivor Arnold Mostowicz. Mostowicz was deported from Łódź to Auschwitz II-Birkenau and eventually to Gross Rosen concentration camp, from which he was freed in May 1945. The photographs used in Jabłoński's film were taken by Walter Genewein, the chief accountant of the ghetto and a member of Nazi party, and their perspective is therefore a contentious one inasmuch as it is the result of what Ulrich Baer has discussed as the 'apparently total correspondence between the photographer's perspective and the incontestable authority' of the Nazi state (2002: 131).[17] In *Tango of Slaves*, as we have seen in Chapter Four, the survivor is taken back to 1940s Warsaw by archival images that appear more effective that the present-day sites in exhuming memories and establishing a spatial and temporal connection with life in the ghetto. In *Photographer*, Mostowicz's testimonial performance reflects the opposite dynamic interplay between the past and present. As Brad Prager suggests, Mostowicz hardly recognises the ghetto in Genewein's photographs, and his response to the sight of old photographs of Bałuty seen through the eyes of a perpetrator is unsettling; these images 'represent the last days of tens of thousands of Jews, who were never seen again', and yet their use in *Photographer* is ultimately 'engaged with the issue of photography's limited ability to record history' (2015: 209–10). The temporal layering of the film, its juxtaposition of past and present, is also achieved by means of the combination of the interview with Mostowicz with a series of zooms and panning shots of the photographs that appear to set in motion the slides taken by Genewein. On its own, as the film makes abundantly clear, the photographic evidence is not evidence per se and, as Prager suggests, rather than substantiating each other, the testimony and the photographic image 'are flawed and insufficient, and one can be called upon to question and undercut the other' while the former can undermine 'the apparent evidence conveyed through the photographs' (2015: 214). In Jabłoński's documentary, these images fade into the black-and-white footage of the same buildings and streets filmed in the 1990s; the familiar juxtaposition of black-and-white archival images and full-colour present-day footage is here reversed. The traditional reliance on archival images whose lack of colour stands for perceived authority and objectivity is here subverted in a narrative where colour reveals the subjective nature of the archive, and black-and-white film stock aims at attesting the higher reliability of the present-day testimony. But, as Frances Guerin has argued, 'the film does not simply challenge the authenticity of Genewein's perspective on the past; it casts its own vision in 1998 as only one version of the past we must continue to seek out' (2012: 154–5).[18] Accordingly, film can use archival images not to provide an apparently objective view of the past but rather to seek out the past from its multitude of versions. In this quest for what is long gone, the opposition between archival images and present-day footage is central to the documentary narrative of the city of Łódź under Nazi occupation and emerges from a series of films which are based on personal journeys to the city and on a consistent use of present-day spaces and locations.

A wealth of archival photographs and footage of the ghetto existed even before Genewein's slides were exhibited for the first time at the Jewish Museum in Frankfurt in 1992. Such material had already been used in films such as *Łódź Ghetto* (Alan Adelson and Kate Taverna, 1989), an expository documentary account of the ghetto, its history and its people.[19] This film is based on a wide variety of sources and combines colour and black-and-white archival films and photographs, including some of those taken by Grossman and Ross, with a voice-over narration based on a polyphony of voices emerging from diaries and memoirs written by men and women who lived in the ghetto. Punctuated with footage of the derelict buildings of the Bałuty district filmed in the late 1980s, *Łódź Ghetto* opens with present-day street scenes and with a shot filmed from the front of a bus running along Nowomiejska Street towards Wolności Square in the centre of Łódź. As the bus enters the square and turns right towards Legionów Street, present-day footage is replaced by a scene filmed in the 1940s from the front of a tram, following the exact same route towards a Wolności Square occupied by military vehicles and German troops. This highly significant transition from the present into the past inscribes the events which took place during the war in the built environment of the city in the 1980s; it establishes a connection between past events and present-day locations by means of editing, with a single cut taking the viewer back in time while maintaining the same precise location (Fig. 5.3).

Figure 5.3 *Łódź Ghetto* (Alan Adelson and Kate Taverna, 1989).

This type of transition informs other documentary narratives of the city of Łódź and filmic journeys to the site of its ghetto, including *Song of the Łódź Ghetto* (David Kaufman, 2011), an expository documentary which focuses on the music of the ghetto street singer Jankiel Herszkowicz and on the present-day performances of his songs by the Jewish music group Brave New World.[20] Largely based on archival photographs and partly on sequences shot in Bałuty in 2010, *Song of the Łódź Ghetto* includes a scene filmed in the building where Herszkowicz lived during the war. Łucja, a granddaughter of the musician, sings one of his street lyrics, 'Getto Getunia', as she enters the courtyard of that apartment block and establishes a site-specific spatial connection with the past by means of the memorialisation of her grandfather's music. Just as in Warsaw, the courtyards of the old buildings once inhabited by the Jews are recurring spaces in documentaries about Łódź during the Holocaust and, as we shall see, the type of scene included in *Song of the Łódź Ghetto* is reminiscent of other cinematic return journeys to the city. Survivors and members of the postgeneration walk under the entrance of apartment blocks tied to their family history and raise their heads once in the courtyards in order to recognise, or to encounter for the first time, the façades of buildings which are often empty, derelict or rundown. In their use of present-day locations such as these courtyards and their juxtaposition of archival material and contemporary footage, expository documentaries like *Photographer, Łódź Ghetto* and *Song of the Łódź Ghetto* thus use tropes that recur in personal documentaries based on the juxtaposition of past and present images, and whose narrative evolves by means of a cinematic exploration of the built environment of Łódź.

These return journeys to a city once known and the exploration of its districts on foot while recalling events which took place on its streets enacts an understanding of memory as that concept defined by Nora as a phenomenon 'in permanent evolution, open to the dialectic of remembering and forgetting, unconscious of its successive deformations, vulnerable to manipulation and appropriation, susceptible to being long dormant and periodically revived' (1989: 8). Accordingly, the exploration of the streets of Łódź by Holocaust survivors and their families triggers a relationship between postmemory and sites of memory tied to the perpetually present experience of the past in the minds and the eyes of those who return, and of those who can now anchor to the built environment of the city those familial histories that had previously belonged to myth. In Sarin and Smalley's documentary *So Many Miracles*, discussed in Chapter Three, Israel Rubinek returns to Łódź on his way to his *shtetl* Pińczów with his wife Frania and his son Saul. Rubinek lived in Łódź at the beginning of the war, before moving back to Pińczów in order to stay with his grandparents and with Frania. The Łódź sequence of the film is bound to a particular event which took place towards the end of 1939 when, hungry and exasperated, Rubinek decided to join other men and women who broke the curfew imposed by the Germans and sought food in a local bakery. Most of them were caught by the Nazis, but he managed to escape while others were killed. In the Łódź sequence of *So Many Miracles*, Rubinek's voice-over recalls this episode while the camera captures him sitting at the entrance of the building at 39 Narutowicza Street, a street that remained outside the boundaries of the ghetto and where Rubinek lived before the war. The return to the city allows Rubinek to experience a vivid recollection of the events which took place on that day, and to bridge the gap between past and present. Narutowicza Street was empty on that day in 1939, and it still appears quiet and silent on the day of filming. As Rubinek sits, visibly distressed, at the entrance to the building, his memories become bound to an eternal present – it is again 1939, and the fear he had felt on that day returns to haunt him in what becomes a twice-lived experience. The street is in the midst of renovation, and the Collegium Anatomicum of the University of Łódź can be seen in the background while the hand-held camera provides a point-of-view shot

Figure 5.4 *So Many Miracles* (Katherine Smalley and Vic Sarin, 1987).

from Rubinek's perspective as he walks circumspectly along Narutowicza Street. This non-fictional restaging of the events of that distant day at the beginning of the war helps Rubinek to establish a closer proximity with the past and, by reflection, it articulates a sense of identification in the perspective of the film's viewer (Fig. 5.4). While in *Loving the Dead* fears of a repetition of violence were activated by objects returning from the past, this sequence of *So Many Miracles* avoids archival footage and consists of a spatial experience of memories, where the actions which took place in 1939 are re-enacted on site; the reminiscences of fear that emerge from Narutowicza Street in this sequence are ultimately bound to the absence of the dead, of those who were not able to avoid capture.

While Israel Rubinek left the city just before the establishment of the ghetto, Holocaust survivors Celia and Morris Elbaum lived there for years. They moved to the USA after the war and returned to Poland in 2006 with their children and grandchildren. Their postmemory journey is accounted for in the documentary *How Much to Remember: One Family's Conversation with History*, directed by the Elbaum's daughter-in-law Nina Koocher in 2006. The family travel to their *shtetl* Łask, to the death camps in Treblinka, Chełmno and Auschwitz II-Birkenau, and to Łódź, where in 1942 Celia and Morris were deported with 758 other Jews from Łask after the liquidation of the smaller ghetto in their hometown.[21] The Elbaums arrived at the ghetto in Bałuty on 1 September 1942, after an excruciating twenty-five-mile journey on a cattle wagon which took almost three days. *How Much to Remember* introduces the history of the ghetto with a long panning shot of the windows of a building that survived the war. Nina Koocher's voice-over narration gives an account of Morris Elbaum's life in the ghetto, where he worked in the soup kitchen; archival images of the ghetto's communal kitchens and factories illustrate this account in an expository mode. Similarly, when he recalls the liquidation of the ghetto in August 1944, archival images of those days are used to illustrate the story. The use of photography and this relentless accumulation of archival material can be seen as an example of the type of repetition that, as Marianne Hirsch suggests, 'connects the second generation to the first, in its capacity to produce rather than screen the effect of trauma that was lived so much more directly as compulsive repetition by survivors and contemporary witnesses' (2012a: 108).[22] As the film references this type of visual archive, Elbaum passes on the knowledge of the events which took place in the ghetto and his own personal history to the postgeneration by means of the identification of three significant locations on the map of the city. First, he locates the parish house of the Church of the Assumption of the Blessed Virgin Mary; during the war this was the location of the police criminal unit, the so-called Kripo, or Kriminalkommissariat Getto, at 8 nKościelna Street (Fig. 5.5). He recalls that he saw men and women taken there, but they were never released from a site associated with fear and pain in the memory of the survivor. He later identifies the old apartment where he last saw his siblings, a location intrinsically related to the idea of loss and to the act of loving the dead. Like Mira Hamermesh, Elbaum is excluded from a site of familial memory and, as he looks up at the apartment's window from the street, he transmits the intimate meaning of that location to the postgeneration that accompanies him on the trip. Finally, and again like Hamermesh in *Loving the Dead*, Elbaum visits the Jewish cemetery of Łódź and finds, with the help of a custodian, the graves of his father and one of his brothers, who both died before the war. As he visits these sites with his children and grandchildren Elbaum transfers familial knowledge to a postgeneration for whom his testimony can anchor stories heard since childhood to the built environment of Łódź, and can allow transgenerational identification by means of those processes of post-memory associated with a spatial experience of the past. In this context, the rundown apartment block and the cemetery overgrown with weeds, grass and bushes mark the irrevocable break originated by the disappearance of Łódź's Jewry, and their physical state of abandon contributes to

Figure 5.5 *How Much to Remember: One Family's Conversation with History* (Nina Koocher, 2006).

emphasising the feeling of loss articulated in Elbaum's words and his exploration of the city, and ultimately reflected in what Nora describes as a process of spatialisation based on 'remnants of experience still lived, in the warmth of tradition, in the silence of custom, in the repetition of the ancestral' (1989: 7).

As discussed in Chapter One, the Jews who survived the camps often became victims of Polish anti-Semitism. Equally tragic were the many suicides of survivors, whether immediately or several years after the war. Maria Ginsberg-Rabinowicz worked as a doctor in the ghetto hospital and, on learning that her daughter had been killed, she took her own life after her return to Łódź from the camps in 1945 (cf. Gilbert, 1986: 812). Street singer Jankiel Herszkowicz, whose life and music is the subject of *Song of the Łódź Ghetto*, was deported from Łódź and survived Auschwitz II-Birkenau and a labour camp in Braunschweig, Germany. He returned to Łódź after the war and committed suicide on 25 March 1972, shattered by the difficulties Jews still encountered in post-war Poland. While Rubinek's memories in *So Many Miracles* precede the sealing of the ghetto and Elbaum's account in *How Much to Remember* reflects life in captivity, in other cinematic journeys to the city survivors have walked the streets of

Łódź while recalling the years that saw the death of Ginsberg-Rabinowicz and Herszkowicz, among many others. The Jewish presence in post-war Łódź before the anti-Semitic campaign of the late 1960s is recounted in Slawomir Grünberg's *Shimon's Returns* (2014) and *The Peretzniks* (2010), two documentaries informed by the ongoing feeling of persecution that characterised life in the city and focusing on the schools which were attended by the orphans of the Holocaust. As we have seen in Marian Marzynski's films set in Warsaw, hopes for the survival and rebirth of Jewish Poland were dashed in the post-war years by widespread anti-Semitism and the resulting emigration to Israel. And yet, in the account provided in these films, what emerges is also a brief period of hope for the Jews, decimated in numbers but claiming back a life in the country.

What also emerges from *Shimon's Returns* and *The Peretzniks* is a topographical shift from the location of the ghetto in Bałuty to the Sródmiescie district, where the new Jewish schools were established. In *Shimon's Returns*, Shimon Redlich visits the sites of his childhood and his youth, including the places where he was sheltered from the Nazis; his itinerary includes Lviv, where he briefly visits the Market Square used as a location in *Boris Dorfman a Mentsh* and *Return to My Shtetl Delatyn*, the towns of Brzeżany, Rai and Narajów in the Ternopil province of Ukraine, and Łódź, where he was taken after the war. The sequences filmed in Łódź open with the image of a tram heading to the suburb of Helenówek, a site associated with the Jewish history of the city. At 15 Krajowa Street there was an orphanage which was run by Chaim Rumkowski before the war, and which became a shelter for child survivors of the Holocaust in 1945.[23] The Yiddish–Polish film *Unzere Kinder* (*Our Children*, Natan Gross and Shaul Goskind, 1948) was filmed on location at the orphanage in Helenówek. Redlich, who briefly lived there after the war, appeared in that film when he was a child and, while it does not contain present-day footage of this location, *Shimon's Returns* uses archival footage from *Our Children* in juxtaposition with images of the survivor's journey to Eastern Europe.

By 2014 the city centre of Łódź had been renovated and, as Redlich walks along Piotrkowska Street and Próchnika Street, this district is presented as lively and thriving, with only fading scars left by the events of the 1940s. In order to reconnect with the past Redlich visits the buildings where his apartment, his school and his youth movement were located, the core of his life in Łódź. These places are located on Rewolucji 1905 Street, formerly Południowa Street, which after the war was predominantly Jewish; the only surviving synagogue of Łódź and the Jewish School were located at civic numbers 28 and 29, while the buildings nearby held accommodation

Figure 5.6 *Shimon's Returns* (Slawomir Grünberg, 2014).

for students and teachers. Redlich, who lived here until 1950, enters the building, speaks with an elderly resident who remembers the school, and visits the courtyard where he used to play and where Polish children are playing today (Fig. 5.6). As he observes that several buildings are derelict and abandoned, Redlich says that the place resembles a cemetery; his experience of this location is one that thus implies continuity of the past into the present and a life lived not as a series of separate events but, as Lowenthal puts it, as an experience which 'incorporates the quality of duration, the passage of time' (1975: 9). Redlich visits his former first-floor apartment and the old couple who now live there. The woman, who was born in 1931 in Odessa, joins Redlich in singing a Russian song before being shown a photograph from his childhood taken on a Rewolucji 1905 Street covered in snow. This photograph is a remnant of a long-gone time that Redlich has held on to during his journey through various life states of being, or, as Lowenthal puts it, through the experience of 'voyage into the unknown guided by our assurance of continuity' (1975: 10). Unlike the painful memories of the city during the German occupation emerging from *So Many Miracles* and *How Much to Remember*, Redlich's account of his youth in Łódź is nostalgically anchored to the buildings where he lived after his familial world was destroyed and before a new wave of persecution was to force him to another displacement. In the course of a process which combines the exploration of the sites and the use of relics, Redlich experiences that type of past which, as Lowenthal suggests, 'is not only recalled; it is incarnate in the things we build and the landscapes we create' (1975: 6), whether that be a physical landscape or a landscape of the mind, constructed and unfolded by means of the repeated processes of journeying and remembering.

In *Shimon's Returns*, anti-Semitism is only hinted at in a shot showing a Star of David drawn across graffiti celebrating the football team ŁKS Łódź, made by supporters of rival team Widzew Łódź in order to mock their opponents. Apart from this exception, what emerges otherwise is a city that welcomes Redlich's return and a journey where nostalgia pervades the act of remembering. This reading of the film is confirmed in the sequence where Redlich encounters a woman he knew at school and who moved to Israel in 1957, where he found her again thanks to a radio announcement. The pair visit Piotrkowska Street, first on foot and then on a rickshaw, and remember the vibe of the place in the late 1940s and early 1950s, when they used to walk down this thoroughfare to reach the school located in Południowa Street or to go to the movies. An old photograph of their classmates brings memories alive as they recall the names of their friends and the addresses where they lived. As Marianne Hirsch suggests, photographs may be 'the only material traces of an irrecoverable past', and as such they 'derive their power and their important cultural role from their embeddedness in the fundamental rites of family life' (1997: 5). For orphans of the Holocaust such as Redlich, the rites of family life were the rites of the Jewish school, and this photograph can be read as a familial trace of the past, of a new family that replaced the one obliterated in the Holocaust. Redlich does not use the photograph to exhume the world which was erased by the Nazis, but rather to unlock the memories of a smaller and more private world that survived the war and ended with the Jews' departure from Poland in the post-war years.[24] The image triggers his own memories of long-gone days that can be understood in terms of those 'symbolic replicas of departed scenes' which, according to Lowenthal, answer the need for 'tangible reminders of things we have done, places we have been, views we have seen' (1975: 8).

The cultural vitality of Jewish schools such as that attended by Redlich temporarily suggested that there was going to be a future for the Jews in Poland. However, pupils educated at these schools were to leave the country soon after their graduation as a result of widespread anti-Semitism. This is the picture that emerges from another documentary about a Jewish school in Łódź, Grünberg's *The Peretzniks*. Originally located at 49 Kilińskiego Street, and transferred to 13 Więckowskiego Street in the 1950s, the Yitskhok L. Peretz School was established in 1945 and, following a steady decline in enrolment after the opening of the Polish border in 1956 and mass emigration to Israel, it closed down in 1969.

Grungberg's film addresses the history of this institution and the memories of its former students. By means of a series of testimonies gathered in Israel and other countries, it provides a powerful image of these individuals' loss of a shared past landscape. Like *Shimon's Returns*, *The Peretzniks* anchors to abandoned buildings and to long-gone institutions the memories of an attempt to rebuild Jewish life in Poland after the Holocaust, its short-lived and constantly threatened success, and its end. In the opening sequence of the film, Jadwiga Kwiatkowska-Tarkowska, a former Polish literature teacher at the school, enters an empty classroom and reads from a register the names of the last 'Peretzniks'; each name is accompanied by a photograph of the student from the 1950s and followed by a short talking-head interview with the former pupils of the Peretz School. They all left Łódź, and most of them settled in Israel or the USA. Their absence from the classroom also stands for the absence of the new generation of Polish Jews who were expected to take their place, while their contribution to this sequence implies a sense of discontinuity with the past, an acceptance of the deprivation of their own landscape of memory:

> Those deprived of their own past landscapes may suffer self-imposed amnesia. Sheer survival may require prisoners and forced migrants to relinquish memories of a past that would contrast too poignantly with the present, but rejection often destroys their sense of purpose and personal worth; without the past they cannot prevision a future worth having. (1975: 15)

Lowenthal's reading of the loss of one's past landscapes is one that identifies the 'Peretzniks' with the forced migrants whose memories are at odds with the present of the place. And yet these former students have achieved a sense of worth and belonging elsewhere, and the city of their youth has faded into a memory to relinquish – despite, or because of, its limited connections to the lived experience of the present. Their testimonies combine regret for what is lost with a powerful bond that has survived the school itself and the diaspora of its pupils. Ultimately, while they might have been displaced from the familial sites of their youth, the interviewees are experiencing a sort of amnesia which departs from Lowenthal's definition: vivid memories are illustrated and triggered by the use of archival images, including personal photographs and film footage, and what is excluded from these testimonies is the darker side of experience, the persecution still suffered after the war ended.

Grünberg uses footage from a fiction film about the war, Janusz Morgenstern's *Ambulans* (*Ambulance*, 1962), including performances by the pupils of the Peretz School who, like Shimon Redlich in *Our Children*, were cast in various roles. In Israel, the former students watch the film again on a computer screen and recall the time of its shooting while identifying themselves and others in the images. In its attempt to exhume memories, *The Peretzniks* also employs archival footage from the 1920s and 1930s in order to introduce the recent history of the city, and images from the immediate post-war years to contextualise the activity of the Peretz School and other institutions (including the orphanage in Helenówek, where *Our Children* was filmed and where Redlich spent the immediate post-war years). Additionally, Henryk Grynberg, the protagonist of Paweł Łoziński's *Birthplace*, is interviewed about his time at Helenówek, while archival photographs and footage are used to provide a visual referent to the writer's memories. Grynberg remembers that in 1946, after the pogrom in Kielce – discussed in Chapter One with a focus on Marcel Łoziński's *Witnesses* – a fence was created to protect the children from anti-Semitic attacks. Young Jews who grew up during the war thus experienced a new threat, reminiscent of the destruction of their world; similarly, the fence around Helenówek evokes images of the brick wall that separated the Jews from the rest of the population in the ghetto in Łódź.

The Peretzniks anchors the task of recalling these difficult times to the built environment of the city, to a past landscape still vivid in the minds of former students. Present-day footage of the building of the former school in Kilińskiego Street reveals a derelict site whose state of abandonment is similar to that of Redlich's school in Rewolucji 1905 Street. Most interviews are recorded remotely; only one of the Peretzniks, Heniek Chmielnicki, returns to Łódź and visits the building. He stands in its courtyard and at the main entrance, walks again along Kilińskiego Street and recalls his time at school with nostalgia and regret for what has been lost (Fig. 5.7).[25] Like Hamermesh, Redlich, Rubinek and Elbaum in the documentaries previously investigated, Chmielnicki achieves closer proximity to the past by means of a physical exploration of the site, the courtyard that was at the centre of life in the school and at the core of his memories. Derelict, rundown or refurbished, the tenement houses of Łódź associated with Jewish history play an important role in the films hitherto discussed, inasmuch as these buildings can be seen as still witnesses of the events which took place in the city during the war. Their connection with the people who inhabited them in the years after the Jews left the city will be discussed in the final section of this chapter, in relation to the use of locations in Pavel Štingl's television documentary *Bałuckie getto* (*The Ghetto in Bałuty*, 2008).

In the documentaries addressed in this chapter, the surviving buildings of the ghetto in the Bałuty district are consistently juxtaposed with personal

Figure 5.7 *The Peretzniks* (Slawomir Grünberg, 2010).

memories and archival images of the sites. The same type of juxtaposition of present-day and archival images was central to an art installation displayed on 18 May 2013 at the Festival of Four Cultures in Łódź, an event that celebrates Polish, German, Russian and Jewish cultural influences on the city. At 17 Piotrkowska Street, as part of the fourth edition of the festival, Tomasz Bergmann presented his video installation *Litzmannstadt – Bałuty*, which uses photographs of the Łódź ghetto taken during the Nazi occupation by Mendel Grossman and Henryk Ross, selected by Dariusz Dekiert and accompanied by the music of Mikołaj Trzaska and DJ Lenar. These photographs portray streets, squares and buildings in the city, with a particular focus on the market square in Bałuty and the areas around Zgierska Street, Lutomierska Street, Łagiewnicka Street and the Church of the Assumption of the Blessed Virgin Mary. By means of a series of complex juxtapositions of these archival images with photographs of the city taken in recent years, *Litzmannstadt – Bałuty* inscribes the past into the present and defines the buildings of Łódź as the silent witnesses of the persecution of the Jews. Carefully taken from the exact same location from which the archival images were captured in the 1940s, these contemporary views of the city emphasise the continuity of the past into the present with significant attention to a built environment that has remained largely unchanged. Conspicuously absent, however, are the Jews who were killed after their photographs were taken.

The buildings of Bałuty are sites where, as Nora suggests, history besieges, deforms, transforms, penetrates and petrifies memory; they are 'no longer quite life, not yet death, like shells on the shore when the sea of living memory has receded' (1989: 12). Their past existence has a continuity in a present where the tenements have survived the war largely intact: unlike Warsaw's, the ghetto in Łódź did not stage an uprising against the Nazis and was spared total destruction. Amongst other changes to the urban fabric of Bałuty, *Litzmannstadt – Bałuty* points at the disappearance of the wooden bridges linking the two sections of the ghetto and the rise of a number of taller post-war buildings next to the nineteenth- and early twentieth-century apartment blocks. Archival photographs dissolve into the city of today, and vice versa; places occupied by men, women and children in the old images of Łódź cross-fade into photographs of the same sites, now empty or occupied by a new generation of Poles. The Jews of Bałuty, photographed during everyday activities or while marching to Radogoszcz, or Radegast, station – the place from which they were deported to the city and then taken to the death camps – thus dissolve and reappear like ghosts in a series of juxtapositions emphasising their physical destruction.

Bergmann's *Litzmannstadt – Bałuty* employs an approach to the interaction between past and present in the urban fabric of the city echoing the strategies used by Štingl in *The Ghetto in Bałuty*, a documentary that combines the testimonies of survivors and bystanders with the present-day spatial experience of the buildings of the former ghetto. Both Bergmann's installation and Štingl's documentary enact a relation to the time of the occupation which, inasmuch as it signals a fracture from the past while highlighting the sameness of place, juggles with what Nora calls 'illumination of discontinuity' on the one hand and 'retrospective continuity' on the other (1989: 16). The houses have survived while their inhabitants have not; but rather than existing as dead shells of long-gone lives, these buildings now belong to the Poles who live there and who have their own memories and experience of them. In *The Ghetto in Bałuty*, continuity and discontinuity with the past are at the centre of an interplay based on a juxtaposition of archival images and present-day photographs and footage; this material is integrated with interviews with Polish residents filmed on location and remote testimonies given by survivors. Štingl uses interviews with a number of Czechs who were deported to the Bałuty district of Łódź in order to tell the story of the ghetto and to illustrate the ways in which the present is still informed by the past, by the persecution of the Jews of the city and of those who were taken here from other parts of occupied Europe. *The Ghetto in Bałuty* uses key locations in the process of establishing an ongoing actuality for the events of 1939–45, and in an attempt to decipher the ways in which the Holocaust is still inscribed in the built environment of the city.[26] Poverty, neglect and unhealthy living conditions in contemporary Bałuty ambivalently provide a thematic continuity with the past while highlighting a more profound discontinuity between the experience of the survivors and those of the later residents; uncertainty about the future is presented as a recurring concern for the Poles of Bałuty, while the Jewish survivors imply that there was a sense of doom and foreboding in the ghetto, a certainty about being on the brink of annihilation. As this ambivalence unfolds, the film uses its locations as sites of memory in order to block the act of forgetting, and in its repetitive shots of apartment blocks, windows, doors, staircases and courtyards, what ultimately emerges from these images is one of the affirming purposes of Nora's concept: the revelation of that ongoing attempt 'to capture a maximum of meanings in the fewest signs' that is at the centre of all spatial processes of memorialisation here investigated (1989: 19).

In a sequence of *The Ghetto in Bałuty*, a local fortune-teller interviewed by Štingl at her place of business explains her view that Bałuty has witnessed good and bad times, and that its buildings and streets are the main witnesses of a past that is rarely talked about and yet not forgotten. In this bizarre location we find the essence of the film, its attempt to bear witness by focusing equally on human subjects and their dwellings. Like *Litzmannstadt – Bałuty*, Štingl's documentary uses this built environment to dig into the past of the city and, additionally, it allows site-specific memories to emerge from the testimonies of the witnesses while the accounts reported by current inhabitants provide connections with the present. The film opens with a car ride along the streets of the former ghetto. A Czech survivor, Marie Alesova, is on the back seat of the car and observes the surviving pre-war buildings along Zgierska Street, the thoroughfare that used to divide the ghetto into two sections, while the car passes below the space that would have been occupied by the wooden bridge built near Lutomierska Street in order to connect the two parts of the ghetto. The car drives north towards the Bałucki Rynek, the market square whose buildings once contained Jewish and German public offices. The driver points at the building at 25 Łagiewnicka Street and explains that it used to have a large clock on its façade which determined the schedule of everyday life in the ghetto. The car finally stops at the Holocaust memorial built on the site of Radegast station. Czesław Bielecki's monument appears in front of the vehicle, and the driver follows the long wall of the Tunnel of the Deported and stops near the original building of the station. It was from exactly this spot that over 200,000 Jews from Poland and other countries were deported to Chełmno and Auschwitz II-Birkenau. While in Jabłoński's *Photographer* the cameras panned over a series of details from colour slides of Radegast station taken by Walter Genewein in the 1940s, in this sequence of *The Ghetto in Bałuty* present-day footage replaces archival imagery and consigns this site to the terrain of memorial space. Unlike other locations in the film, the place is deprived of an ongoing actuality in its monumentalisation, no longer a station but a reminder of the destruction of the Jews who lived in the ghetto.

Along with a large section of the city's Jewish population, Austrian, German, Luxemburger and Czech Jews lived in the ghetto and were eventually deported to the death camps. In the autumn of 1941, over 5,000 Jews were taken from Prague to Łódź; half of them did not survive the winter, and no more than 276 of them were still alive after the war. Štingl filmed a series of talking-head interviews with a group of survivors, including Vera Arnstejnova, Maja Randova, Libena Hajkova and Mario Petrovsky; their testimonies include stories about the arrival in the ghetto, work and everyday life, poverty and hunger, loss and deportations to the camps. As they articulate an interplay with the accounts of those who now live in their former houses, the testimonies of these survivors address the sense of surprise and disbelief experienced on their arrival in Łódź, provide details about the events that preceded the departure from Prague, list the items they decided to bring with them and assess the widespread and misguided belief that life would improve once they reached Poland.[27] Archival pictures of the ghetto are edited in combination to these testimonies and are used throughout the film to illustrate the oral histories of the survivors. As they also serve the purpose of linking the interviews, which are recorded remotely in the Czech Republic, to the present-day footage of Bałuty, these testimonies are often detailed and preoccupied with everyday struggles and events rather than with the broader issues of trauma and memory. Nora has argued that in the contest of witnessing past events, 'the less extraordinary the testimony, the more aptly it seems to illustrate the average mentality' (1989: 14). The testimonies presented in *The Ghetto in Bałuty*, in their quotidian tone, reveal the average experience of the ghetto and that manner of becoming accustomed to the destruction which also characterised Szymon Srebrnik's aforementioned account, in *Shoah*, of life in captivity.

Following the first group of interviews with the survivors, present-day footage of the buildings of the former ghetto shows adults and children going about their everyday activities in what appears as a rundown and poor district of Łódź, a pocket of urban neglect on the map of the city. The camera explores the interior of one of these buildings, and anti-Semitic graffiti can be seen near the staircase; supporters of Widzew Łódź football club have used the derogative word 'Yid' and a drawing of the Star of

Figure 5.8 *Bałuckie getto* (*The Ghetto in Bałuty*, Pavel Štingl, 2008).

David to mock rival team ŁKS Łódź (Fig. 5.8).[28] A Polish man explains that he was born and grew old in that building; as he looks outside from one of the windows on the staircase, two archival photographs from the early 1940s, representing a courtyard seen from a similar elevated position, are added to this scene, illustrating the way in which the present can give way to the past. The film returns to the present with footage of the courtyards of Bałuckie accompanied by the accounts of local Polish residents, who remember when Jews used to sell herrings in Nad Łódką Street and recall other Jewish stores located at the corner of Bazarowa Street and Lutomierska Street.[29] The topographical specificity of this account also contributes to establishing a connection between past and present by evoking a void that belongs to a shared experience of the built environment of Bałuty. The film establishes a link between accounts of the living conditions in the ghetto and present-day poverty by juxtaposing images of the family's children with archival photographs of the ghetto's children and with a survivor's account of health issues, starvation and terrible hygiene standards. Štingl's camera enters one of the old buildings of the ghetto and captures domestic scenes of an apartment occupied by a large family living in poverty in the cramped space; other scenes of destitution are filmed in and outside the buildings of Łagiewnicka Street, where chronically unemployed residents are shown buying alcohol, drinking, smoking and watching daytime television. Often embarrassed by the state of their dwellings, the interviewees explain that most former residents have emigrated, relatives and friends have been lost and families who have lived in the building for generations will soon have to leave.[30]

The Ghetto in Bałuty enacts other juxtapositions of archival images and present-day footage, maintaining the interplay between continuity and change that characterises many of the Holocaust narratives hitherto discussed. Several sequences provide examples of this type of juxtaposition; an interview with a survivor, who recalls that Poles bought goods from the Czechs and sold them on the market in the ghetto, is followed by archival images of the market, which are then juxtaposed with present-day footage of a small local market in Bałuty at which Poles sell cheap clothing and other goods in a rundown space covered by graffiti.[31] Another juxtaposition of past and present emerges in a sequence where a survivor's account about her work in a bra factory is followed by archival images of the ghetto's factories, and by a present-day interview with a Polish tailor who is struggling to make a living out of his trade. In the following sequence the children of Bałuty are entertained at a puppet theatre, and these images are followed by archival pictures of the ghetto's children accompanied by the soundtrack made by the voices of the puppeteers recorded in the present. These audio and visual incursions of the past into the present and of the present into the past, the thematic connections between the accounts of those who died or survived the Holocaust and those who live and struggle in present-day Bałuty, are the strategies used in this documentary in order to articulate a site-specific discourse on the inscription of memory in the built environment of Łódź. In doing so, the film reflects upon what Nora discussed as a transition 'from the idea of a visible past to an invisible one, from a solid and steady past to our fractured past; from a history sought in the continuity of memory to a memory cast in the discontinuity of history' (1989: 17). The transition articulated by Nora is here filtered through several layers of time: the memories of the city that existed before the Holocaust, the trauma of captivity in the ghetto during the war, the attempt to rebuild a Jewish community after the war and contemporary Łódź, with its fading traces of a fractured and discontinuous past. The cinematic city reflects these phases by means of the intertwining of archival images and location shooting, and addresses the intricacy of the process of capturing memories anchored to a built environment, continuously elaborated through the connection between past events and their actuality. Processes of memorialisation concerning cities like Lviv and Łódź, as well as Warsaw and Kraków, need to be placed in a continuum of events which began before the war, continued during the German occupation and have persisted to a present day that has not yet done away with the past. As we shall see in the final chapter, a different discourse should be made for those cities of death that were created for the purpose of the extermination of the Jews and that were built, used and erased in the space of a few years.

Notes

1. In regard to the use of Lviv's sewers as hiding places, *SS-Gruppenführer* Fritz Katzmann noted in 1943: 'The Jews tried every means to evade evacuation. They not only attempted to escape from the ghetto, but hid in every imaginable corner, in pipes, in chimneys, in sewers, and canals. They built tunnels under the hallways, underground; they widened cellars and turned them into passageways; they dug trenches underground, and cunningly created hiding places in lofts, woodsheds, attics, and inside furniture' (in Gilbert, *The Holocaust: The Jewish Tragedy*, p. 580).
2. Penz and Lu, 'Introduction: What is Urban Cinematics?'.
3. Approximately 100,000 Jews lived in Lviv when the Nazis occupied the city on 29 June 1941. The month of November saw the first large-scale murder operation in the city and the establishment of a Jewish residential quarter which was to become the ghetto. Between the summer of 1942 and the autumn of 1943, almost the entire Jewish population of the city was exterminated by means of murder operations and deportations to the death camps in Sobibór and Bełżec and to the Janowska concentration camp, on the outskirts of Lviv (Miron, *The Yad Vashem Encyclopaedia*, pp. 437–43).
4. The controversies related to the role played by Ukrainians in the destruction of the Jews of Lviv are related to a series of events which took place during the war. For example, between 25 and 27 July 1941, local Ukrainians seized thousands of men and women and took them to a prison where at least 2,000 of them were murdered. The excuse for the pogrom was the killing of the Ukrainian nationalist Simon Petlura by Shalom Schwartzbard, which took place in Paris in 1926 (Gilbert, *The Holocaust: The Jewish Tragedy*, p. 173).
5. This documentary also uses the house once inhabited by Yiddish writer Shalom Aleichem as one of its locations, and thus situates Jewish cultural heritage on the map of the city.
6. Lefebvre, *The Production of Space*.
7. The town of Kagul was renamed Cahul after the war.
8. It is only in a very private and personal scene that Dorfman shares family photographs of his mother, his father and other relatives; however, these images are bound to his roots in Bessarabia rather than to the city of Lviv.
9. Despite the presence of recurring scenes showing various cultural and recreational activities taking place in the Jewish centre Hesed Arieh, Dorfman observes that young men and women do not want to be associated with their Jewish heritage.
10. The monument is situated near the bridge under which the gate into the

ghetto known as 'the Gate of Death' was situated; from this place the Jews of Lviv were taken to their execution, never to be seen again.

11. *SS-Obersturmbannführer* Adolf Eichmann visited Lviv in 1941 as part of a trip to Eastern Europe during which he witnessed the extermination of the Jews. At his trial in 1961 he recalled his arrival to the station: 'I came to Lviv and saw for the first time a charming picture – the railway station which was built in honour of the sixtieth year of the reign of Franz Josef; and since I always find pleasure in that period, maybe because I heard so many nice things about it in my parents' home – the relatives of my stepmother were of a certain social standing. It was painted yellow and I remember it, I remember that the date was inscribed on the wall. This for the first time drove away these terrible thoughts which had never left me since Minsk, this was the first time I could forget' (in Gilbert, *The Holocaust: The Jewish Tragedy*, p. 167).
12. Most of the Jews deported to Siberia survived the war and eventually returned to the city of Lviv.
13. Hamermesh, *The River of Angry Dogs.*
14. Žižek, *Looking Awry*; Žižek, *The Puppet and the Dwarf.*
15. Hirsch, 'Objects of Return'.
16. See Bourla, 'Shaping and Reshaping Memory'.
17. Baer, *Spectral Evidence.*
18. Guerin, *Through Amateur Eyes.*
19. The ghetto has been the subject of an increasing number of films from the early 1980s and only a couple of documentaries in the previous decades. The French film *Le temps du ghetto* (*The Time of the Ghetto*, Frédéric Rossif, 1961) included archival footage filmed in Wolborska Street, Jakuba Street and Wschodnia Street in Łódź, but was in fact a documentary about the ghetto in Warsaw, where this footage was thought to have been filmed (Tomasz Majewski (ed.), *Time of the Litzmannstadt Ghetto: Film Images; Inferno in* the *Promised Land*, Łódź: Marek Edelman Dialogue Center, p. 29). *Litzmannstadt Ghetto* (Daniel Szylit and Irena Kukulska, 1965) was one of the earliest documentaries about the ghetto, and for many years it remained one of very few. Fifteen years later, *Image Before My Eyes* (Joshua Waletzky, 1980) included footage of the ghetto in Łódź and was followed by a feature-length documentary on the ghetto, *The Story of Chaim Rumkowski and the Jews of Łódź* (Peter Cohen and Bo Kuritzen, Sweden, 1982). More recently, documentaries have focused on individual survivors in a number of films, including *Mostowicz* (Małgorzata Andrzejewska-Psarska, 1998), *Nie oplataj mnie . . .* (*To Stay Alive*, Piotr Zarębski, 2000), *My Łódź is No More: The Story of Yosef Neuhaus* (Zvi Nevo, 2009), *Aj waj* (Joanna Satanowska, 2014), *Litzmannstadt Ghetto. Piekło na Ziemi Obiecanej* (*Litzmannstadt Ghetto: Inferno in* the *Promised Land*, Mariusz Olbrychowski, 2009), *Aspangbahnhof 1941. Geschichte einer Frauenfreundschaft* (*Aspangbahnhof 1941. A Story of a Female Friendship*, Angelika Brechelmacher, 2014), and *Linie 41* (*Line 41*, Tanja

Cummings, 2015). Other films have focused on the deportations from the ghetto to the death camps: *Radegast Station* (Małgorzata Burzyńska-Keller, 2003), *Memoriał Radegast Bahnhof* (*Memorial Radegast Station*, Małgorzata Burzyńska-Keller, 2009), *Radegast* (Borys Lankosz, 2008) and *Likwidacja 08.1944* (*Liquidation 08.1944*, Marek Miller and Michał Bukojemski, 2009). Other aspects of life and death in the ghetto have been explored in *Obóz cygański w Łodzi* (*The Gypsy Camp in Łódź*, Jarosław Sztandera, 2004), and in *Z głębokości wołam* (*From* the *Depths I Call*, Wojciech Gierłowski, 2005) and *Oddajcie mi swoje dzieci* (*Give Me Your Children*, Piotr Weychert and Piotr Perz, 2014), two documentaries focusing on the deportation of Jewish children and the actions of Chaim Rumkowski.

20. The role of music in the ghetto and in pre-war Łódź is also explored in *Zamir: Jewish Voices Return to Poland* (Rob Cooper and Eric Stange, 2000), a documentary about the Zamir Chorale of Boston's trip to Eastern Europe. This choral group was founded in 1969 and traces its lineage to the Hazomir Jewish Society for Literature and Music of Łódź, which was founded in 1899.
21. On 24 August 1942, the Jews of Łask were led to the Church of the Immaculate Conception of the Blessed Virgin Mary and held for three days. After a selection, 760 Jews were sent to Łódź. The remaining 3,500 Jews of Łask were deported and murdered in Chełmno (Miron, *The Yad Vashem Encyclopaedia*, p. 389).
22. Hirsch, *The Generation of Postmemory*.
23. The Helenówek refuge was originally run by the Jewish Committee and, soon after the war, was taken over by the Polish State.
24. Other photographs used in the film show Redlich standing next to the Citroën of his uncle, who was, according to him, the only Jewish taxi driver in the city. Another photograph shows him posing with his dog Diana. These images also contribute to the process of remembrance discussed above.
25. Heniek also visits the second site of the school, in Więckowskiego Street, which has changed less than the building in Kilińskiego Street and is in better condition overall.
26. For example, the film introduces the viewer to a building near the market square which was used by the Gestapo during the war for interrogation and imprisonment. It is a now a tattoo parlour where tattoos are created in what used to be cell number thirteen, which still retains some of its original features.
27. A survivor explains that it was only in the moment when the Czechs were marched to the Łódź ghetto and noticed the lack of hygiene and the starved look on the faces of its people that they realised their expectations had been wrong.
28. Later in the film, two young men are filmed making this graffiti and being reprimanded by other locals.
29. This is followed by a sequence filmed during the Easter Day procession,

a reminder of the Catholic identity of the area, held outside the Church of the Assumption of the Blessed Virgin Mary. These images imply that there are no Jews in this area today, and that the neighbourhood is entirely Christian.

30. Hints of anti-Semitism emerge in this sequence when a local man claims that Jews are coming back to reclaim their flats and buildings, and are asking for rents that Poles cannot afford.
31. During this sequence, a Polish woman explains that the heating system is poor and she does not like winter; a thematic association is established by the use of photographs of the ghetto during this season, the harshest time of the year for the Jews of Bałuty. The interplay between past and present continues when the film shows a Polish wedding reception in the courtyard and juxtaposes these images with an archival photograph showing a newlywed Jewish couple in the ghetto.

CHAPTER 6

A Tale of Two Cities of Death: Treblinka and Oświęcim

'The earth beneath my feet was coarse and sharp: filled with the fragments of human bone.'

— Martin Gilbert, *The Holocaust: The Jewish Tragedy*

The documentaries discussed in the previous chapters have addressed the ways in which the destruction of the Jews resulted in the annihilation of countless communities and displaced millions of men, women and children from their *shtetlekh* and their neighbourhoods, while creating new kinds of places where the victims were concentrated, exploited and eventually murdered. This chapter presents a topographical shift in focus from the places inhabited by the Jews before and during the war to the spaces designed for their extermination in the context of what should not be understood as one event, but rather as a succession of small- and large-scale actions that brought Eastern European Jewry to its destruction. Within the myriad of events constituting the Holocaust a continuity can be established between the early pogroms and the death marches which followed the liberation of the camps, between the burning barn in Jedwabne and the four crematoria of Auschwitz II-Birkenau, and between all the crime scenes that swallowed the Jews of Poland. The Holocaust in the territories of the Second Polish Republic occurred in a variety of locations and by means of various ways of execution, including shooting, hanging and the use of gas vans and gas chambers operating either with exhaust fumes or with the cyanide-based pesticide Zyklon B. In the west, Chełmno extermination camp operated from December 1941 to March 1943 and again from June 1944 to January 1945; between 152,000 and 340,000 Jews were killed here. In the east, between October 1941 and November 1943, as many as two million Jews were murdered in the death camps Bełżec, Sobibór and Treblinka during the German mass-murder operation known as Aktion Reinhard.[1] In March 1942 the first gas chamber at Auschwitz II-Birkenau became operational, and by November 1944 at least 1,100,000 people, mostly Jews, were killed in this killing factory. Hundreds of thousands of children, men and women were also murdered in concentration camps such as Majdanek, near Lublin, and Stutthof, near Gdańsk, in particular during operations such as Aktion Erntefest, the mass shooting of 43,000 Jews which took place on 3 November 1943 in the territory of the General Government.

The five largest killing centres in occupied Poland (Chełmno, Bełżec, Sobibór, Treblinka and Auschwitz II-Birkenau) have had a different reflection and a varied presence in the moving image. After the war and as early as in 1947, when Wanda Jakubowska's drama *Ostatni etap* (*The Last Stage*) was released, Auschwitz II-Birkenau became the preferred location of Holocaust cinema and a topographical embodiment of the extermination. Since then, fiction films set and often shot in the Silesian camps abounded and similarly a large number of documentaries have been made in the grounds of Auschwitz I and Auschwitz II-Birkenau. These documentaries often incorporate photographs taken by the perpetrators while the gas chambers were still fully operational, and footage filmed after the liberation of the camps. The death camps of Aktion Reinhard, on the other hand, were dismantled by the Nazis before the end of the war and there is very limited, almost nonexistent, visual material in the archives about the events that took place in the eastern killing centres; in combination with the fact that only a small number of individuals survived these camps, the lack of visual referents has resulted in a comparatively small number of films using Bełżec, Sobibór and Treblinka as locations. Filmed in Serbia in 1987, Jack Gold's *Escape from Sobibór* is the only fiction film set in Sobibór, whereas Bełżec and Treblinka have never been used as locations in fiction cinema. A significant number of documentaries, however, have addressed the events that took place during Aktion Reinhard, with a particular focus on the uprisings in Sobibór and Treblinka.

Shoah contains an interview recorded in Sobibór with Jan Piwonski, a former assistant pointsman at the local railway station; in 1979, Lanzmann also filmed a conversation with Sobibór survivor and insurgent Yehuda Lerner in Jerusalem, which was not included in the final cut of *Shoah* but, accompanied by present-day footage of Sobibór, was later used in his documentary *Sobibór, October 14, 1943, 4 p.m.* (2001). This is arguably the most celebrated of a small number of cinematic accounts of the uprising in Sobibór based on location shooting and interviews with survivors, and including the following titles: *Past and Present, History Falsified* (Thomas and Dena Blatt, 1987), *Vosstanie v Sobibore* (*The Uprising in Sobibór*, Pavel Kogan and Lily Van Den, 1990), *Z królestwa śmierci* (*From the Realm of Death*, Urszula Hasiec and Grzegorz Michalec, 2008), *Sobibór: the*

Plan, the Revolt, the Escape (Karen Lynne and Richard Bloom, 2010) and *Escape From a Nazi Death Camp* (Hereward Pelling, 2014).[2] Szymon Zin's *Bełżec* (2004) and Guillaume Moscovitz's *Bełżec* (2005) are the only documentaries that exclusively focus, in an expository manner, on the first camp of Aktion Reinhard; this scarcity is plausibly explained by the fact that most death-camp documentaries are based on contemporary testimonies of survivors, and Chaim Hirszman and Rudolf Reder, the only two known Bełżec survivors, died in 1946 and 1968 respectively.[3] A larger cohort of documentaries has been filmed in Treblinka, after Bełżec and Sobibór the third death camp to be built during Aktion Reinhard, and will be discussed in the first section of this chapter. The second part of the chapter concludes this book's journey to Poland with a reflection on the use of the town of Oświęcim and the sites of the camps Auschwitz I and Auschwitz II-Birkenau as locations in documentary films concerned with the transmission of knowledge and the relationship between memory, history and place.

In documentary cinema, the soil of the camps in Treblinka and Oświęcim provides the spatial focus for investigations evolving along two timelines: the events of the 1940s and the post-war world. The temporal and spatial interplay articulated in documentary films is an answer to the challenge posed by the partial or total disappearance of traces; for example, Lanzmann's detached long shots of the countryside in Treblinka, as Brad Prager has argued, emphasise the attempt to fill the silence and to rationalise the disjunctions imposed by the chronological gap between the war and the time of filming (2015: 27). The landscapes of *Shoah* often lack physical traces of the events, and yet the spatially connected testimonies gathered by Lanzmann in juxtaposition with these long shots contribute to articulating an understanding of a remote past that becomes part of an alien present. Similarly, *Shoah*'s unassuming tracking shots, taken from a moving car driving along the streets of Oświęcim, reveal a site of memory where past events require re-elaboration in the present by means of the act of remembering. Among those who remember, Holocaust survivor Otto Dov Kulka has used the expression 'metropolis of death' in relation to the camps in Oświęcim, in an attempt to reach 'beyond the experience of the world of Auschwitz' and to articulate a metaphor representing a place which, in Kulka's reflective memory, expands 'into a world order that would change the course of human history' (2013: xxii).[4] Accordingly, the cinematic exploration of the *metropoleis* of death of Treblinka and Oświęcim in *Shoah* will guide the following discussion of the ways in which these two sites have been used, at times consistently and at times in flashes, loops and leaps, in documentaries made after Lanzmann's own journey to Poland at the end of the 1970s, and their emergence from oblivion by means of that particular awareness of the void which can only be achieved in the attempt of filling it. This chapter thus looks at the relationship between spaces that were created for the purpose of the Final Solution and the marks they left on rural and urban landscapes after the war; in particular, it focuses on survivors' return journeys to their sites of persecution and their places of mourning, to those green fields that used to be muddy hells where, to paraphrase Primo Levi, the Jews knew no peace, fought for a crust of bread, died by a yes or no, without hair and without name, with empty eyes and cold wombs, and yet sometimes survived with the strength to remember.[5]

Treblinka

Previous chapters have looked at the absences left by the murdered Jews in the villages and cities of Poland, including Otwock (*Tell Me Why*), Suchowola (*Everyone Had Their Own Jew*), Brańsk (*Shtetl*), Opatów (*Paint What You Remember*), Pińczów (*So Many Miracles*) and Warsaw (*Tango of Slaves*). The Jews of these particular cities and villages, the relatives of Marzynski, Ziv, Rubinek, Kirshenblatt, Jurek and other survivors, were all killed at the extermination camp in Treblinka. In these documentaries, Treblinka is a threatening absence, an invisible presence whose name evokes the deepest fears and the most profound sense of loss, mourning and grieving. Similarly, in Sławomir Grünberg and Tomek Wiśniewski's short documentary *Castaways* (2013), Treblinka does not appear as a location and yet the name of the death camp pervades its narrative and its testimonies. The film is set in Łapy, a small town between Białystok and Treblinka whose 630 pre-war Jewish residents, a fifth of the overall population, were murdered by the Nazis. The cattle trains taking the Jews of the Białystok region to Treblinka would slow down as they passed through this town, and several children were reported to have been thrown from the wagons through the small windows of the carriages. *Castaways* includes present-day scenes filmed in Łapy as well as interviews with Polish bystanders Jerzy Rydzewski, Mieczyslaw Francke and Mieczyslaw Lapinski among others; it also uses archival photographs of the station taken during the war, with visible Nazi flags and members of the SS and Wehrmacht. Like Lviv-based documentary *Boris Dorfman a Mentsh*, Grünberg and Wiśniewski's film includes repeated shots of the railway station, trains and tracks in a way that is evocative of the work of Lanzmann; the panning of the camera on these tropes of Holocaust documentary cinema summons visions of the exhausting journey to Treblinka,

Figure 6.1 *Castaways* (Sławomir Grünberg and Tomek Wiśniewski, 2013).

the extermination of the Jews cramped in the cattle trains, the death of an entire pre-war world and its survival in the memory of the living (Fig. 6.1).

Castaways shares *Shoah*'s obsessive focus with the imagery of railroad transport which originated from Lanzmann's first visit to Treblinka in 1978, when the filmmaker was transfixed by the presence of regular train traffic on the same tracks that had brought the Jews to their death during the Holocaust: 'Treblinka was nothing but a ghost station: as I stood petrified on the platform, attempting to come to terms with the enormity of what I was witnessing, trains passed, some hurtling straight through, others stopping to load and unload passengers' (2012: 473). In *Shoah*, Lanzmann juxtaposed this location with the testimonies of survivors, bystanders and perpetrators, including former *SS-Unterscharführer* Franz Suchomel, the man who tells Lanzmann that if Auschwitz II-Birkenau was a factory then Treblinka was a very primitive and yet well-functioning assembly line of death. The immediate post-war image of the sites of these two death camps reflects this distinction, with barracks, workshops and other buildings surviving at least partly intact in Oświęcim and an eerie forest clearing in Treblinka, where the Nazis almost succeeded in concealing all evidence of the genocide which took place there. Their attempt failed. In September 1944 Soviet Russian writer Vasily Grossman, who was one of the journalists accompanying the scouts of the Soviet Army and who collected some of the first eyewitness testimonies from the Eastern Front, entered the land where the camp had once stood, and in 1946 he published a long article on the discovery of Treblinka:

> The earth ejects crushed bones, teeth, bits of paper and clothing; it refuses to keep its awful secret. These things emerge from the unhealed wounds in the earth. There they are – the half-rotten shirts of the slain, the trousers, shoes, tarnished cigarette-cases, the tiny cogwheels of watches, penknives, shaving brushes, candlesticks, children's shoes with red pompons, towels with Ukrainian embroidery, lace underwear, scissors, thimbles, corsets, and trusses. . . . Pervading everything is the nauseating stench of corruption, a stench that neither fire nor sunshine, rain, snow or wind have been able to overcome. And hundreds of tiny forest flies swarm over the decaying fragments of clothing and paper. (1946: 407)[6]

Grossman's article was used at the Nuremberg Trials as evidence against the Nazis and contributed to revealing the horrors of Treblinka to a Western Europe that struggled to absorb the development of the Final Solution on the Eastern Front, and was more inclined to focus on the concentration camps freed by the American and British forces in the territories of the Reich, including Dachau, Mauthausen-Gusen and Belsen, or the death camp in Poland where Western European Jews were murdered, Auschwitz II-Birkenau. Among those who paid attention to the revelations about Treblinka emerging from the Nuremberg Trials was French filmmaker Jean-Pierre Melville, whose war drama *Le Silence de la mer* (1949) made the first reference in cinema to the third Aktion Reinhard death camp: towards the end of the film a German lieutenant asks an SS officer about Treblinka, a name that in 1949 meant nothing to most Europeans. As the camera tracks in and then back on a portrait of Adolf Hitler placed on the SS officer's desk, the lieutenant's voice over reads a report about the mass executions of the Jews in Treblinka by means of exhaust fumes. And yet, despite this early reference, for years the reality of Treblinka was largely ignored both inside and outside Poland, in public debate as well as in film. When Holocaust historian Martin Gilbert visited the site in 1959, Treblinka still looked like the desolate place evoked by Grossman thirteen years earlier:

> From Treblinka village we proceeded for another mile or two, along the line of an abandoned railway through a forest of tall trees. Finally we reached an enormous clearing, bounded on all sides by dense woodland. Darkness was falling, and with it, the chill of night and a cold dew. I stepped down from the cart on to the sandy soil: a soil that was grey rather than brown. Driven by I know not what impulse, I ran my hand through that soil, again and again. The earth beneath my feet was coarse and sharp: filled with the fragments of human bone. (1986: 17)

In the same year *SS-Untersturmführer* and Treblinka commander Kurt Franz was arrested in Düsseldorf, where he had worked as a cook since 1949, and the dreadful reality of Treblinka began to emerge from obscurity. After the arrest of Kurt Franz, which was followed by the arrest of

SS-Hauptsturmführer and Treblinka commander Franz Stangl in 1967, the Treblinka trials which took place in Düsseldorf in 1964–5 and 1970–1 revealed the horrors of Aktion Reinhard to the world and resulted in the two former commanders being sentenced to life imprisonment (Donat, 1979: 296–316).[7]

Between the making of *Le Silence de la mer* and the filming of *Shoah* thirty years later, the site of the camp was monumentalised and declared a national place of martyrdom on 10 May 1964. Only the accounts of the eyewitnesses and forensic evidence have helped historians to understand the layout of the camp; there is no footage of Treblinka, and just a handful of photographs from Kurt Franz's unauthorised album, cruelly titled *Schöne Zeiten* ('Good Times'), which was retrieved only after his arrest on 2 December 1959, exists. Thousands of men and women survived the camps in Oświęcim, while only seventy individuals are known to have survived Treblinka, and only a handful of them wrote memoirs about their experience in the camp.[8] In spite of the difficulties in visualising Treblinka, Lanzmann's *Shoah* aimed at letting the death camp re-emerge from darkness by bringing its past horrors to the present and to reality. Post-war images of Treblinka, such as those produced by Lanzmann or emerging from a larger cohort of documentaries, reveal no physical evidence of the ways in which the site was used during the war. As Ulrich Baer suggests, images of former camps and killing grounds are often saturated with markers of the Holocaust, including ruins, barbed wire and memorial stones (2002: 66). However, defined by its deprivation of any physical remnant of the extermination process, the cinematic image of Treblinka has been articulated in two directions: on the one hand the site is contextualised in its present-day monumentalised state, and on the other the countryside surrounding the memorial area is portrayed as a place that has remained largely unchanged in the post-war years. According to Baer, such images 'force us to see that there is nothing to see there, and they show us that there is something in a catastrophe as vast as the Holocaust that remains inassimilable to historicist or contextual readings' (2002: 66). Baer is specifically discussing here the photographs of concentration and death camps taken by Dirk Reinartz and Mikael Levin as a challenge to our 'reliance on historical context as an explanatory framework' (2002: 67). The appearance of Treblinka in film also hints to such a challenge, and yet, by means of juxtaposing present-day footage with the testimonies of bystanders and survivors or with postmemory-based reflections, this is an image that uses space as a means of introspection and thus integrates the limited information provided by the landscape itself and by mere historical contextualisation.[9]

Claude Lanzmann filmed on location at the site of the gas chambers and at the village of Treblinka, two miles away from the camp. On his visit to the region, the filmmaker had a shattering revelation born out of simple logic: 'A man who was sixty in 1978 [Lanzmann writes in his autobiography] would have been twenty-four in 1942, someone who was seventy now would then have been in the prime of life. A fifteen-year-old boy in 1942 would now be about to turn fifty' (2012: 472). This realisation helped Lanzmann to create a complex film where, as Sue Vice has argued, the 'focus is on the past only as it makes itself felt in the present, at least, the present time of the film in the 1970s and 1980s' (2011: 39).[10] During his visit, the filmmaker realised that the witnesses of the genocide were all around him and that invaluable insight on the events could have been gained by interviewing the Poles who saw the Jews being brought to their death. Lanzmann spoke with Czesław Borowi and other local bystanders in the vicinity of Treblinka's railway station, which was still in operation at the end of the 1970s. He also interviewed Henryk Gawkowski, the man who drove the trains taking the Jews to the camp, at his home in Małkinia Górna, on the other bank of the Bug River. These interviews are recorded in the present of the film and contribute to articulating a journey in time to the extermination period in 1942–3.

The second strategy employed by Lanzmann to establish a continuity between the past and the present consists of a series of interviews with two survivors, recorded remotely and then edited with shots of the memorial on the site of the camp and train traffic between the villages of Małkinia Górna, Treblinka, Poniatowo and Wólka Okrąglik.[11] Richard Glazar and Abraham Bomba were both members of the *Sonderkommando* work unit and were interviewed by Lanzmann in Basel (Switzerland) and Tel Aviv (Israel) respectively. As he sits on a balcony overlooking the Mittlere Brücke on the Rhine River, Glazar provides an account of the burning pyres of Treblinka and recites the words of a song sung by a prisoner who had been an opera singer: 'My God, my God, why hast Thou forsaken us? We have been thrust into the fire before, but we have never denied Thy Holy Law.' Accompanied by Glazar's voice-over, the film location changes to the snowy landscape of Treblinka and its memorial stones, with a circular panning shot of the area taken from the granite monument that stands where the gas chambers stood. A similar temporal transition is provided in one of the most widely discussed scenes of the film, which begins with Gawkowski driving the old locomotive from Małkinia Górna to Treblinka. Gawkowski wears a driver's uniform and cap, leans from the window, makes a gesture by drawing his finger across his throat. At this point, Bomba's voice-over begins the account of the deportation, the arrival at Treblinka and the selection process. The location changes briefly to Tel Aviv before returning to Treblinka with a shot filmed from the rear seat of the car driven by Lanzmann as it approaches the railway station. Lanzmann places the events narrated by Bomba and Glazar in the present by editing their accounts with images of present-day Treblinka, and by juxtaposing two narratives taken in different countries in the process of anchoring past events to the specific site of the camp. In these long sequences, Lanzmann's camera pans over cattle trains and rural scenes, memorial stones and muddy roads, and jumps on an anachronistic locomotive running through the Polish countryside.

As Sue Vice has argued, the witnesses interviewed in *Shoah* seem 'to undergo a collapse of temporal boundaries, and at the same time the spectator experiences a closing of the gap between the *mise en scène* and the scenes of the past that they can only imagine' (2011: 46). The result of this process has brought Treblinka back from obscurity and has contributed to inscribing the site of the death camp in the topography of the extermination of the Jews in collective knowledge. Since *Shoah*, Treblinka has appeared as a location in a number of documentaries including *Never Forget to Lie*, a film already discussed in connection to its journey to Warsaw and Kraków. In this film, Marian Marzynski, his cousin Ed Herman and his wife Halina drive along provincial road 627 between the towns of Ostrołęka and Sokołów Podlaski and reach the village of Treblinka and, eventually, the site of the death camp. During Aktion Reinhard, Herman's grandfather, who had been deported from the Warsaw Ghetto, escaped from a train on its way to the camp, but he was eventually captured by the Nazis and murdered. Various shots of the stones at the memorial and the surrounding forests contribute to establishing a connection with past events in a way that is reminiscent of Lanzmann's filming at the site. However, Lanzmann notoriously refused to use archival images, whereas Marzynski includes a photograph of Herman's grandfather taken in the 1930s and used by the member of the postgeneration to establish a familial link with the place. This undertaking signals a thematic difference between *Never Forget to Lie* and *Shoah*, a film that aims at chiselling the Holocaust in its collective dimension rather than focusing on one individual killing. What *Never Forget to Lie* and *Shoah* share is the use of a landscape where the absence of traces requires the filmmaker to integrate the site-specific experience of the memorial area of Treblinka with a series of strategies aimed at establishing a connection with the past.[12]

Other documentaries articulated an interplay between location shooting in Treblinka, the direct testimonies of survivors, the inclusion of archival material and postgenerational connections to the sites of annihilation. Tim

Gray's *A Promise to My Father* (2010) uses Kurt Franz's photographs of Treblinka to illustrate the family history of Holocaust survivor Israel Arbeiter as he returns to Poland and Germany from the United States, where he moved after the war. Arbeiter is accompanied in this postmemory journey by his nephew Matthew Fritz. Their itinerary takes them to Warsaw and to the family *shtetl* Płock, where they visit the marketplace and search unsuccessfully for a candlestick that was buried by Arbeiter during the war in the basement of a house in the former ghetto district. In 1942 he was deported to the ghetto in Starachowice and then to the Soldau concentration camp in Działdowo, north-central Poland, while his parents and siblings were murdered in Treblinka. *A Promise to My Father* includes a short visit to the site of the camp late one evening, with Arbeiter commemorating his family as he stands near the granite monument erected on the site of the gas chambers. For this survivor, Treblinka is a place of mourning and a location he did not directly experience during the war; this phase of the journey is thus less concerned with passing on knowledge, and instead relates to his attempt to find some kind of closure by visiting the place where his relatives were murdered and to reach an intimate proximity to the dead.

A process of postmemory is also at the heart of *Finding Leah Tickotsky: A Discovery of Heritage in Poland* (Sarah Golabek-Goldman, 2010), a documentary which combines present-day images of the Treblinka memorial reminiscent of Lanzmann's shots with archival images of Jews who were murdered at the camp. *Finding Leah Tickotsky* is an account of the journey undertaken in 2007 by the filmmaker, a Stanford University student who had taught English in the village of Zakliczyn, to the places where her family lived before the Holocaust, including Jedwabne, Jasionówka, Łomża and Białystok.[13] This postmemory journey also brought Golabek-Goldman to Treblinka, the site of the extermination of many members of her family. Accompanied by the sound of a flute, the short sequence filmed at the death camp opens with a characteristically peaceful view of the forest near the site of the gas chambers; this is followed by a shot of the Bug River taken from the bridge which had also been filmed by Lanzmann in the 1970s. At the site of the camp, Golabek-Goldman identifies the stone for the town of Jasionówka and lights a candle for that community in search of a postgenerational closure (Fig. 6.2). Accompanied by Sarit Hadad's song 'Shema Israel', her walk between the memorial stones and various shots of the site are superimposed on photographs of Jews taken in interwar Poland. These archival photographs thus articulate an association between life in the *shtetlekh* and death in the camp, whereas the lack of such images in *Shoah* aims at neutralising the chronological gap between

Figure 6.2 *Finding Leah Tickotsky: A Discovery of Heritage in Poland* (Sarah Golabek-Goldman, 2010).

the events and at delineating the Holocaust as a phenomenon that is still ongoing in a present day, where a Jewish barber in Tel Aviv is repeating the actions, now staged for the camera, that he was forced to perform in Treblinka.

In the above-mentioned and much-discussed sequence from *Shoah*, German-born Abraham Bomba recalls the arrival of a transport from his hometown Częstochowa and has an emotional breakdown at the memory of an encounter with two women he knew in happier days.[14] The fate of the Jews of Częstochowa, a Polish city located on the Warta River, who were murdered in Treblinka also pervades Michał Nekanda-Trepka's *Jakby to było wczoraj* (*As if it were yesterday*, 2005), a documentary in which Holocaust survivor Sigmund Rolat returns to Częstochowa and visits the places of his childhood as well as the site of the forced Nazi labour camp in the armament factories and workshops of HASAG.[15] As in Grünberg and Wiśniewski's *Castaways*, the location that is conspicuously absent from this documentary is Treblinka, the final destination of the Jews of Częstochowa, including many members of Rolat's family. The third Aktion Reinhard camp is evoked here in the words and the tears of a witness who never set foot in the camp, but whose father, Henryk

Rosenblatt, was killed during the Treblinka uprising of August 1943. In documentaries such as *Castaways* and *As if it were yesterday*, a space created by the Nazis for the Final Solution and which operated with devastating strength for barely fifteen months becomes the absent locus of the memory of the extermination in the words of the witnesses. The name of Treblinka pervades these narratives, and yet it evokes a liminal space located along the railway tracks crossing Łapy or Częstochowa, the embodiment of an invisible and fractured past cast in the continuity of memory and chiselled in the discontinuity of the history of the Polish Jews.

Samuel Willenberg was also deported from Częstochowa to the third Aktion Reinhard camp, from which he escaped during the 1943 revolt, and eventually became the last survivor of Treblinka. He died in 2016. Willenberg appears in several documentaries that make use of the site of the death camp as a key location, including Michał Nekanda-Trepka's *Ostatni świadek* (*The Last Witness*, 2002), a film focusing on Willenberg's role in the Treblinka uprising, an event narrated against the background of today's life in the countryside around the site of the camp.[16] *The Last Witness* opens with present-day scenes filmed in Israel and followed by archival footage filmed in the 1930s showing a Jewish marketplace and street life in an unidentified location. Willenberg is first seen sitting on a train on his way to Haifa in the company of his grandchild, and this scene precedes unspecified footage of Jews taking their belongings to one of the Polish ghettos. Before the sequences of Willenberg's journey to Poland, Nekanda-Trepka includes a juxtaposition of archival footage of interwar Poland with present-day footage of Mount Carmel, Israel, thus establishing a spatial and temporal connection between two landscapes of Jewish heritage and history. In the following sequence Willenberg has returned to Poland and is travelling to Opatów (where he observes the space left empty by a *mezuzah* on the doorpost of a former Jewish home) and to his hometown Częstochowa. The journey to Poland also includes Willenberg's visit to Treblinka, which is introduced with a shot of a road sign reminiscent of those filmed by Lanzmann over twenty years earlier (Fig. 6.3). By 2002 the train station was no longer in operation and yet, whereas the documentaries discussed above are almost exclusively concerned with the site of the camp, *The Last Witness* places Willenberg's testimony in a landscape which includes the local farms and barns, where Poles engage in conversations with the survivor, and the trackbed of the disused railway, along which Willenberg walks from the former station to the site of the camp. As he stands near the memorial stones and the monument resembling one of the cremation pits, Willenberg describes his arrival at the camp, the moment he saw the *Lazarett* and the burning

Figure 6.3 *Ostatni świadek* (*The Last Witness*, Michał Nekanda-Trepka, 2002).

pyres, his selection as a member of the *Sonderkommando* and the time he spent cutting women's hair or sorting the belongings of those who were murdered.[17]

In an attempt to reflect upon the role of mediation in the dynamics of cultural memory, this visit is briefly juxtaposed with Willinberg's journey to Masada, Israel, where a Jewish mass suicide allegedly followed the Roman siege of 73–74 CE, in a thematic connection between an event which belongs to ancient Jewish history and the suicidal revolt in Treblinka. In doing so, *The Last Witness* articulates a confrontation between traumatic histories and memories converging here in recognition of an interplay between disparate acts of remembrance, and reflecting Michael Rothberg's description of multidirectional memory as a mutual constitution and overlap of distinct historical events (2009: 179). As the memory of Treblinka is subject to a process of borrowing, adaptation and modification that contextualises its being in multiple geographical and chronological directions, Nekanda-Trepka's camera tracks over the memorial stones in a way which is again reminiscent of *Shoah* while Willenberg gives an account of his role in the revolt and his successful escape. The itinerary presented in *The Last Witness* continues to the rural villages of Wólka Okrąglik and Jakubiki, where Willenberg sought help after the revolt and where he now meets a farmer who gave shelter to three Jews who escaped from Treblinka. He also identifies the place where he spent his first night as a free man, and meets the man who helped him back in 1943.[18] This sequence articulates a discourse on the decisions taken by Poles who helped Jews on the run from the Nazis, their fears of German retaliation and the moral dilemmas they encountered in making decisions such as sheltering or reporting the escapees. The mark left by the Holocaust on the memories of these Poles thus contributes to a multidirectional shift from a vertical reading of the Holocaust as part of history of the Jews to a horizontal reading of the Final Solution as a transcultural geographical phenomenon that has its soil in the Polish countryside as well as in the Israeli mountains seen in the previous sequence. More specifically, Willenberg's account in *The Last Witness* has contributed to placing Treblinka on the map of documentary filmmaking and integrated information provided by Lanzmann's exploration of the sites of camp in *Shoah*. The duality of this landscape, monumental and rural, is inscribed in films that trace a topography of extermination which contributes to redefining the Holocaust as a spatially diverse and complex phenomenon whose archival imagery is, in most instances, incomplete and out of reach. After its first evocation in Melville's *Le Silence de la mer*, the name and the site of Treblinka went into cinematic oblivion until the release of *Shoah*, a documentary in which the death camp emerged as a location where the distance between past and present is abolished, and in which witnesses and survivors are turned into actors performing for Lanzmann's camera. During the ensuing three decades Treblinka has remained absent from fiction films while playing an important role in a number of Holocaust documentaries, where the monumentalised emptiness of the site is used to experience the past and to articulate processes of postmemory, or evoked as a threatening void, a place of mourning and grieving.

Oświęcim

The name of Auschwitz has commonly been used as a term standing for the entirety of the Holocaust, whereas more specifically it stands for a network of labour and death camps established by the Nazis in the town of Oświęcim, in Lesser Poland, and its environs. Liberated by the Red Army in the winter of 1945, this metropolis of death included forty-five satellite camps and the three large camps: Auschwitz I, Auschwitz II-Birkenau and Auschwitz III-Monowitz.[19] Auschwitz I is associated with the imprisonment and murder of a heterogeneous group of prisoners mainly composed of Poles and also including a significant number of Jews; Auschwitz II-Birkenau, with its four main crematoria, is a site of the extermination of Polish Jews as well as Italian, French, Dutch and Hungarian Jews, among other nationalities. Despite the Germans' attempt to conceal all traces of the genocide, Auschwitz I and Auschwitz II-Birkenau (hereafter referred to as Auschwitz and Birkenau) survived the war at least partly intact and, unlike the Aktion Reinhard's killing centres in Eastern Poland, they became sites of memory where the process of anchoring past events to the present could be facilitated by the persistence of the landscape and its built environment.

Tim Cole has discussed Auschwitz and Birkenau as they emerge from survivors' testimonies based on return journeys to the camps in terms of 'a series of interconnected micro-sites rather than a homogenous memorial landscape' and has advocated the necessity of understanding the survivors' experience by means of a 'dynamic relationship between landscape and memory' (2013: 102).[20] This section of the chapter looks at the ways in which Auschwitz and Birkenau, and specifically certain spaces within these two camps, have been used in documentary cinema from the filming of *Shoah* in the 1970s to today, with particular attention to films focusing on return journeys to the camps undertaken by Holocaust survivors. In Auschwitz, recurring locations include the gate bearing the inscription 'Arbeit Macht Frei', the barracks, the reconstructed gas chamber and the crematorium; in Birkenau they comprise the second *Judenrampe* (the unloading ramp), the surviving wooden barracks in the former Quarantine Block, the brick barracks in the former women's section, the main gate and watchtower, the Kanada warehouse facilities for the belongings of the victims, the ruins of the four crematoria, the site of the extermination pits and the pyres. The investigation of these spaces is built upon Cole's categorisation of the material and symbolic landscape of Auschwitz and Birkenau in relation to three main groups of sites: the ruins of the gas chambers and crematoria at Birkenau, which are visited for the first time by the survivors and which belong to the dead, and not to those who left the camp alive; the barracks in Auschwitz and Birkenau, which are bound to the experience of the survivors and to their personal Holocaust histories; the gateways and other formerly Nazi-controlled places where survivors re-enact their original arrival and departure from the camp (2013: 104). As we shall see, in documentary films these locations see the return of survivors engaged in the process of passing on their knowledge to the postgeneration while mourning those who have died in the camps and appropriating places from which they were previously excluded.[21]

Documentary accounts of journeys to Oświęcim combine the different temporalities embodied in their itineraries, in the memories they exhume and in their use of archival material. Alain Resnais' pivotal Holocaust documentary *Night and Fog*, which was written by French poet and Mauthausen-Gusen survivor Jean Cayrol, anticipated later films with its intertwining of archival photographs and contemporary footage filmed in the autumn of 1955 in Auschwitz and in Birkenau. Resnais used archival images from various camps, including the Westerbork transit camp in the Netherlands and the Majdanek camp near Lublin, in juxtaposition with present-day footage of the barracks, watchtowers, barbed-wire fences and ruined gas chambers in Auschwitz and Birkenau filmed in Eastmancolor; he thus established a spatially loose temporal connection between the events of the years 1940 to 1945, during which the camps were operational, and the present time of the film in 1955. Forty years later, Hans Fels and Kees Hin's poetic documentary *Auschwitz-Birkenau 1940–1945–1995* articulated a more specific temporal and spatial connection between the period 1940–5 and the time of the film in 1995. The spatiality of these two documentaries evolves differently and, whereas *Night and Fog* loosely locates Auschwitz in occupied Europe, *Auschwitz-Birkenau 1940–1945–1995* specifically situates the camps in the town of Oświęcim. In the process of juxtaposing present-day footage of the camps and the town with archival material from the 1940s, Fels and Hin's documentary reveals a spatial connection between two timelines and travels beyond the spaces created or adapted by the Nazis in the process of the Final Solution, into the everydayness of the pre-existing and surviving town of Oświęcim.

Auschwitz-Birkenau 1940–1945–1995 opens with nocturnal views of Auschwitz after a snowstorm, which include recurring visual tropes of Holocaust cinema such as the barbed-wire fence, the brick walks, the barracks, the gates and the watchtowers of the camp. These images are followed by daytime footage of the train station, with food kiosks, passengers and musicians playing jazz music at a local bar (Fig. 6.4). A multi-layered soundtrack, largely composed of music and of male and female voices reciting the names of victims, accompanies images of the *Judenrampen* and the surviving barracks in the former Quarantine Block of that camp filmed from the gate building. These images anticipate the thematic juxtaposition of shots of the human hair of the victims on display at Auschwitz with a short scene filmed at the hairdressing salon at the railway station. Similarly, archival footage of the Jewish children of Birkenau showing the numbers tattooed on their arms is thematically combined with present-day footage of the Polish children of Oświęcim singing in their classroom. In one of the scenes that follows, a long shot of the thoroughfare Romana Mayzla

Figure 6.4 *Auschwitz-Birkenau 1940–1945–1995* (Hans Fels and Kees Hin, 1995).

along the marketplace, looking towards the Church of the Assumption of the Blessed Virgin Mary, is accompanied by a camera movement taking the viewer to a clothing shop at 21 Rynek Główny where a woman is trying on an evening dress; this scene is followed by an archival photograph showing the arrival of Hungarian Jewish women at Birkenau. Another juxtaposition is provided by a panning shot of the prosthetic limbs of the victims on display at the Auschwitz museum and a short present-day scene showing a man trying on shoes at a local shop. Towards the end of the film, the camera pans over the buildings of Auschwitz and over an open window where a couple are sitting on a bed kissing. This image is juxtaposed with archival photographs of corpses in Birkenau and with footage from the 1940s showing a woman and an emaciated child moving towards the camera – a scene immediately followed by a present-day re-enactment performed by a Polish woman and a child.

By means of these juxtapositions, which evoke those articulated in *The Ghetto in Bałuty*, *Auschwitz-Birkenau 1940–1945–1995* establishes a temporal connection between past and present, as well as a spatial relationship between Oświęcim as a town in Lesser Poland and Auschwitz as the abstracted site of the destruction of the Jews. With a focus on the topographical specificity of the camps in Oświęcim, *Auschwitz-Birkenau 1940–*

1945–1995 thus elaborates a spatial and temporal discourse where past and present intertwine in three main locations including Auschwitz, Birkenau and the town centre. By providing a geographically localised reading of the events, *Auschwitz-Birkenau 1940–1945–1995* inscribes the Oświęcim camps in the broader landscape of the Holocaust and departs from an understanding of 'Auschwitz' and the sole, or the primary, location of the genocide. Fels and Hin's documentary is thus reminiscent of the spatial and temporal connections between the camps, the Jewish cemetery, the streets and the railway station of Oświęcim, with its freight and passenger train traffic, articulated by Lanzmann in *Shoah* by means of a series of juxtapositions with the testimonies of bystander Helena Pietyra, who lived in Oświęcim before, during and after the war, and survivors Paula Biren, Rudolf Vrba and Filip Müller, who are interviewed remotely in Cincinnati, New York and Tel Aviv respectively.[22] In *Shoah*, Oświęcim is introduced with a tracking shot filmed from a car driving along Piastowski Bridge towards the Church of the Assumption of the Blessed Virgin Mary, a location also seen in *Auschwitz-Birkenau 1940–1945–1995*. A second tracking shot of the streets of Oświęcim is preceded by similar images filmed from a car in Włodawa, another town which saw its Jewry disappearing in the fire of the Holocaust. Lanzmann thus develops the theme of the void left by the murdered Jews across the Polish towns where they lived as an element of continuity between two locations physically separated by over 250 miles. Through these juxtapositions Lanzmann seeks a space that belongs to the past as well as to the present, and which stands for the entirety of the Holocaust while being geographically specific; accordingly, as Hannah Pollin-Galay suggests, the locations of *Shoah* can be seen 'as a metaphor for estrangement and silence in Holocaust memory', resulting in a cognitive absence that situates the genocide 'outside the perimeter of ordinary space' (2013: 27).[23] Like *Auschwitz-Birkenau 1940–1945–1995*, *Shoah* thus articulates an experience of the inconceivable emphasised by an apparent triviality of quotidian images of Oświęcim that evoke the destruction of the Jews and are emphatically juxtaposed with a slow tracking shot filmed at the entrance of Birkenau that mimics the arrival of a truck or train to the camp.

The most detailed testimonies about the Oświęcim camps in *Shoah* are given by Slovakian survivors Vrba and Müller. The interview with Vrba, who worked in the *Aufräumungskommando* in Birkenau,[24] was filmed in Central Park and other locations in New York and is juxtaposed with long shots and tracking shots of Birkenau, including the remains of Crematorium II, which was blown up in the revolt of 7 October 1944; the *Judenrampe*; the quarantine barracks filmed from the main building; and a series of long shots of the railway tracks and train traffic in the Oświęcim area. Former *Sonderkommando* Müller was interviewed in Israel, and his testimony is located in Oświęcim by means of the juxtaposition of his voice-over narration and the snowy landscape filmed by Lanzmann on the sites of the camps, including the *Sonderkommando* cell in Block 11, the brick barracks over which Lanzmann's camera pans repeatedly, the Black Wall where executions took place, the gas chamber and crematorium in Auschwitz, the watchtowers, the *Judenrampe*, the barbed-wire fences and the ruins of Crematorium II in Birkenau.[25] After *Shoah*, the editing techniques used by Lanzmann to locate in Oświęcim testimonies recorded elsewhere have been adopted and reinvented by other filmmakers. For example, Andrzej Wajda's *Pamiętam* (*I Remember*, 2002) is constructed on the testimonies given by Leszek Allerhand, Stanislaw Jonas, David Efrati and Henryk Mandelbaum, four Birkenau survivors who are interviewed remotely in their homes in Poland, Israel and the USA. Wajda places their accounts in Oświęcim by means of interlacing the talking-head interviews with footage of Auschwitz and Birkenau taken during the March of the Living, the yearly educational program which brings Jewish students from the USA, Israel and other countries to the sites of the Holocaust in Poland. In a discussion of such heritage journeys, Erica Lehrer has argued that the iconicity of the camps combined with the widespread presence of 'barbed wire, electrified fences with concrete pilings, and the monotone grey, unpainted walls of municipal structures' can give the traveller 'an uncanny sense of actually travelling into the wartime past one has come to contemplate' (2012: 221).[26] The documentaries addressed in this chapter use these tropes and travel to these locations in order to articulate survivors' return journeys to the sites of their persecution, to account for postmemorial explorations and, more recently, to investigate the phenomenon of mass tourism in Oświęcim.[27]

As Tim Cole suggests, the camps are 'experienced by survivors as more than simply a passive landscape that is visited to enact a series of rituals of mourning, guiding and revenge' (2013: 121). These rituals have been captured in documentaries filmed in Auschwitz and Birkenau, two lingering presences in a group of cinematic journeys addressed in the previous chapters and in their articulation of a dynamic relationship between memory and place in the context of narratives of return where soil, ruins and buildings can unlock and exhume long-buried painful memories. In Imielska's *Tell Me Why*, Auschwitz survivor Jurek visits the Yad Vashem Holocaust History Museum in Jerusalem and stands in front of a large photograph of the entrance to Birkenau, in a journey that does not physically take him to the camp and whose spatiality is mediated by an archival image. An actual return journey is instead seen in Koocher's *How Much to Remember*, which includes a short sequence filmed at the entrances of Auschwitz and Birkenau, where the filmmaker's mother-in-law was interned during the war. In *Loving the Dead*, Hamermesh's journey to Poland continues from Łódź to Birkenau, where the filmmaker's father was killed. The railway sign of the Oświęcim station anticipates a sequence filmed on the grounds of Birkenau on a foggy day and showing Hamermesh as she walks along the *Judenrampe*, the place where her father would have disembarked from a cattle car reaching the camp from the Radegast station in Łódź. An actor playing the role of her father's ghost stands near the ramp, wearing a coat and holding a suitcase; in the following scene, now naked, he stands next to barbed-wire fence, his vulnerability emphasised by the foggy vastness of the camp and by its emptiness (Fig. 6.5).

While deserted spaces and structured absences have regularly characterised the landscapes of the camps filmed during these return journeys, mass tourism has affected the sites increasingly in the past thirty years and has had an impact on certain cinematic representations of these locations. The touristic character of the present-day camp can be observed in the short documentary *Branko: Return to Auschwitz* (Topaz Adizes, 2013), a film focusing on Hollywood producer Branko Lustig's return journey to Auschwitz and Birkenau to celebrate the *bar mitzvah* he could never have as a young man. Lustig's account is juxtaposed to his visit to various locations, crowded with tourists and including the gate bearing the inscription 'Arbeit Macht Frei', the former brothel in Block 24 at Auschwitz and the *Judenrampe* in Birkenau.[28] The polyphony of voices emerging from these

Figure 6.5 *Loving the Dead* (Mira Hamermesh, 1991).

documentaries provides individual topographies of a space that, at once crowded with tourists characterised by deeper absences, has acquired an iconic role in the visual memory of the Holocaust. Accordingly, films such as *Tell Me Why*, *How Much to Remember*, *Loving the Dead* and *Branko: Return to Auschwitz* articulate an experience of return where Oświęcim is 'not simply a site, a place, a town, a topography' but rather, as Griselda Pollock suggests, an event that 'signifies an encounter with death, and as such signifies a stupefying absence, the destroyed millions who signified furthermore, the destruction of one of the civilizations of Europe' (2003: 176).[29]

Documentary accounts of return journeys to the camps can articulate a dynamic engagement with locations that lie beyond ordinary topographies both in spatial and temporal terms. *A Promise to My Father*, a film already discussed in relation to its use of Treblinka as a location, provides a useful example of this articulation of site-specific encounters with memory and death. After Arbeiter's visit to the Aktion Reinhard camp, the film introduces Auschwitz with an archival photograph of the 'Arbeit Macht Frei' gate followed by present day images of the gate, the barbed-wire fence, the barracks, the interiors of the gas chamber and the crematorium. As we shall see, other documentaries have used the gate and the crematorium as iconic Holocaust locations and yet, as Debórah Dwork and Robert Jan van Pelt have explained, Crematorium I in Auschwitz was reconstructed after the war 'to speak for the history of the four crematoria at Birkenau' (1994: 239),[30] whereas the infamous gate did not belong to the experience of the Jews brought to Oświęcim for enslavement and extermination:

> The inscribed arch did not have a central position in the history of Auschwitz. First, it played no role in the Judaeocide. Arriving at the Auschwitz train station, the Jews were marched or taken by truck to Birkenau; later a spur rail line was laid and the transports went there directly. Furthermore, although the arch was the main gate to Auschwitz I in 1941, in the expansion program the following year it became an internal structure separating the original camp from the extended domain. (1994: 237)

Moreover, whereas Birkenau was created by the Nazis for the purpose of extermination, Auschwitz was the result of the conversion of sixteen preexisting buildings that had once served as army barracks during and after the Habsburg occupation of south-western Poland. Documentary images of the barracks at Auschwitz can thus provide a multidirectional reading of the camp as a site of Jewish, Christian and Polish martyrdom, open to, as Andrew Charlesworth suggests, 'different interpretations and malleable to the needs of state power and religious forces' (1994: 579).[31]

The visit to the camps illustrated in *A Promise to My Father* continues to Birkenau, to its surviving barracks and to its *Judenrampe*, and thus re-establishes a coherent topography of the Judaeocide as opposed to the broader category of Nazi crimes. As he stands on the *Judenrampe* and embodies the role of expert and guide, Israel Arbeiter shows the number tattooed on his forearm to a group of Czech students and tells them about his internment, thus becoming one of those survivors who, according to Cole, 'perform their testimony and reinhabit these places with their authoritative stories' (2013: 112). Arbeiter was deported to Oświęcim from the Soldau concentration camp, Działdowo, in 1943 and eventually transported to the concentration camp in Stutthof, 340 miles north of Oświęcim, towards the end of the war. His return journey to Birkenau includes locations associated with his imprisonment in the camp as well as places he is visiting for the first time. As he walks along the railway tracks while archival photographs illustrate his memories of the selection process, Arbeiter looks at the open gate under the main watchtower and observes that it would normally have been closed when the camp was operational. Whereas the building has remained largely unchanged, the simple discrepancy between the view of a wide-open gate and the memory of an insurmountable barrier provokes a sense of alienation in the survivor's experience of the camp, which he overcomes by providing a detailed account about his arrival at Birkenau. Arbeiter was selected for manual labour and was made to follow other inmates along the main street of the camp, the *Lagerstrasse*, where he now returns and follows his own steps to the men's section of the camp (Fig. 6.6). Here he seeks a personal

Figure 6.6 *A Promise to My Father* (Tim Gray, 2010).

connection with the altered site and identifies the exact spot of his bunk within the perimeter of the scattered remains of Barrack 28, where he spent most of his time in Birkenau. Cole has observed that the camp was architecturally subdivided into separate sections and thus 'survivors had geographically limited experiences of the camp' (2013: 113). However, Arbeiter worked a rolling wagon emptying toilets throughout the entire camp and had more freedom of movement than other inmates, a freedom which brought him to see the waiting area outside Crematorium V and the men, women and children who were soon to be gassed. In *A Promise to My Father*, he walks along the Ringstrasse to the ruins of that crematorium and to the areas where pyres and mass graves were located. He also visits the building known as 'die zentrale Sauna', where the prisoners' clothing was disinfected in steam rooms and where the photographs of those who were murdered are now on display. As it articulates a dynamic relationship between past and present and between space and memory, *A Promise to My Father* thus focuses on a man who slowly overcomes the disorientation that regularly affect the survivors of a camp that today bears only a vague resemblance to the place of their interment.

Beyond the changes to the built environment, as Cole suggests, spatial disorientation affects multiple senses (2013: 121): the terrible smell of human flesh being burnt in the pyres lingers in the memories of the survivors, and so do the noises, the orders shouted by the men of the SS and the *Kapos*. The disappearance of the past, according to Gary Weissman, complicates the experience of visiting Birkenau on account of 'the post-war museumification of the site, the deterioration of what has been preserved, and the absence of the horrific past reality that, on some level, one anticipates encountering there' (2004: 173). The disorientation caused by the process of memorialisation of the site can be observed in the course of the return journeys to the camps undertaken by survivors and members of the postgeneration that are portrayed in James Moll's *The Last Days* (1998). This documentary specifically addresses the extermination of the Hungarian Jews in Birkenau, and is based on the testimonies of a group of Holocaust survivors including Bill Basch, Irene Zisblatt, Renee Firestone, Alice Lok Cahana and Tom Lantos.[32] While most interviews are recorded remotely and connected to the events by means of extensive and topographically coherent use of archival photographs and footage of the camp, *The Last Days* also includes sequences filmed during postmemory journeys made by the survivors and their children to their familial sites of life and death. Irene Zisblatt returns to her *shtetl* Polena and to the town of Mukacheve, where she was deported at the beginning of the war; Renee Firestone returns to Uzhhorod, the town where she grew up.[33]

Figure 6.7 *The Last Days* (James Moll, 1998).

The concentration camps in Dachau and Bergen Belsen are visited by Bill Basch and Alice Lok Cahana respectively, whereas Oświęcim sees the return of Firestone and Cahana.

Moll introduces Birkenau as a location with a zooming shot on an archival photograph of its main building, an image that then fades to a present-day long shot of the same place taken from the *Judenrampe* (Fig. 6.7). Alice Lok Cahana walks along the railway tracks with her son Michael and provides an account of the arrival and the selection process juxtaposed with archival images of the events and with present-day footage taken inside a barrack. Cahana also visits the ruins of the latrine in Birkenau, and this location unlocks a very personal memory: it is the location where she celebrated Sabbath with her sister and other children who prayed and sang Hebrew songs during their imprisonment. The second journey to Oświęcim recorded in *The Last Days* sees Renee Firestone returning to the camp to seek closure during a visit that reopens old wounds. After walking under the 'Arbeit Macht Frei' gate, she sees the files documenting her arrival and the internment in the camp, as well as records for her father and her sister Klara, who was the subject of medical experiments.[34] Firestone also lights a candle and prays at the ruins of Crematorium V, a site that she could not have experienced during her imprisonment but which embodies a familial connection because her mother was murdered there. As Cole suggests, the ruined gas chambers and crematoria are sites of closure where family members are 'finally mourned and symbolically laid to rest' (2013: 107). Firestone and Cahana's visits to Birkenau thus exemplify the two main tendencies revealed by such narratives of return:

on the one hand site-specific memories emerge from the renewed experience of spaces lived by the survivors during their imprisonment, while on the other hand, the process of mourning is anchored to locations that did not belong to the survivors' direct experience of the camp.

The crematoria are often framed as sites of closure and mourning as well as sites of resistance and resilience associated with their explosion during the rebellion of October 1944. Accordingly, Steve Prankard's documentary *Following in Felix's Footsteps* (2016) uses the crumbling buildings of Birkenau's crematoria in relation to the theme of resistance to the Nazis' genocidal plans. This film combines a loose use of archival photographs from various concentration camps, including Buchenwald, with survivor Felix Opatowski's return journey from Canada to the sites of his youth in Łódź, to the memorial at Radegast station and finally to the camps in Oświęcim and Mauthausen-Gusen. In 1944, Opatowski took part in the plot to blow up the crematoria at Birkenau and helped smuggle dynamite from Auschwitz III-Monowitz. His account is given on the sites of the ruins of crematoria II, IV and V during a visit to the camps which includes both sites that were experienced by the survivor, and places from which he was excluded during his internment. In Auschwitz, like Firestone in *The Last Days*, Opatowski walks under the 'Arbeit Macht Frei' gate and visits the so-called neutral zone before the electrified fence, where he was given the task of clearing ice, snow and the corpses of inmates who committed suicide by throwing themselves against the barbed wire. In Birkenau, Opatowski visits the surviving barracks in the Quarantine Sector while giving an account of his imprisonment; he also walks to sites beyond his experience of the camp, including the ruins of Bunker Two, or the 'White House' (a specially adapted farmhouse where Jews were murdered in four temporary gas chambers which were in operation between 1942 and 1944), and the locations of the ditches and pyres on the outskirts of the camp (Fig. 6.8). Sites of death that were unfamiliar to the prisoner during Felix's time in Oświęcim thus feature prominently in this documentary and articulate a discourse on resistance built on the image of the ruins of the crematoria, providing an answer to the misconceived claim that the Jews walked passively to their deaths.

Survival as a form of resistance is also at the core of the testimony provided by Polish-British Holocaust survivor Kitty Hart-Moxon in a series of films about her internment in Birkenau, including *Kitty: Return to Auschwitz* (Peter Morley, 1979) and *One Day in Auschwitz* (Steve Purcell, 2015).[35] In these documentaries, Hart-Moxon returns to various sites including the *Judenrampe*, the ruined crematoria, the surviving barracks in the Quarantine Sector and in the women's section of the camp, the

Kanada section and the location of the pyres and pits in the silver birch forest. As Griselda Pollock has argued, throughout Hart-Moxon's visits to Birkenau two temporalities collide by means of a use of landscape itself as a concrete link between past and present (2003: 184); Hart-Moxon's memories populate this landscape in a present where grass has grown where only mud could previously be seen, silence has replaced noise and chaos has given way to calm. In both *Kitty: Return to Auschwitz* and *One Day in Auschwitz*, Hart-Moxon's testimony activates a process of postmemory in which the visit to the camps allows members of the post-generation – her son in the earlier film, and two young women in the latter – to engage with the past and to anchor their previous knowledge to the physical environment of the camp. In the course of this process, they share and absorb Hart-Moxon's attempt to revive and intertwine memory to ruins, scattered remains and repeated itineraries.

Morley's *Kitty: Return to Auschwitz* opens with a sequence filmed in Birmingham and including scenes filmed at a local branch of the supermarket chain Safeway, where Hart-Moxon is queuing at the tills; at the studio where she works as a radiologist; and during an interview recorded at her apartment. This sequence, which at first appears incongruous in the context of a Holocaust documentary, contributes to the establishment of a connection between everyday life in Britain in the 1970s and the extraordinary events which took place in Poland in the 1940s. Family photographs from the 1930s are used in the following scene to bridge this spatial and temporal gap and to illustrate the narration provided by a male voice-over commentary. Hart-Moxon was imprisoned in Birkenau in 1943 at the age of sixteen, survived internment and eventually moved

Figure 6.8 *Following in Felix's Footsteps* (Steve Prankard, 2016).

Figure 6.9 *Kitty: Return to Auschwitz* (Peter Morley, 1979).

to Birmingham after the war. In 1979, she decided to visit Oświęcim and pass on her knowledge to her son David. The film follows them to Birkenau, a location which is introduced with shots of the barbed-wire fence, the main watchtower and the *Judenrampe*. Hart-Moxon's immediate response to the site is a sense of alienation caused by the discrepancy between the emptiness of the place and her memories of the crowded camp, where over thirty members of her family were murdered. Crane shots illustrate the vastness of the camp, empty apart from the two figures walking on the ground where the barracks used to stand and where only the brick chimneys now remain (Fig. 6.9). The pair move along the railway tracks in the direction of the former women's section of the camp, and eventually head towards the crematoria. As in *A Promise to My Father*, the visit continues to the exact spot where the selection process took place along the *Judenrampe* and near the Lagerstarsse. Hart-Moxon identifies Block 20, where she stayed during her imprisonment; Block 25, where people were taken before being executed in the gas chambers and which she recognises because of the barred windows; and Block 12, the hospital for infectious disease where her mother worked during her captivity. As they also visit the latrines, the bath blocks and the wooden barracks of the Quarantine Sector, Hart-Moxon explains that in order to survive she would get food and items of clothing from the dead, hence emphasising the theme of survival as the epitome of resistance to the obliteration.

The visit continues to the location of the Kanada warehouse, where the belongings of victims were processed and shipped to Germany and where Kitty worked during most of her time at the camp. These locations belong to her experience of the camp, whereas the final part of the itinerary brings her to spaces that were beyond her own experience: Crematorium IV, from where she explains that she would hear the screams of those who were being murdered, the ruins of the earlier gas chambers known as the White House and the Red House, and the burial sites, where she identifies fragments of bones and human ashes. *Kitty: Return to Auschwitz* thus constructs an itinerary that begins at the familiar sites of the survivor's experience of the camp and concludes at the sites of mourning in an attempt to obtain a closure that always seems to elude the survivors. Thirty-six years after the making of Morley's film, *One Day in Auschwitz* provides a similar itinerary which also includes these two types of locations in Birkenau and reveals that, after many return journeys to the camp, a complete sense of closure is still beyond reach. Hart-Moxon gives her testimony as she visits once again the places where she lived and those she feared, now in the company of sixteen-year-old Lydia Hollingsworth and Natalia Smith, two young women who share Hart-Moxon's age at the time of her imprisonment and to whom she is not directly related. In 1979 the survivor's task was to pass on her knowledge to her son; after twenty-five more years, the process of transmission of knowledge is extended to a postgeneration that absorbs Hart-Moxton's experience by means of identification. In both films the transmission of knowledge, inscribed on the physical experience of the sites of persecution, is directly articulated on the basis of the relationship between Hart-Moxton and her fellow travellers. This type of postgenerational connection conjures images from other films and other landscapes: from the *shtetl* to the ghetto and to the camps, processes of transmission of knowledge captured in documentaries tell a story of memories impressed on minds and places, of resistance to the act of forgetting, of the understanding of a destruction which unfolded in a myriad of locations, and of that shared experience of journeying in time and in space which unfolds in the films investigated in *Journey to Poland*.

Notes

1. Named after *SS-Obergruppenführer* Reinhard Heydrich, who was killed in Prague on 27 May 1942 by Czech and Slovakian soldiers, Aktion Reinhard was the codename of the Nazi plan to mass-murder the entire Jewish population of the General Government district of German-occupied Poland (see Arad, *Bełżec, Sobibór, Treblinka*). The statistics used in this chapter are based on Gilbert, *Routledge Atlas of the Holocaust* (Fourth Edition).
2. *Past and Present, History Falsified, The Uprising in Sobibór, From* the *Realm*

of Death, and *Sobibór: the Plan, the Revolt, the Escape* are based on interviews with men and women who escaped Sobibór in October 1943, including Thomas Blatt, author of the memoir *From the Ashes of Sobibór: A Story of Survival* (Evanston, IL: Northwestern University Press, 1997). In *From the Realm of Death*, Blatt also returns to his *shtetl* Izbica, where he visits the Jewish cemetery and the house where he spent his childhood. In addition to these films, *Land der Vernichtung* (*Land of Annihilation*, Romuald Karmakar, 2004) was shot with a mini DV camera at the sites of the death camps in Bełżec, Sobibór, Treblinka and Majdanek as an aide-memoire to conceptualise a feature film about Polizeibataillon 101, a major perpetrator of the Holocaust in Eastern Poland. Additionally, Nina Koocher's *How Much to Remember: One Family's Conversation with History*, a documentary already discussed in Chapter Five in relation to its postmemory journey to Łódź, contains a long sequence filmed during a group visit to the site of the killing centre in Chełmno. Another documentary about the ghetto in Łódź that includes a sequence filmed in Chełmno is Cummings' *Linie 41*.

3. Moscovitz's *Bełżec* is filmed on location on the site of the only major death camp in Poland that was not included in Claude Lanzmann's *Shoah*. *Bełżec* includes interviews with local bystanders and with a younger generation of Poles and, unlike Lanzmann's work, it makes sporadic use of archival images.
4. Kulka, *Landscapes of the Metropolis of Death*.
5. 'You who live safe/In your warm houses/You who find, returning in the evening/Hot food and friendly faces/Consider if this is a man/Who works in the mud/Who does not know peace/Who fights for a scrap of bread/Who dies because of a yes or a no/Consider if this is a woman/Without hair and without name/With no more strength to remember/Her eyes empty and her womb cold/Like a frog in winter'. In Levi, *Survival in Auschwitz*, p. 11.
6. Grossman, 'The Treblinka Hell'.
7. Donat, *Death Camp Treblinka*.
8. Among a small number of memoirs written by Treblinka survivors are Chil Rajchman's *Treblinka: A Survivor's Memory* and Richard Galzar's *Trap with a Green Fence: Survival in Treblinka*. Rajchman's book was written in Yiddish in Warsaw towards the end of the war and only published in 2009, while Galzar's memoir was written immediately after the war and first published in German in 1992. As early as 1944, Jankiel Wiernik published *Rok w Treblince* (*A Year in Treblinka*), a clandestine booklet printed by the Jewish National Committee (Żydowski Komitet Narodowy) which was translated into English in the following year by the American Representation of the General Jewish Workers' Union of Poland. Samuel Willenberg's memoir *Revolt in Treblinka* was first published in Hebrew in 1986 and in English in 1992. Hershl Sperling also wrote a memoir, which was found in his briefcase in 1989 just after his suicide in Glasgow. It was reproduced in Mark S. Smith's book *Treblinka Survivor: The Life and Death of Hershl Sperling*.

9. An account of the recent excavations and the forensic evidence emerging from the ground of Treblinka is provided in the documentary *Treblinka: Hitler's Killing Machine* (Alex Nikolic-Dunlop, 2014).
10. Vice, *Shoah.*
11. Additionally, Lanzmann employs the same strategy when he combines an interview with *SS-Unterscharführer* Franz Suchomel secretly recorded at the Hotel Post in Braunau am Inn, the town where Adolf Hitler was born, with an aerial view of Treblinka and shots of the train crossing the bridge on the Bug. Lanzmann also interviews Alfred Spiess, a prosecutor at the Treblinka trial whose account accompanies other shots of present-day Treblinka.
12. Among other films discussed in previous chapters, Nina Koocher's documentary *How Much to Remember: One Family's Conversation with History*, about a postmemory journey to the Bałuty district of Łódź she undertook with her parents-in-law, also includes a short sequence filmed at the site of the camp in Treblinka. Koocher's hand-held camera films the stones of the same post-war memorial which were captured by Lanzmann on a snowy winter day almost thirty years earlier.
13. The title of the film refers to the fact that Golabek-Goldman discovered the gravestone of her great-great-grandmother, Leah Tickotsky, at the Jewish cemetery in Jasionówka.
14. Sue Vice, among other viewers, has suggested that Bomba's story is in fact a displaced story about himself and an encounter with his own wife and sister in Treblinka (Vice, *Shoah*, pp. 56–7).
15. HASAG: Hugo Schneider Aktiengesellschaft Metallwarenfabrik.
16. Willenberg also told his story in Gerardo Stawsky's *A Pesar de Treblinka* (*Despite Treblinka*, 2002), Chris Lethbridge's *Nazi Hunters: Death Camp Commandant* (2010), Christophe Cognet's *Parce que j'étais peintre* (*Because I Was a Painter*, 2013) and Adam Kemp's *Death Camp Treblinka: Survivor Stories* (2013). The latter is an expository documentary based on Willenberg's testimony and that of another survivor, Kalman Taigman. Willenberg returned to Treblinka with the film crew while Taigman, like Bomba in *Shoah*, was interviewed remotely in Tel Aviv. *Death Camp Treblinka* includes location shooting, interviews with scholars such as David Cesarani, oral testimonies, archival footage, the photographs from Kurt Franz's album and the famous image of the smoke and fire that followed the riot taken by Lieutenant Franciszek Ząbecki, a stationmaster in the village of Treblinka, and rare archival images of the site in 1944 as it was discovered by the Red Army's scouts. The film focuses on a journey from Willenberg's hometown, Częstochowa, which we see both in archival images and in the present-day shooting, to Warsaw and Treblinka, where he walks with his daughter on the site of the memorial. In a remarkable comment made as the camera shows the countryside around Treblinka, he remembers that as the deportation train passed through the same forest in 1943 the children of the Warsaw Ghetto saw a forest for the first time in their lives.

17. The *Lazarett* was a barracks surrounded by a barbed-wire fence where sick and elderly prisoners were killed just after their arrival at the camp. In this sequence, Willenberg also remembers the first time he saw Kurt Franz and his St Bernard dog Barry, which was instructed to assault prisoners; the arrival of a transport from Radomsko; and the moment when he recognised the coat that belonged to his sister.
18. Later in the film, Willenberg and the farmer walk along the Bug River and the survivor also speaks with local women and men on the streets of the villages where he went in hiding after his escape, including Kosów Lacki, Sterdyń and Kostki. *The Last Witness* ends with the account of his return to Warsaw, his emotional reunion with his father and the memories of his dead sisters, of whom photographs from the 1930s are shown in the final sequence of the film.
19. Auschwitz had been converted from pre-war military barracks, whereas Birkenau was a vast purpose-built concentration and extermination complex. Monowitz was the labour camp attached to a IG Farben factory where Primo Levi was imprisoned.
20. Cole, 'Crematoria, barracks, gateways'.
21. These spaces have also been used in television reports such as CNN's *Voices of Auschwitz* (2015), among many others.
22. Lanzmann also interviewed Armando Aaron and other surviving Jews from Corfu, Greece, who experienced deportation to Oświęcim and whose relatives were murdered in Birkenau; 1,600 Jews from Corfu were deported by the Nazis, and only 122 survived the camp. Aaron's testimony is recorded on the streets of the small island and juxtaposed with images of trains running across the countryside in Poland. During the interview, Lanzmann's camera reveals the old buildings of Corfu, a world apart from Oświęcim. Rather than a juxtaposition of testimony and site, what the viewer sees here is the incongruity of a Mediterranean location like Corfu juxtaposed with the camps in Poland, and the film thus articulates a reflection on the geographical extent of the Nazi Final Solution. Other documentaries have looked at specific national groups of Jews who were deported to Birkenau; for example, Ruggero Gabbai's *Memoria. I sopravvissuti raccontano* (*Memory: Survivors Speak*, 1997) is based on the testimonies of several Italian Jewish men and women who survived the Holocaust, including Shlomo Venezia, Romeo Salmonì, Nedo Fiano, Ida Marcheria and Leone Sabatello, and who are brought back to the camp in order to provide their accounts of the background of the ruined railway tracks, barracks, chimneys and crematoria of Birkenau.
23. Pollin-Galay, 'The Holocaust is a Foreign Country'.
24. The *Aufräumungskommando* was composed of a group of prisoners responsible for sorting the belongings of the victims killed in the gas chambers.
25. Recently addressed in a celebrated fiction film such as László Nemes's *Son of Saul* (*Saul Fia*, 2015), the *Sonderkommando* is also the subject of Michał Bukojemski's short documentary *Sonderkommando* (2005), an account of the

work undertaken by those Jews who were forced to aid with the disposal of gas-chamber victims in Birkenau. In this film, archival photographs are accompanied by a male voice-over reading the depositions of survivors from the *Sonderkommando*, including Ya'akov Gabai, Josef Sackar, Leon Cohen, Shlomo Dragon, Henryk Tauber and Shaul Chasan. Performing as a guide and as an expert, former member of the *Sonderkommando* Henryk Mandelbaum, who participated in the rebellion of 7 October 1944, is followed by Bukojemski's camera to the ruins of the four crematoria, to the pits and to the two temporary gas chambers known as the Red House and the White House. *Sonderkommando* is part of a series of five documentaries made for the Auschwitz-Birkenau Museum by Michał Bukojemski. The collection *Z Kroniki Auschwitz* (*From the Auschwitz Chronicle*, 2005) also includes *Najdłuższy Apel* (*The Longest Roll Call*), *Orkiestra* (*Orchestra*), *Rampa w Birkenau* (*The Platform in Birkenau*) and *Miłość* (*Love*). Each film combines present-day filming in Auschwitz and Birkenau with archival photographs, drawings and the voices of actors reciting lines from survivors' memoirs.

26. Lehrer, 'Relocating Auschwitz: Affective Relations in the Jewish-German-Polish Troika'.
27. For instance, Benstock's *The Holocaust Tourist*, a film which has already been discussed in Chapter Four, includes various scenes of tourists visiting the camps and taking photographs at the gate and at the gas chamber of Auschwitz and by the surviving barracks in Birkenau. The film raises questions regarding the reasons behind mass tourism on the sites of the extermination and tourists' varied responses to the exploration of the camps. Philippe Mora's personal documentary *Three Days in Auschwitz* (2015) also reveals the significant presence of tourists in the camps.
28. In *A Journey Back* (Brian McKenna, 1985), various locations, including the *Judenrampe* and Crematorium IV in Birkenau, feature in another visit to the camps undertaken by a well-known survivor: director, writer, teacher and producer at the Actors' Studio Jack Garfein.
29. Pollock, 'Holocaust tourism'.
30. Dwork and van Pelt, 'Reclaiming Auschwitz'.
31. Charlesworth, 'Contesting Places of Memory'.
32. *The Last Days* also includes interviews with Dario Gabbai, a Greek Jew who was a member of the *Sonderkommando*, and Randolph Braham, a Romanian Jew who survived the Holocaust in a soviet camp for POWs.
33. Formerly part of Hungary, the towns of Polena, Mukacheve and Uzhhorod are now in the Ukraine.
34. Her mother was gassed immediately after her arrival at Birkenau, and no records were taken.
35. Hart-Moxon has also told her story in *The Psychology of Neo-Nazism: Another Journey by Train to Auschwitz* (Mark Cousins and Mark Forrest, 1993), *Death March: A Survivor's Story* (David Nelson, 2002) and *Story of*

a Lifetime: Kitty Hart-Moxon (Chris Buckler, 2013), three documentaries filmed in Birkenau and in various other locations in Poland, including the city of Lublin.

Epilogue: New Routes

Isuchar Moshe Szwarc was born near the market square of Zgierz, a town located just north of Łódź, in February 1859. He was considered one of the most erudite and wisest men in the community, and on his eightieth birthday in 1939 the Jewish press in Poland published numerous articles in his honour. A few months later, the Nazis burnt his library while he collapsed and died of a heart attack. Nobody could attend Szwarc's funeral, as he was hastily buried by the Red Cross (cf. Shtockfish, Kanc and Fisher, 1975–86: 486).[1] Zgierz was renamed Görnau by the Nazis between 1943 and 1945, and its former *rynek* is now named after Pope John Paul II. Over seventy years after the death of Szwarc, the journey to Łódź undertaken by Holocaust survivor Natan Grossmann in Tanja Cummings' documentary *Linie 41* (*Line 41*, 2015) would begin on this square, the place where in 1940 the Jews of Zgierz were assembled before being deported to the ghettos in Głowno and Bałuty. While in Zgierz, Grossmann identifies the house where he lived with his family and which they rented from a wealthier Polish family. From this location the survivor travels to Łódź, where his parents perished and from where his brother was deported to Chełmno, and visits various sites in the city, including the *rynek* and the courtyards of Bałuty, Zielna Street, Tokarzewskiego Street, Radegast Station, Staromiejski Park and the Jewish cemetery. Towards the end of *Line 41*, Grossmann observes ironically that he was fortunate to be deported to Birkenau because the alternative, Chełmno, offered no chance of survival. Indeed, only a handful of people survived this camp, including Lanzmann's witness Szymon Srebrnik; *Line 41* returns to the locations of *Shoah* in Chełmno and repeats Lanzmann's car ride from the church where the Jews were imprisoned to the Rzuchow forest, where they would arrive already dead inside the gas vans. As Cummings' film suggests, thirty years after the release of *Shoah* the cinematic landscapes of Poland are still informed by repetitive itineraries across the landscapes where the Jews were exterminated. More specifically, *Line 41* is named after the tram line that crossed the ghetto in Bałuty through a fenced-off throughway and that is used as a recurring motif in the documentary. Germans and Poles rode every day on the tram carriages, which became, for those who were trapped in the ghetto, a reminder of the world from which they had been excluded; so near and yet so distant. The tram line is at the core of Cummings' investigation: 'The tram remains a mystery [the director's voice-over explains] – it embodies a curse of indifference. Mechanical. Thoughtless. Nothing holds it back.' Like Lanzmann's train continuing its journey on the old railway tracks, the trams of Łódź filmed in the present day repeat their ride across a city where painful memories are inscribed in its buildings and in its absences. With a similar concern for recurring patterns, itineraries and tropes, this book has investigated the ways in which the geography of the Holocaust locates memory, postmemory, history and their representations in material space and place, and follows dynamics inscribed in spatial and temporal routes, chiselled in the built environment and its archival image, aimed at passing on the knowledge and at finding closure.

Journey to Poland has followed an itinerary which started in the places inhabited by the Jews before the Holocaust, including the *shtetlekh* and the neighbourhoods where they had lived, worked, eaten, slept and prayed until the annihilation; and it has continued to the spaces created by the Nazis for the purpose of the Final Solution, with a particular focus on the *metropoleis* of death in Treblinka and Oświęcim. *Journey to Poland* has thus investigated the spaces contained within the borders of the Second Polish Republic, the territories where Lanzmann built the geography of *Shoah* and where most of the events associated with the Final Solution unfolded. And yet, other spaces west, east and south of Poland belong to the broader topography of the Holocaust, and documentary cinema has extended its reach to the sites of memory of the Jews of France, Italy, Netherlands, Belgium, Hungary, Bulgaria, Greece, Ukraine, Lithuania, Latvia and Estonia, among other countries. For example, Ron Steinman's *My Grandfather's House: The Journey Home* (2003) and Pearl Gluck's *Divan* (2003) can be read as non-fiction road movies, taking members of the postgeneration from the USA to their ancestral homes in Lithuania and Hungary respectively. The so-called Holocaust by bullets, the extermination of one and a half million Jews in Eastern Europe at the hands of the *Einsatzgruppen*, is explored in Romain Icard's film *Shoah par balles: l'histoire oubliée* (*Shoah by Bullets: Forgotten History*, 2008) and its journey to the sites of the executions in Ukraine. The concentration camps in the territories of the Reich are explored in documentaries such as Rex Bloomstein's *KZ* (2016), which was filmed at the site of the Mauthausen-

Gusen camp (Austria) and engages with young visitors' response to the exploration of the place. Theresienstadt, the concentration camp built for the Jews of German-occupied Czechoslovakia, is the focus of Claude Lanzmann's *The Last of the Unjust* (2013), and the main location of a significant number of documentaries concerned with narratives of memory and postmemory unfolded on the background of this specific location.[2] A study of the spatial and temporal dynamics articulated in these films would develop the present *Journey to Poland* into a *Journey to Occupied Europe*, framed through the lenses of documentary cinema and shaped by an image of the transnational ramifications of the Final Solution.

New directions in the spatial approach to the study of film and the Holocaust could eventually take into account different types of films. Whereas this journey has focused on the documentary landscapes of the Holocaust, occasional references to fiction films and their creative use of locations have been made: Gold's *Escape from Sobibór* was set in the Aktion Reinhard's death camp and filmed in Serbia, while Spielberg's *Schindler's List* and Polanski's *The Pianist* located the ghettos of Kraków and Warsaw on the 'wrong' side of the Vistula, thus prioritising architectural verisimilitude over topographical accuracy. Holland's *In Darkness* recreates Lviv by means of filming in various locations including Warsaw, Berlin and Łódź, three cities that own their specific Holocaust narratives.[3] The topographical creativity of these films should not necessarily be seen as a shortcoming, and in itself provides tools for articulating a discourse on the landscapes of the extermination of the Jews in Eastern Europe which is beyond the scope of this book, but should be seen as a fruitful new direction in the exploration of film, space and the Holocaust. Recent dramas seem to confirm the potential of such spatial investigation. Paweł Pawlikowski's *Ida* (2013) is an eerie road movie which takes the viewer across a sparse, dark and traumatised Polish landscape characterised by the same absences discussed throughout this book in relation to documentary accounts of the Holocaust. In its locations, including the former *shtetl* Szczebrzeszyn and the city of Łódź, the story of a nun who discovers her own Jewish identity as an orphan of the Holocaust echoes the narrative of documentaries such as Paweł Łoziński's *Birthplace* and their elaboration of loss developed during journeys across the Polish countryside. László Nemes' Hungarian drama *Saul fia* (*Son of Saul*, 2015) is set in Birkenau, and yet the film avoids all recognisable landmarks in its relentless pursuit of a member of the *Sonderkommando* and his quest to find a burial place for a Jewish boy. The dark, cramped spaces of the crematoria and the barracks speak of Birkenau as well as all other death camps, while the Jewish boy becomes the *unknown victim* of the genocide, standing for all those who have been killed. *Son of Saul* reinvents the use made by Spielberg of the Talmudic discussion implying that whoever saves a life saves the entire world; there are no lives to be saved in the crematorium, and offering a decent burial to one of the dead is all one can hope for in a place that is death itself.

Future research in the field of the Holocaust and film should advocate a spatial focus on the events that constitute the genocide, aimed at an understanding of the complexities of the Final Solution, a phenomenon too often reduced to a linear narrative evolving in a few well-known spaces with a straightforward temporality that puts an end to it in January 1945. *Journey to Poland* has attempted to trace a topography of life and death by means of a study of a polyphony of voices and a mosaic of images emerging from a conspicuous group of documentaries that ultimately reframes the spatial and temporal dimensions of the Holocaust. This spatial approach to the study of the intertwining between film, history and memory raises at least one fundamental methodological question. To what extent should a scholar engage with the physical exploration of the sites of memory, including the locations of the films discussed in the present space-based enquiry? Most studies of film are not concerned with this question, and visits to film studios or locations in the context of other scholarly approaches to cinema are rarely part of the methodology. A spatial reading of film requires a different approach, though. Specifically, the study of film and the Holocaust has travelled far in the psyche and arguably in timid steps towards the actual landscapes of the life and death of European Jewry. And yet it is still difficult to assess the necessity of visiting the places discussed in a spatial investigation such as that presented in this book. What would have been different in these six chapters had I not visited most of the locations investigated? The empirical knowledge of a certain space can facilitate the process of recognising film locations and itineraries. And I think this would have been a different book had I not done so. Or perhaps very little would have changed in the text itself; and yet I would not have wanted to write this book at all, had I not seen the fragments of the ghetto wall in Warsaw; had I not felt guilty for being thirsty during a visit to Birkenau; had I not seen anti-Semitic graffiti in Podgórze; had I not walked by the Ner river in Chełmno and seen fragments of Jewish gravestones paving the way in Treblinka; had I not been overexposed to the Polish summer heat in Płaszów; had I not spent days exploring Jewish cemeteries, crumbling synagogues and empty marketplaces in the villages of Eastern Poland and Ukraine; had I not stood outside the Łódź cemetery at the very beginning of Shabbat on a Friday evening; and had I not travelled to Bełżec, Sobibór and, beyond the topographical borders of this book, to Ponary, Rumbula and Babi Yar. I scheduled the itineraries of these journeys while planning the structure of this book, and wrote part of it while travelling in Eastern Europe. I have gained geographical knowledge, but beyond the uncomfortable stupor and the realisation that beauty exists in places associated with endless suffering, I do not have a grand philosophical view about the Holocaust to share with the reader. What I have now is a view over what is left of the Golden Rose Synagogue and a manuscript that is a map, unfolded through film.

Lviv, 14 July 2016

Notes

1. Shtockfish et al., *Sefer Zgierz, mazkeret netsal le-kehila yehudit be-Polin*, p. 486.
2. Documentaries about Theresienstadt include Amir Bar-Lev's *The Fighter* (2000), Malcolm Clarke's *The Lady in Number 6: Music Saved My Life* (2013), Frank Heimans' *Paradise Camp* (1986), Zuzana Justman's *Voices of the Children* (1999), Pavel Štingl's *A Story about a Bad Dream* (2000), Malcolm Clarke and Stuart Sender's *Prisoner of Paradise* (2002) and Doug Shultz's *Defiant Requiem: Voices of Resistance* (2013).
3. Fictional and documentary landscapes of the Holocaust in the city of Lublin and on the site of the concentration camp of Majdanek are the subject of my article 'The Cinematic City and the Destruction of Lublin's Jews'.

Bibliography

Adorno, Theodor W. [1951] (1981), 'Cultural Criticism and Society', in *Prisms*, trans. Samuel and Shierry Weber, Cambridge, MA: MIT Press, pp. 17–34.

Arad, Yitzhak (1999), *Bełżec, Sobibór, Treblinka: The Operation Reinhard Death Camps*, Bloomington: Indiana University Press.

Ashworth, G. J. (2002), 'Holocaust Tourism: The Experience of Kraków-Kazimierz', *International Research in Geographical and Environmental Education* vol. 11, no. 4, pp. 363–7.

Ashworth, G. J., and J. E. Tunbridge (1996), *Dissonant Heritage: Managing the Past as a Resource in Conflict*, Chichester: Wiley.

Ashworth, G. J., and J. E. Tunbridge (1999), 'Old Cities, New Pasts: Heritage Planning in Selected Cities of Central Europe', *Geojournal* vol. 49, no. 1, pp. 105–16.

Avisar, Ilan (1988), *Screening the Holocaust: Cinema's Images of the Unimaginable*, Bloomington: Indiana University Press.

Baer, Ulrich (2002), *Spectral Evidence: The Photography of Trauma*, Cambridge, MA: MIT Press.

Bar-Itzhak, Haya (2012), 'A Materialised Settlement and a Metaphysical Landscape in Legends of Origin of Polish Jews', in Julia Brauch, Alexandra Nocke and Anna Lipphardt (eds), *Jewish Topographies: Visions of Space, Traditions of Place*, Farnham, Surrey: Ashgate Publishing, pp. 161–80.

Barmatz, Zeev (2013), *Heroism in the Forest: The Jewish Partisans of Belarus*, Glil Yam: Kotarim International Publishing.

Baron, Jaimie (2013), *The Archive Effect: Found Footage and the Audiovisual Experience of History*, London and New York: Routledge.

Bartov, Omer (1996), *Murder in Our Midst: The Holocaust, Industrial Killing, and Representation*, New York and London: Oxford University Press.

Bartov, Omer (2008), 'Eastern Europe as the Site of Genocide', *Journal of Modern History* vol. 80, no. 3, pp. 557–93.

Bourla, Lisa (2015), 'Shaping and Reshaping Memory: the Łódź Ghetto Photographs', *Word & Image: A Journal of Verbal/Visual Enquiry* vol. 31, no. 1, pp. 54–72.

Browning, Christopher R. (2001), *Ordinary Men: Reserve Police Battalion 11 and the Final Solution in Poland*, London and New York: Penguin Books.

Bruzzi, Stella [1997] (2006), *New Documentary: A Critical Introduction*, London and New York: Routledge.

Burleigh, Michael (2000), *The Third Reich: A New History*, London: Pan Macmillan.

Charlesworth, Andrew (1994), 'Contesting Places of Memory: The Case of Auschwitz', *Environment and Planning D: Society and Space* vol. 12, pp. 579–93.

Charlesworth, Andrew, and Michael Addis (2002), 'Memorialization and the Ecological Landscapes of Holocaust Sites: The Cases of Płaszów and Auschwitz-Birkenau', *Landscape Research* vol. 27, no. 3, pp. 229–51.

Cinquegrani, Maurizio (2016), 'The Cinematic City and the Destruction of Lublin's Jews', *Holocaust Studies: A Journal of Culture and History* vol. 22, no. 2–3, pp. 244–55.

Cinquegrani, Maurizio (2017), 'The Cinematic *Shtetl* as a Site of Postmemory', in François Penz and Richard Koeck (eds), *Cinematic Urban Geographies*, Basingstoke: Palgrave Macmillan, pp. 137–54.

Clarke, David B. (1996), 'Holocaust Topologies: Singularity, Politics, Space', *Political Geography* vol. 15, no. 6–7, pp. 457–89.

Cole, Tim (2013), 'Crematoria, Barracks, Gateways. Survivors' Return Visits to the Memory Landscapes of Auschwitz', *History and Memory* vol. 25, no 2, pp. 102–31.

Cole, Tim (2016), *Holocaust Landscapes*, London and New York: Bloomsbury.

Desbois, Patrick (2009), *The Holocaust by Bullets: A Priest's Journey to Uncover the Truth Behind the Murder of 1.5 Million Jews*, Basingstoke: Palgrave Macmillan.

Donat, Alexander (ed.) (1979), *Death Camp Treblinka: A Documentary*, New York: Schocken Books.

Dwork, Debórah, and Robert Jan van Pelt (1994), 'Reclaiming Auschwitz', in Geoffrey H. Hartman (ed.), *Holocaust Remembrance: The Shapes of Memory*, Oxford: Blackwell, pp. 232–51.

Eliach, Yaffa (1998), *There Once Was a World: A 900-Year Chronicle of the Shtetl of Eishyshok*, New York: Little, Brown and Company.

Galzar, Richard (1995), *Trap with a Green Fence: Survival in Treblinka*, Evanston, IL: Northwestern University Press.

Giaccaria, Paolo, and Claudio Minca (2016), 'Introduction: Hitler's Geographies, Nazi Spatialities', in P. Giaccaria and C. Minca (eds), *Hitler's Geographies: The Spatialities of the Third Reich*, Chicago: University of Chicago Press, pp. 1–18.

Gilbert, Martin (1986), *The Holocaust: The Jewish Tragedy*, London: Harper Collins.

Gilbert, Martin (2009), *The Routledge Atlas of the Holocaust*, London and New York: Routledge.

Ginzburg, Carlo (1992), 'Just One Witness', in Saul Friedländer (ed.), *Probing the Limits of Representation: Nazism and the 'Final Solution'*, Cambridge, MA: Harvard University Press, pp. 82–96.

Gross, Jan (2001), *Neighbours: The Destruction of the Jewish Community in Jedwabne, Poland*, Princeton, NJ: Princeton University Press.

Grossman, Vasily (1946), 'The Treblinka Hell', in *The Years of War (1941–1945)*, Foreign Languages Publishing House: Moscow.

Guerin, Frances (2012), *Through Amateur Eyes: Film and Photography in Nazi Germany*, Minneapolis: University of Minnesota Press.

Haggith, Toby, and Joanna Newman (eds) (2005), *Holocaust and the Moving Image: Representations in Film and Television since 1933*, London: Wallflower.

Haltof, Marek (2012), *Polish Film and the Holocaust: Politics and Memory*, New York and Oxford: Berghahn Books.

Hamermesh, Mira (2004), *The River of Angry Dogs*, London: Pluto Press.

Hansen, Miriam Bratu (2001), '*Schindler's List* Is Not *Shoah*: Second Commandment, Popular Modernism, and Public Memory', in Barbie Zelizer (ed.), *Visual Culture and the Holocaust*, London and New York: Continuum, pp. 127–51.

Hilberg, Raul (1985), *The Destruction of European Jews*, New York: Holmes and Meier.

Hilberg, Raul (1993), *Perpetrators Victims Bystanders: The Jewish Catastrophe 1939–1945*, New York: Harper Perennial.

Hirsch, Joshua (2003), *Afterimage: Film, Trauma, and the Holocaust*, Philadelphia: Temple University Press.

Hirsch, Marianne (1997), *Family Frames: Photography, Narrative, and Postmemory*, Cambridge, MA: Harvard University Press.

Hirsch, Marianne (2008), 'The Generation of Postmemory', *Poetics Today* vol. 29, no. 1, pp. 103–28.

Hirsch, Marianne (2012a), *The Generation of Postmemory: Writing and Visual Culture After the Holocaust*, New York: Columbia University Press.

Hirsch, Marianne (2012b), 'Objects of Return', in Jakob Lothe, Susan Rubin Suleiman and James Phelan (eds), *After Testimony: The Ethics and Aesthetics of Holocaust Narrative for the Future*, Columbus: Ohio State University Press, pp. 198–220.

Hirsch, Marianne, and Leo Spitzer (2003), '"We Would Not Have Come Without You": Generations of Nostalgia', in Katharina Hodgkin and Susannah Radstone (eds), *Contested Pasts: The Politics of Memory*, London: Routledge, pp. 79–95.

Hoffman, Eva (2004), *After Such Knowledge: Memory, History and the Legacy of the Holocaust*, New York: Public Affairs.

Huyssen, Andreas (1993), 'Monument and Memory in a Postmodern Age', *The Yale Journal of Criticism* vol. 6, no. 2, pp. 249–61.

Insdorf, Annette (1989), *Indelible Shadows: Film and the Holocaust*, Cambridge and New York: Cambridge University Press.

Kerner, Aaron (2011), *Film and the Holocaust: New Perspectives on Dramas, Documentaries, and Experimental Films*, London and New York: Bloomsbury Academic.

Khevin Goldberg, Hadassa (1957), 'The Riots of the Eve of Yom Kippur', in Kh. Shteynberg, M. Vonkhotsker, Y. Levin and Y. Tsaban (eds), *Sefer Sukhovola* ('Book of Suchovola'), Jerusalem and Tel Aviv: Memorial Library of Jewish Communities, p. 159.

Kirshenblatt-Gimblett, Barbara (1995), 'Introduction', in Mark Zborowski and Elizabeth Herzog (eds), *Life Is With People: The Culture of the Shtetl*, New York: Schocken, pp. ix–xlviii.

Kirshenblatt-Gimblett, Barbara (2001), 'The Popular Arts of American Jewish Ethnography', in Deborah Dash Moore and Ilan Troen (eds), *Divergent Jewish Cultures: Israel and America*, New Haven: Yale University Press, pp. 155–92.

Knowles, Anne Kelly, Tim Cole, and Alberto Giordano (eds) (2014), *Geographies of the Holocaust*, Bloomington and Indianapolis: Indiana University Press.

Koch, Gertrud (1989), 'The Aesthetic Transformation of the Image of the Unimaginable: Notes on Claude Lanzmann's *Shoah*', trans. by Jamie Owen Daniel and Miriam Hansen, *October* vol. 48 (Spring), pp. 15–24.

Kugelmass, Jack, and Jonathan Boyarin (eds) (1998), 'Introduction', in *From a Ruined Garden: the Memorial Books of Polish Jewry*, Bloomington: Indiana University Press, pp. 1–48.

Kulka, Otto Dov (2013), *Landscapes of the Metropolis of Death: Reflections on Memory and Imagination* (trans. Ralph Mandel), London: Allen Lane.

Laarse, Rob van der (2013), 'Archaeology of Memory: Europe's Holocaust Dissonances in East and West', in Dirk Callebaut, Jan Mařik and Jana Maříková (eds), *Heritage Reinvents Europe*, EAC Occasional Paper, no. 7, Budapest: Archaeolingua, pp. 121–130.

LaCapra, Dominick (1998), *History and Memory after Auschwitz*, Ithaca: Cornell University Press.

Lanzmann, Claude (2007), 'Site and Speech: An Interview with Claude Lanzmann about *Shoah*', with Marc Chevrie and Hervé Le Roux, in Stuart Liebman (ed.), *Claude Lanzmann's* Shoah*: Key Essays*, Oxford and New York: Oxford University Press, pp. 37–49.

Lanzmann, Claude (2012), *The Patagonian Hare*, London: Atlantic Books; first published in France as *Le lièvre de Patagonie*, Paris: Gallimard.

Lefebvre, Henri [1974] (1991), *The Production of Space*, trans. Donald Nicholson-Smith, Oxford: Blackwell; first published as *La production de l'espace*, Paris: Anthropos.

Lehrer, Erica (2012), 'Relocating Auschwitz: Affective Relations in the Jewish-German-Polish Troika', in Kristin Kopp and Joanna Nizynska (eds), *Germany, Poland and Postmemorial Relations: In Search of a Livable Past*, New York: Palgrave Macmillan, pp. 213–38.

Levi, Primo [1947] (1996), *Survival in Auschwitz*, New York: Simon and Schuster; first published in Italian as *Se questo è un uomo*, Turin: Biblioteca Leone Ginzburg.

Levy, Richard S. (ed.) (2005), *Antisemitism: A Historical Encyclopaedia of Prejudice and Persecution (Volume One)*, Santa Barbara, CA: ABC-CLIO.

Lowenthal, David (1975), 'Past Time, Present Place: Landscape and Memory', *Geographical Review* vol. 65, no. 1, pp. 1–36.

Lowenthal, David (1985), *The Past Is a Foreign Country*, Cambridge: Cambridge University Press.

Mandel, Naomi (2001), 'Rethinking "After Auschwitz": Against a Rhetoric of the Unspeakable in Holocaust Writing', *Boundary 2* vol. 28, no. 2, pp. 203–28.

Michman, Dan (2011), *The Emergence of Jewish Ghettos During the Holocaust*, Cambridge: Cambridge University Press.

Miron, Guy (2010), *The Yad Vashem Encyclopaedia of the Ghettos During the Holocaust*, Jerusalem: Yad Vashem.

Nichols, Bill (1991), *Representing Reality: Issues and Concepts in Documentary*, Bloomington: Indiana University Press.

Nichols, Bill (1994), *Blurred Boundaries: Questions of Meaning in Contemporary Culture*, Bloomsbury: Indiana University Press.

Nora, Pierre (ed.) (1984), *Les Lieux de Mémoire: La République*, Paris: Gallimard (Bibliothèque illustrée des histoires).

Nora, Pierre (1989), 'Between Memory and History: Les Lieux de Mémoire', *Representations* no. 26, *Special Issue: Memory and Counter-Memory*, pp. 7–24.

Olin, Margaret (1997), 'Lanzmann's *Shoah* and *the* Topography of *the* Holocaust Film', *Representations* no. 57, pp. 1–23.

Orlicki, Józef (1983), *Szkice z dziejów stosunków polsko-zydowskich, 1918–1949* ('Sketches of the History of Polish–Jewish Relations'), Szczecin: Krajowa Agancja Wydawnicza.

Pankiewicz, Tadeusz (1947), *Apteka w getcie krakowskim*, Kraków: Wydawnictwo Literackie; trans. into English as *The Cracow Ghetto Pharmacy* by Henry Tilles for the Holocaust Library, New York, 1987.

Penz, François, and Andong Lu (2011), 'Introduction: What is Urban Cinematics?', in François Penz and Andong Lu (eds), *Urban Cinematics: Understanding Urban Phenomena through the Moving Image*, Bristol: Intellect Books, pp. 7–19.

Pettitt, Joanne, and Vered Weiss (2016), 'Introduction', *Holocaust Studies: A Journal of Culture and History* vol. 22, no. 2–3, special issue: *Tracing Topographies: Revisiting the Concentration Camps Seventy Years after the Liberation of Auschwitz*, pp. 141–50.

Pollin-Galay, Hannah (2013), 'The Holocaust is a Foreign Country: Comparing Representations of Place in Lithuanian Jewish Testimony', *Dapim: Studies on the Holocaust* vol. 27, no. 1, pp. 26–39.

Pollock, Griselda (2003), 'Holocaust Tourism: Being There, Looking Back and the Ethics of Spatial Memory', in David Crouch and Nina Lübbren (eds), *Visual Culture and Tourism*, Oxford: Berg, pp. 175–89.

Prager, Brad (2015), *After the Fact: The Holocaust in Twenty-First-Century Documentary Film*, London and New York: Bloomsbury Academic.

Rajchman, Chil [2009] (2012), *Treblinka: A Survivor's Memory*, London: Maclehose Press; first published as *Je suis le dernier Juif*, Paris: Le Livre de Poche.

Reimer, Robert C. (2000), *Cultural History through a National Socialist Lens: Essays on the Cinema of the Third Reich*, Rochester, NY: Camden House.

Rhodes, Richard (2003), *Masters of Death: The SS-Einsatzgruppen and the Invention of the Holocaust*, London: Vintage.

Rothberg, Michael (2009), *Multidirectional Memory: Remembering the Holocaust in the Age of Decolonization*, Redwood City, CA: Stanford University Press.

Saxton, Libby (2008), *Haunted Images: Film, Ethics, Testimony and the Holocaust*, London: Wallflower.

Schulz, Bruno [1934–7] (2008), *The Street of Crocodiles and Other Stories*, trans. Celina Wieniewska, London and New York: Penguin Books.

Shandler, Jeffrey (2014), *Shtetl: A Vernacular Intellectual History*, New Brunswick, NJ: Rutgers University Press.

Shtockfish, David, Sh Kanc and Z. Fisher (eds) (1975–86), *Sefer Zgierz, mazkeret netsal le-kehila yehudit be-Polin* ('Memorial Book Zgierz'), Tel Aviv: Zgierz Society.

Smith, Mark S. (2010), *Treblinka Survivor: The Life and Death of Hershl Sperling*, Stroud: The History Press.

Sontag, Susan (1989), *On Photography*, New York: Anchor Doubleday.

Spector, Shmuel, and Geoffrey Wigoder (eds) (2001), *The Encyclopaedia of Jewish Life Before and During the Holocaust: A–J*, New York: New York University Press.

Spence, Jo, and Patricia Holland (eds) (1991), *Family Snaps: The Meaning of Domestic Photography*, London: Virago.

Steinlauf, Michael C. (1997), *Bondage to the Dead: Poland and the Memory of the Holocaust*, New York and Syracuse: Syracuse University Press.

Stone, Daniel (1996), 'Jewish Immigration from Poland Before World War Two', in John J. Bukowczyk (ed.), *Polish Americans and Their History: Community, Culture, and Politics*, Pittsburgh: University of Pittsburgh Press, pp. 93–120.

Taylor, Richard (1998), *Film Propaganda: Soviet Russia and Nazi Germany*, London and New York: I. B. Tauris.

Vice, Sue (2011), *Shoah*, London: BFI and Palgrave Macmillan.

Wachsmann, Nikolaus (2016), *KL: A History of the Nazi Concentration Camps*, London and New York: Abacus.

Walker, Janet (1997), 'The Traumatic Paradox: Documentary Films, Historical Fictions and Cataclysmic Past Events', *Signs* vol. 22, no. 4, pp. 803–25.

Walker, Janet (2012), 'Moving Testimonies: "Unhomed Geography" and the Holocaust Documentary of Return', in Jakob Lothe, Susan Rubin Suleiman and James Phelan (eds), *After Testimony: The Ethics and Aesthetics of Holocaust Narrative for the Future*, Columbus: Ohio State University Press, pp. 269–88.

Weissman, Gary (2004), *Fantasies of Witnessing: Post-war Efforts to Experience the Holocaust*, Ithaca: Cornell University Press.

Wiernik, Jankiel (1944), *Rok w Treblince*, Warsaw: Żydowski Komitet Narodowy.

Willenberg, Samuel [1986] (1992), *Revolt in Treblinka*, Warsaw: Zydowski Instytut Historyczny; first published in Hebrew by Israel's Ministry of Defense.

Williams, Linda (1991), 'Mirrors Without Memories: Truth, History, and the New Documentary', *Film Quarterly* vol. 46, no. 3, pp. 9–21.

Žižek, Slavoj (1992), *Looking Awry: An Introduction to Jacques Lacan through Popular Culture*, Cambridge, MA, and London: MIT Press.

Žižek, Slavoj (2003), *The Puppet and the Dwarf*, Cambridge, MA, and London: MIT Press.

Filmography

A Pesar de Treblinka (*Despite Treblinka*), Gerardo Stawsky. Uruguay: Universidad ORT Uruguay, 2002. 90 minutes. Location: Montevideo (Uruguay).

Aj waj, Joanna Satanowska. Poland: National Film School in Łódź, 2014. 14 minutes. Location: Łódź.

Apteka pod Orłem (*Under the Eagle Pharmacy*), Krzysztof Miklaszewski. Poland: TVP, 2006. 45 minutes. Location: Kraków.

Aspangbahnhof 1941. Geschichte einer Frauenfreundschaft (*Aspangbahnhof 1941. A Story of a Female Friendship*), Angelika Brechelmacher. Austria: Verlag Grenzen Erzaehlen, 2014. 69 minutes. Location: Łódź.

Auschwitz-Birkenau 1940–1945–1995, Hans Fels and Kees Hin. Netherlands: Fels and Hin, 1995. 12 minutes. Location: Oświęcim.

Back to Gombin, Minna Packer, 2002. USA: Packer Productions. 56 minutes. Location: Gąbin.

Bałuckie getto (*The Ghetto in Bałuty*), Pavel Štingl. Poland: TVP Kultura, 2008. 87 minutes. Location: Łódź.

Bełżec, Szymon Zin. Poland: Bełżec Memorial Museum, 2004. 62 minutes. Location: Bełżec.

Bełżec, Guillaume Moscovitz. France: VLR, 2005. 92 minutes. Location: Bełżec.

Boris Dorfman a Mentsh, Gabriela von Seltmann and Uwe von Seltmann. Germany: Apfelstrudel Media Berlin, 2014. 55 minutes. Location: Lviv (Lithuania).

Branko: Return to Auschwitz, Topaz Adizes. USA: The New York Times's Op-Docs, 2013. 10 minutes. Location: Oświęcim.

Campo di Fiori, Michał Nekanda-Trepka. Poland: Telewizja Polska, 2012. 28 minutes. Location: Warsaw.

Castaways, Sławomir Grünberg and Tomek Wiśniewski. USA and Poland: LogTV, 2013. 27 minutes. Location: Łapy.

Chutor Konne, Michał Nekanda-Trepka. Poland: Studio Filmowe Everest, 2007. 25 minutes. Location: Konne (Białystok).

Death Camp Treblinka: Survivor Stories, Adam Kemp. UK: BBC, 2013. 58 minutes. Location: Treblinka.

Death March: A Survivor's Story, David Nelson. UK: BBC, 2002. 62 minutes. Location: Oświęcim.

Escape From a Nazi Death Camp, Hereward Pelling. USA: PBS, 2014. 56 minutes. Location: Sobibór.

A Film Unfinished, Yael Hersonski. Israel and Germany: Oscilloscope Pictures, 2010. 89 minutes. Location: Warsaw.

Finding Leah Tickotsky: A Discovery of Heritage in Poland, Sarah Golabek-Goldman. USA: Sarah Golabek-Goldman, Mona Golabek and Phyllis Pollak, 2010. 48 minutes. Locations: Zakliczyn, Jedwabne, Jasionówka, Łomża, Białystok, Treblinka.

Following in Felix's Footsteps, Steve Prankard. USA: SC Group, 2016. 80 minutes. Locations: Łódź, Oświęcim.

Fotoamator (*Photographer*), Dariusz Jabłoński. Poland: Apple Film Productions, Broadcast AV, TVP1, Arte, Canal+ Polska, 1998. 52 minutes. Location: Łódź.

Hiding and Seeking: Faith and Tolerance After the Holocaust, Menachem Daum and Oren Rudavsky. USA: PBS in association with Independent Television Service, 2002. 85 minutes. Locations: Zdunska Wola, Działoszyce, Bronów.

The Holocaust Tourist, Jes Benstock. UK: Technobabble, 2006. 10 minutes. Locations: Oświęcim, Kraków.

How Much to Remember: One Family's Conversation with History, Nina Koocher. USA and France: Nina Koocher and Josephine Productions, 2006. 57 minutes. Locations: Chełmno, Oświęcim, Łódź.

Image Before My Eyes, Joshua Waletzky. USA: Docurama, 1980. 88 minutes. Location: Łódź.

Inheritance, James Moll. USA: PBS and USC Shoah Foundation Institute, 2006. 75 minutes. Locations: Kraków, Płaszów.

Jakby to było wczoraj (*As if it were yesterday*), Michał Nekanda-Trepka. Poland: Telewizja Polska, 2005. 45 minutes. Location: Częstochowa.

A Journey Back, Brian McKenna. Canada: CBC, 1985. 57 minutes. Location: Oświęcim.

Każdy miał swojego Żyda (*Everyone Had Their Own Jew*), Tomasz Wisniewski. USA and Poland: LogTV and Tomasz Wisniewski, 2014. 32 minutes. Location: Suchowola.

Kitty: Return to Auschwitz, Peter Morley. UK: Yorkshire Television, 1979. 83 minutes. Location: Oświęcim.

Land der Vernichtung (*Land of Annihilation*), Romuald Karmakar. Germany: Cinekarmakar, 2004. 140 minutes. Locations: Sobibór, Treblinka, Bełżec, Majdanek.

The Last Days, James Moll. USA: Ken Lipper and June Beallor, 1998. 87 minutes. Locations: Oświęcim (Poland); Dachau and Bergen Belsen (Germany).

The Legacy of Jedwabne, Slawomir Grünberg. USA and Poland: LogTV, 2005. 56 minutes. Location: Jedwabne.

Likwidacja 08.1944 (*Liquidation 08.1944*), Marek Miller and Michał Bukojemski. Poland: Contrastudio, 2009. 16 minutes. Location: Łódź.

Linie 41 (*Line 41*), Tanja Cummings. Germany: European Association for East-West Rapprochement, 2015. 101 minutes. Location: Łódź.

Litzmannstadt - Bałuty, Tomasz Bergmann. Poland: Festiwal Łódź 4 Kultur, 2013. 41 minutes. Location: Łódź.

Litzmannstadt Ghetto, Daniel Szylit and Irena Kukulska. Poland: Wytwórnia Filmów Oświatowych, 1965. 17 minutes. Location: Łódź.

Litzmannstadt Ghetto. Piekło na Ziemi Obiecanej (*Litzmannstadt Ghetto. Inferno in the Promised Land*), Mariusz Olbrychowski. Poland: Time after Time International, 2009. 57 minutes. Location: Łódź.

Łódź Ghetto, Alan Adelson and Kate Taverna. USA: The National Endowment for the Humanities, 1989. 103 minutes. Location: Łódź.

Loving the Dead, Mira Hamermesh. UK: BBC2, 1991. Locations: Oświęcim, Łódź.

Luboml: My Heart Remembers, Aaron Ziegelman. USA: Eileen Douglas and Ron Steinman, 2003. 57 minutes. Location: Luboml.

Memoria. I sopravvissuti raccontano (*Memory. Survivors Speak*), Ruggero Gabbai. Italy: Forma International, 1997. 90 minutes. Location: Oświęcim.

Memoriał Radegast Bahnhof (*Memorial Radegast Station*), Małgorzata Burzyńska-Keller. Poland: City Hall of Łódź, 2009. 20 minutes. Location: Łódź.

Miasteczko Kroke (*The Little Town of Kroke*), Kuba Karys and Natalia Schmidt. Poland: Discovery Historia TVN, 2008. 44 minutes. Location: Kraków.

Miejsce urodzenia (*Birthplace*), Paweł Łoziński. Poland: Studio Filmowe Kronika and Państwowa Wyższa Szkoła Filmowa Telewizyjna i Teatralna, 1992. 47 minutes. Locations: Dobre, Drop, Głęboczyca, Radoszyna.

Mostowicz, Małgorzata Andrzejewska-Psarska. Poland: Verissima, 1998. 102 minutes. Location: Łódź.

My Łódź is No More: The Story of Yosef Neuhaus, Zvi Nevo. Israel: The International School for Holocaust Studies, Yad Vashem, The Hebrew University of Jerusalem, 2009. 40 minutes. Location: Łódź.

Nazi Hunters: Death Camp Commandant, Chris Lethbridge. UK: IMG Entertainment, 2010. 45 minutes. Location: Treblinka.

Never Forget to Lie, Marian Marzynski. USA: PBS Frontline, 2013. Locations: Warsaw, Kraków.

Nie opłataj mnie . . . (*To Stay Alive*), Piotr Zarębski. Poland: Telewizja Polska, 2000. 58 minutes. Location: Łódź.

Nuit et brouillard (*Night and Fog*), Alain Resnais. France: Argos Films, 1955. 32 minutes. Locations: Oświęcim, Majdanek.

Obóz cygański w Łodzi (*The Gypsy camp in Łódź*), Jarosław Sztandera. Poland: National Film School in Łódź, 2004. 20 minutes. Location: Łódź.

Oddajcie mi swoje dzieci (*Give Me Your Children*), Piotr Weychert and Piotr Perz. Poland: Grupa Filmowa, 2014. 22 minutes. Location: Łódź.

One Day in Auschwitz, Steve Purcell. USA: USC Shoah Foundation Institute, 2015. 45 minutes. Location: Oświęcim.

Ostatni świadek (*The Last Witness*), Michał Nekanda-Trepka. Poland: Studio Filmowe Everest, 2002. 51 minutes. Location: Treblinka.

Paint What You Remember, Slawomir Grünberg. USA and Poland: LogTV, 2009. 30 minutes. Location: Opatów.

Pamiętam (*I Remember*), Andrzej Wajda. USA: USC Shoah Foundation, 2002. 57 minutes. Location: Oświęcim.

Parce que j'étais peintre (*Because I Was a Painter*), Christophe Cognet. France and Germany: La Huit and Augenschein Filmproduktion, 2013. 104 minutes. Locations: Israel, France, Belgium.

Past and Present, History Falsified, Thomas and Dena Blatt. USA: Thomas and Dena Blatt, 1987. 23 minutes. Location: Sobibór.

The Peretzniks, Slawomir Grünberg. USA and Poland: LogTV, 2010. 48 minutes. Location: Łódź.

Po-lin. Okruchy pamięci (*Po-lin. Slivers of Memory*), Jolanty Dylewskiej. Poland: Bomedia, 2008. 82 minutes. Locations: Gąbin, Kałuszyn, Kock, Kolbuszowa, Kozienice, Kurów, Raniżów, Sędziszów Małopolski, Sejny, Skierniewice, Sokołów Małopolski, Tykocin, Tyszowce, Zaręby Kościelne, Kraków, Łódź (Poland); Borysław/Boryslav, Nowogródek/Navahrudak, Skidel/Skidzyel, Słonim/Slonim (Belarus); Bolechów/Bolekhiv, Gródek Jagielloński/Horodok (Ukraine).

Powiedz mi, dlaczego (*Tell Me Why*), Małgorzata Imielska. Poland: Studio Filmowe Kalejdoskop, 2005. 45 minutes. Locations: Warsaw, Otwock, Oświęcim, Białystok.

A Promise to My Father, Tim Gray. USA: WWII Foundation, 2010. 55 minutes. Locations: Treblinka, Oświęcim.

The Psychology of Neo-Nazism: Another Journey by Train to Auschwitz, Mark Cousins and Mark Forrest. UK: Tibor Fischer, 1993. 52 minutes. Location: Oświęcim.

Radegast, Borys Lankosz. Poland: Grupa Filmowa Fargo, 2008. 50 minutes. Location: Łódź.

Radegast Station, Małgorzata Burzyńska-Keller. USA: Centre for Jewish History and Culture, 2003. 20 minutes. Location: Łódź.

Return to My Shtetl Delatyn, Willy Lindwer. Netherlands and Israel: AVA Productions and Terra Film Productions, 1992. 60 minutes. Locations: Kraków, Przemysl, Lviv, Stryj, Delatyn, Bolechov.

Return to Poland, Marian Marzynski. USA: WGBH Educational Foundation for PBS, 1981. 59 minutes. Locations: Warsaw, Łęczyca.

Shimon's Returns, Slawomir Grünberg. USA and Poland: LogTV, 2014. 65 minutes. Locations: Łódź (Poland); Berezhany, Rai, Narajów, Lwów (Ukraine).

Shoah, Claude Lanzmann. UK and France: BBC, Historia, Les Films Aleph, Ministère de la Culture de la Republique Française, 1985. 566 minutes. Locations: Sobibór, Treblinka, Oświęcim, Chełmno, Warsaw. Outtake: 'Tadeusz Pankiewicz – Kracow'; story RG-60.5014; film ID: 3220 (60 minutes), Steven Spielberg Film and Video Archive, USHMM.

Shtetl, Marian Marzynski. USA: PBS Frontline, 1996. 180 minutes. Location: Brańsk.

Sobibór, October 14, 1943, 4 p.m., Claude Lanzmann. France: France 2 Cinéma, Les Films Aleph, Why Not Productions, 2001. 95 minutes. Location: Sobibór.

Sobibór: the Plan, the Revolt, the Escape, Karen Lynne and Richard Bloom. USA: Richard Bloom, 2010. 19 minutes. Location: Sobibór.

So Many Miracles, Katherine Smalley and Vic Sarin. USA: Alternative Pictures/CBC/The National Center for Jewish Film, 1987. 58 minutes. Location: Pińczów.

Song of the Łódź Ghetto, David Kaufman. Canada: Sun-Street Productions, 2011. 121 minutes. Location: Łódź.

Story of a Lifetime: Kitty Hart-Moxon, Chris Buckler. UK: BBC, 2013. 29 minutes. Locations: Lublin, Oświęcim.

The Story of Chaim Rumkowski and the Jews of Łódź, Peter Cohen and Bo Kuritze. Sweden: SVT, 1982. 55 minutes. Location: Łódź.

Świadkowie (*Witnesses*), Marcel Łoziński. Poland: Videonowa Warsawa, 1986. 26 minutes. Location: Kielce.

Tango of Slaves, Ilan Ziv. Israel: Tamouz Media co-production with Israel Broadcasting Authority, 1994. 106 minutes. Location: Warsaw.

Le temps du ghetto (*The Time of the Ghetto*), Frédéric Rossif. Belgium: Les films de la Pléiade, 1961. 89 minutes. Location: Łódź.

A Town Called Brzostek, Simon Target. Australia: Handheld Features, 2014. 50 minutes. Location: Brzostek.

There Once Was a Town, Jeffrey Bieber. USA and Israel: WETA and Noga Productions, 2000. 90 minutes. Locations: Eishyshok and Vilnius (Lithuania); Нача and Radun (Belarus).

Three Days in Auschwitz, Philippe Mora. USA: Dripping Paint Pictures, 2015. 55 minutes. Location: Oświęcim.

Treblinka: Hitler's Killing Machine, Alex Nikolic-Dunlop. UK: Furneaux & Edgar/GroupM Entertainment, 2014. 44 minutes. Location: Treblinka.

Два танго (*Two to Tango*), Hesed Arieh. Lithuania: Hesed Arieh, 2006. 19 minutes. Location: Lviv (Lithuania).

Voices from the Attic, Debbie Goodstein. USA: Direct Cinema Limited, 1988. 58 minutes. Location: Urzejowice.

Vosstanie v Sobibore (*The Uprising in Sobibór*), Pavel Kogan and Lily Van Den. Russia: Lily Van Den, 1990. 140 minutes. Location: Sobibór.

Z królestwa śmierci (*From the Realm of Death*), Urszula Hasiec and Grzegorz Michalec. Poland: TVP Lublin, 2008. 26 minutes. Location: Sobibór.

Z głębokości wołam (*From the depths I call*), Wojciech Gierłowski. Poland: Telewizja Polska, 2005. 25 minutes. Location: Łódź.

Z kroniki Auschwitz (*From the Auschwitz Chronicle*), Michał Bukojemski. Poland: Państwowe Muzeum Auschwitz-Birkenau w Oświęcimiu, 2005. Series including: *Sonderkommando*, *Najdłuższy Apel* (*The Longest Roll Call*), *Orkiestra* (*Orchestra*), *Rampa w Birkenau* (*The Platform in Birkenau*) and *Miłość* (*Love*). Approximately 26 minutes for each segment. Location: Oświęcim.

Zamir: Jewish Voices Return to Poland, Rob Cooper and Eric Stange. USA: Zamir Chorale of Boston, 2000. 60 minutes. Location: Łódź.

Index

CPSIA information can be obtained
at www.ICGtesting.com
Printed in the USA
BVHW061555300620
582685BV00003B/28

9 781474 463232